W9-BZV-079

DISCARD

AMERICAN PHAROAH

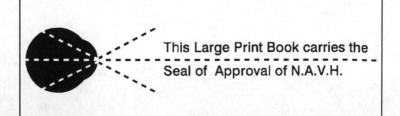

This Large Print Book carries the
Seal of Approval of N.A.V.H.

AMERICAN PHAROAH

THE UNTOLD STORY OF THE TRIPLE CROWN WINNER'S LEGENDARY RISE

JOE DRAPE

THORNDIKE PRESS

A part of Gale, Cengage Learning

GALE
CENGAGE Learning·

Farmington Hills, Mich • San Francisco • New York • Waterville, Maine
Meriden, Conn • Mason, Ohio • Chicago

Copyright © 2016 by Joe Drape.
Additional copyright/credits information is on page 457.
Thorndike Press, a part of Gale, Cengage Learning.

ALL RIGHTS RESERVED $34
The publisher is not responsible for websites (or their content) that are not owned by the publisher.
Thorndike Press® Large Print Biographies and Memoirs.
The text of this Large Print edition is unabridged.
Other aspects of the book may vary from the original edition.
Set in 16 pt. Plantin.

LIBRARY OF CONGRESS CATALOGING-IN-PUBLICATION DATA

Names: Drape, Joe.
Title: American Pharoah : the untold story of the Triple Crown winner's legendary
    rise / by Joe Drape.
Description: Waterville, Maine : Thorndike Press, 2016. | Series: Thorndike Press
    large print biographies and memoirs | Includes bibliographical references.
Identifiers: LCCN 2016015592 | ISBN 9781410491855 (hardcover) | ISBN 1410491854
    (hardcover)
Subjects: LCSH: American Pharoah (Horse) | Race horses—United
    States—Biography.
Classification: LCC SF355.A455 D73 2016 | DDC 798.40092/9—dc23
LC record available at https://lccn.loc.gov/2016015592

Published in 2016 by arrangement with Hachette Books, a division of Hachette Book Group, Inc.

Printed in Mexico
1 2 3 4 5 6 7 20 19 18 17 16

AUG - - 2016

To Mary & Jack
Love you always and forever

CONTENTS

AUTHOR'S NOTE

I was beginning to believe that I was never going to see a horse capture the Triple Crown. I was a kid in the 1970s when Affirmed, Seattle Slew, and Secretariat made sweeping the Kentucky Derby, Preakness, and Belmont Stakes look easy. I was merely a fan then, one who was soon to be transformed into a horseplayer. My father taught me how to read the *Daily Racing Form,* and my mother loved horses and spending an afternoon at the track.

As my career as a journalist progressed and took me on assignments across the country and even the world, I found myself with a lot of downtime. So I went, and still go, to racetracks — at last count, more than ninety in seven countries. They range from a bush track in Rayne, Louisiana, where Cajun farmers race quarter horses and Thoroughbreds for as little as $300, to Royal Ascot, Queen Elizabeth II's track not too far from Windsor Castle in the English countryside. There's the challenge of puzzling over a horse's past performances and deciding if this is his day to win. There is the camaraderie and cockeyed optimism of horseplayers chasing a score. Best of all are the horses — lovely creatures that take my breath away when their strides stretch out effortlessly with their feet barely touching the ground.

Long before I wrote about race horses, I owned them, which helped me appreciate the great costs, great responsibility, and great thrill that come with being part of the sport. Horses are athletes, spectacular ones, and depend on their grooms, trainers, and owners to do right by them. Sometimes that is easier said than done and, as a result, a great deal of my work has focused on what is wrong with what can be a beautiful sport.

Over the past two decades covering horse racing, however, I have never stopped wanting to see a great horse up close, a Triple Crown champion. On seven previous occasions, I have spent a Saturday afternoon in June at Belmont Park hoping that by day's end I would be writing the first draft of history (as journalism is called) about America's twelfth Triple Crown champion. I was heartbroken the first couple of times but eventually learned to manage my expectations.

If I thought the quest for a Triple Crown was futile, what could casual sports fans have possibly thought after thirty-seven years without the sweep successfully competed?

We found out on June 6, 2015, when Victor Espinoza and American Pharoah hit the stretch of that grand old racetrack on Long Island in total command of the Belmont Stakes. Words really cannot summarize the sheer joy and the volume of the noise in which the duo were greeted. It was soul quaking. I've been to Olympics and Super Bowls, World Series and NCAA championships and every kind of sporting event in between, but never have I experienced this kind of communal celebration.

Every single person in attendance wanted the same thing. We wanted American Pharoah to win, to achieve something most thought impossible. We wanted to be able to say that we were there when a great horse made history.

He did, and we can.

CHAPTER ONE:
A BRIEF ENCOUNTER

March 3, 2011

It took them a while to get Littleprincess-emma ready for her date. She was bathed first and then her tail was wrapped in gauze to keep it out of the way. A leather apron, or bite shield, was hung on her neck to protect her from the nibbles and rough nuzzles of her soon-to-be lover. A pair of booties, filled with down and pads, was slipped on her back hooves to soften any kicks aimed at her companion. The moment a mare and stallion meet in the breeding shed to do what comes natural to them is often as violent as it is brief.

On the morning of March 3, 2011, the lucky stud was a horse named Pioneerof the Nile, who not long ago was a talented enough racehorse to win five of his ten starts and earn more than $1.6 million in purses. In fact, he was good enough two springs before to place second in the 135th running of the Kentucky Derby — a result that both teased and tormented his owner, Ahmed Zayat. While Pioneerof the Nile's loss by a length suggested he had the pedigree to become a blue chip, moneymaking stallion, a loss is still a loss and this one was especially painful because it kept Zayat out of the winner's circle of America's greatest race.

For now, however, Pioneerof the Nile was a cheap date, commanding only $15,000 per breeding, and his calendar was hardly full. This was only his second season in the breeding shed, and his offspring were two years away from hitting the racetrack and demonstrating whether they were runners or not.

Littleprincessemma was one of ninety-one mares he was covering this season, or about a third of what the nation's leading sire, Distorted Humor, was doing at WinStar Farm over in Woodford County. In fact, for Zayat, it was pretty much a free date. He owned Littleprincessemma, whom he named for his youngest daughter, Emma. He had bred and raced Pioneerof the Nile before selling 30 percent of his stallion rights to the Vinery, one of the hundreds of horse farms here in the Bluegrass state that had earned Kentucky its reputation as the

Bethlehem of the American Thoroughbred.

The Egyptian-born industrialist had made his fortune selling beer and wine to Muslims and was rapidly investing it here in the horse business. He had recently settled a bitter, costly, and public bankruptcy fight with Fifth Third Bank of Cincinnati, which said he had defaulted on $34 million of loans they made to his racing business, Zayat Stables.

He needed cash and was paring down a stable that at one time numbered 250 horses. He had sold the Vinery its 30 percent share of Pioneerof the Nile for $1.3 million, and in 2010, he sold a more significant percentage of breeding rights of a colt named Eskendereya to Stonestreet Farms for more than $7 million. Shares in stallions were valuable commodities: Pioneerof the Nile may have commanded only $15,000 now per mating but that number could grow exponentially if his offspring started to consistently win big races.

Zayat was hardly alone feeling the squeeze in the horse business. The 2008 recession sent the Thoroughbred industry, along with everything else, into a free fall. Some of the same dynamics that brought down subprime mortgages had gutted the horse business: no-money-down lending and a breeding and sales market based on the assumption of ever-rising prices.

It meant that too many horses were bred, too much money was borrowed to breed them, and now too many people were trying to sell a surplus of horses to people who didn't want them. In short, horsemen (as Thoroughbred breeders and owners fancy themselves) had bet their farms and were losing them.

Now there were more than 300 farms for sale, a 50 percent increase over the previous year, in the four counties that make up horse country in Kentucky: Fayette, Woodford, Bourbon, and Scott.

The banks had bailed out on the industry as well: loans to breed and buy horses had dropped 60 percent to about $400 million from an estimated $1 billion in 2007. The tight credit took its toll — the number of mares bred nationally, like Littleprincessemma, had dropped 35 percent, and the number of stallions standing stud, like Pioneerof the Nile, had fallen by nearly 40 percent.

Horseplayers, the gamblers who are the lifeblood of the sport, were keeping their money in their pockets, too. The North American handle, or amount bet on races, was $11.1 billion, down 30 percent from the $15.4 billion wagered in 2007.

These were scary times, but it mattered little on the March morning Pioneerof the Nile sauntered into the breeding shed at the Vinery for his appointment with Littleprincessemma.

It was spring in the Bluegrass — the most hopeful time of the year for breeders and owners. It was the time when a brief, often expensive, interlude between a mare and a stallion might create a home-run horse. The kind of foal that, four springs from now, might run away with the Kentucky Derby, prevail in the Preakness Stakes, and capture the Belmont Stakes to sweep the three classic races that make up American horse racing's Triple Crown.

Only eleven horses had previously managed to capture Thoroughbred racing's Holy Grail and the last, Affirmed, did so more than three decades ago in 1978. Why so few?

Theories abound but the bottom line is that it takes an exceptional horse and a fair amount of good fortune to navigate a twenty-horse field throughout the mile-and-a-quarter Kentucky Derby course, a distance few are bred for.

In addition, the Derby winner must travel to Baltimore after the toughest race of his life and with only two weeks' rest and defeat another dozen or so — many of them fresh challengers — in the Preakness Stakes, a mile-and-three-sixteenths race.

Finally, three weeks later in New York, the Derby and Preakness champ must pass the "Test of the Champion," as the Belmont Stakes is known, a grueling mile-and-a-half marathon against a field of fresh, accomplished horses — the top finishers from the Derby who have had five weeks of rest as well as a new cast of accomplished rivals that haven't been chewed up on the road to the Triple Crown.

In short, three cities, three tracks, three of the longest distances that horses will ever run are compressed into a five-week schedule.

This pursuit of history begins with each breeding season in barns like this one, with their polished mahogany stalls and shiny brass fittings and rubberized floors. Even if Zayat, or the multitudes of dreamers like him, were unable to conjure up visions of a historic horse, a fast, pedigreed one that was able to pass that trait on to babies would do just fine.

Better perhaps than breeding Triple Crown champs like Secretariat, Seattle Slew, and Affirmed was coming up with the next Storm Cat. He had been more than a home-run horse. He'd been a jackpot horse.

Storm Cat was modestly talented on the racetrack but a legend in the breeding shed. In his peak breeding years, he commanded $500,000 per mating — an act that he performed up to 150 times or more a year.

On the racetrack, he won four of his eight starts, including the Young America Stakes, a Grade 1 or top-rated race. However, in the 1985 Breeders' Cup Juvenile championship, Storm Cat suffered a chipped knee, finishing second to a rival named Tasso. He was never the same on the racetrack and was retired after two more races.

Those are not the results he is remembered by, though. Instead, Storm Cat is revered for his million-dollar pedigree, which continued to throw off hundreds of millions in cash long after he was retired from stallion duties in 2008 at age twenty-five.

Storm Cat came from rich blood. His grandfather, the Canadian-bred champion Northern Dancer, had earned $1 million per mating from 1984 through 1987, and his mother, Terlingua, was a daughter of Secretariat. Over more than twenty years, Storm Cat passed on that class and speed, siring 8 champions and 801 winners, 180 of them worldwide stakes winners that altogether earned more than $128 million in purses.

What he did for the breeding business was even more impressive. Storm Cat's offspring strode through the sales rings like royalty, and rich people lost their heads and often their money. In 2004, a Storm Colt son sold for $8 million; the following year, another one sold for $9.7 million.

In 2009, when Storm Cat's last crop went through the auction ring at the prestigious Keeneland September Yearling Sale in Lexington, Kentucky, the recession was in full bloom, but one of his colts was the sales topper, at $2.05 million.

This colt did not pan out in the breeding shed, but plenty more did — nearly a dozen are now stallions, including one of the world's leading sires, Giant's Causeway, who was already flirting with a $100,000 stud fee.

It was this search for your very own equine ATM machine that was responsible for 100,000 jobs — at racetracks, tack shops, vet hospitals, sales companies, and so on — and more than $4 billion in economic impact that made the Bluegrass the cornerstone of Kentucky's $8.8 billion tourism trade.

Horse racing earned its appellation as the Sport of Kings in Europe, but it *is* America's oldest sport and one that initially appealed to a nation struggling for freedom and independence, a nation that was painfully aware of how hard both were to achieve.

It is a pastime based on competition — my horse is faster than yours. Even better, it invited gambling, another quintessential American pursuit. Like it or not, horse racing is part of the American character. It predates baseball and is the only sport that was ever conducted out of the White House. In the early 1800s, President Andrew Jackson ran a stable from there.

Here in the Bluegrass, any decline the sport was suffering was ignored while the business of building a faster racehorse was left mostly to an international cast of millionaires and billionaires rather than old line royalty. For example:

- Vinery Farms belonged to Tom Simon, a former corporate law attorney in Germany, who also owned part of a Thoroughbred operation in Australia.
- Graham and Antony Beck, South African winemakers, operated Gainesway.
- Juddmonte Farms belonged to mem-

21

bers of the royal family of Saudi Arabia while Darley America was owned by Sheikh Mohammed bin Rashid al-Maktoum, the ruler of Dubai.

- Ashford Stud was the American arm of Coolmore, the Irish-based breeding and racing operation headed by a pair of Irish horsemen and an English gambler and former bookmaker.
- Lane's End Farm was the domain of William S. Farish, a Texas oilman who was appointed by President George W. Bush as the United States ambassador to the Court of St. James.
- WinStar Farm was the vision of Kenny Troutt, the founder of Excel Communications, a Texas-based telecommunications company that used multi-level marketing to pile up a fortune in long-distance phone service.

For centuries, horsemen have leaned on an axiom to characterize a process that is more art than science and is largely dependent on good fortune:

"Breed the best to the best and hope for the best."

It is the heart and soul of the Thoroughbred business: Breeders try to engineer how far and how fast future horses will run by deciphering the bloodlines of generations past. They attempt to create a blue-chip stock that someone wants to own. They know it is as volatile as an Internet start-up and as unpredictable as Hollywood's box office.

Still, they try.

Zayat was among the newest members of this tribe of alchemists. He was not in the breeding shed for Littleprincessemma's assignation with Pioneerof the Nile, but he had more than a hand in what was about to happen.

Besides the fact that he owned both of them, Zayat knew the bloodlines each possessed were potentially blockbuster and would mean the future foal would have as many as eight classic winners in the first five generations of his or her ancestry.

The sire of Pioneerof the Nile, Empire Maker, won the 2003 Belmont Stakes and was successfully passing this stamina down to his offspring as a stallion. Empire Maker's father, Unbridled, captured the 1990 Kentucky Derby and was second in that year's Preakness. He went on to sire a winner of each Triple Crown race. Littleprincessemma's pedigree boasts the 1973 Triple Crown champion, the great Secretariat, along with Northern Dancer, the 1964

Derby and Preakness champ who is considered one of the greatest sires of the twentieth century.

Finally, who was Littleprincessemma's granddaddy? None other than Storm Cat.

In 2007, Zayat paid $250,000 for her as a yearling, but Littleprincessemma's racing career was over after only two races. Her regal bloodlines, however, made her ripe for a career as a broodmare. She was unable to produce a foal in her first breeding, but she delivered one a little over a month ago from another Zayat stallion named Maimonides.

Now Littleprincessemma was dressed and primed to create her second foal. A teaser stallion named Red in an adjacent stall had squealed, whinnied, and in a full throat made it clear to her that she was desirable. The Vinery employed two teasers — the other was named Ralph — for what was a depressing but essential job. They aroused the mare to insure that she was ready to receive a stallion. After all, these were 1,200-pound animals worth millions of dollars and a swift, safe, and successful mating was vital.

Littleprincessemma was built like a sprinter with muscle twined around sturdy bones and a big bottom. She was a chestnut with a blaze on her face and one white sock and one white stocking on her hind legs.

Littleprincessemma raised her tail, squatted, and urinated, a sign that she was ready. There was no relief for Red. His job was done, so he was led out of the barn. Red traded duties with Ralph so neither teaser got terminally discouraged.

In came Pioneerof the Nile. He was a big, rangy horse with a Clint Eastwood walk, athletic but not in a hurry. He already had established himself as something of a prima donna. He preferred peppermints to carrots. He was also sometimes reticent and required a whiff of pheromones from a cup of thawed urine from a mare to get himself interested. Pioneerof the Nile refused to be rushed. He needed some foreplay and did not mind rocking back on his hind legs once, twice, as many as four times before securing his mount and consummating the relationship.

The Vinery's most successful stallion, on the other hand, lived up to his name — More Than Ready — and earned $60,000 a pop to make quick work of the mares. He serviced as many as 150 mares a year. In fact, he was so professional that he was sent to Australia each summer to create even more progeny to race in the Southern Hemisphere.

The cameras were now rolling. With this much money at stake, every moment of Littleprincessemma and Pioneerof the Nile's conjugal visit was videotaped to demonstrate that best practices and safety were observed to preempt any insurance claims.

In the wild, with no one looking, more than 2,000 pounds of horseflesh collide routinely as new life is made. Here the ballet between Littleprincessemma and Pioneerof the Nile was choreographed by a quartet of handlers suited up in helmets and flak jackets and offering whispers of encouragement to an excited stallion and his compliant mare.

There were no sharp corners in sight, the walls were padded thick, and the floor was made of playground rubber. Littleprincessemma leaned against a foam-wrapped chest board so she wouldn't skitter forward. She waited patiently as Pioneerof the Nile snorted and bellowed and pounded out a muted rhythm with his false starts.

Finally, he reared back on his two hind legs and landed not so gently on Littleprincessemma's backside. He did not really need any further help, but the "entering man," as the gentleman charged with ensuring a stallion hits his bull's-eye is known, helped Pioneerof the Nile hit the target.

Talk about a dirty job. He held a breeding roll — a sort of padded baton. It was soft, thick, and wrapped in plastic. He wedged it between Littleprincessemma and Pioneerof the Nile to his colleague on the other side. The stallion bucked and roared. The mare staggered and whinnied. The noise was tornado volume but car crash brief.

The big horse was done.

The entering man whisked a cup beneath Pioneerof the Nile and caught some semen. He handed it off to the stallion manager, who took it to a lab on the other side of a glass window and put it under a high-powered microscope. He estimated the quantity and motility of the sperm and added it to his detailed notes of Littleprincessemma and Pioneerof the Nile's appointment.

She was led out.

He strutted around the ring before being taken back to his paddock. There was another mare waiting for another stud here and at every other breeding farm in the Bluegrass.

This was breeding season in the Bluegrass, after all, which, fittingly, begins around Valentine's Day of each year.

It would be eleven months before Zayat

would know if this coupling that looked so good on paper resulted in a healthy foal. It would take two more years after that to get this horse to the racetrack.

There would be a championship season, a near career-ending injury, and enough twists and turns from the good, the bad, and the ugly sides of horse racing to put the words *Triple Crown* on the tip of the tongues of sports fans, racing fans, and even the general public.

For five glorious weeks America's oldest sport would return to the center of the nation's consciousness.

What no one suspected was that a brief encounter in the Bluegrass on a March morning in 2011 would give us a horse for the ages.

CHAPTER TWO:
GROUNDHOG DAY

February 2, 2012

It was about 11:00 p.m. on February 2, 2012, when Dr. Tom VanMeter got the call from his farm manager telling him Little-princessemma's water had broken and she was ready to drop her baby. Dr. VanMeter pulled his boots on and made his way to the foaling shed, or Stork Barn as he liked to call it, on top of the hill of his Stockplace Farm. He had 800 acres here just ten miles down the road from another of Kentucky's most revered landmarks, Rupp Arena, which was named for legendary basketball coach Adolph Rupp and was the home of the Kentucky Wildcats. Fast horses, bourbon, and the Big Blue were more than obsessions in the Commonwealth of Kentucky; they were woven into the fabric of every born-and-bred Kentuckian who believed himself a true hardboot. VanMeter believed he was a hardboot by bloodlines as

29

well. He was a seventh-generation Kentuckian whose family had done all sorts of ranching, raised cattle, grew cotton, and bred horses. Back in 1901, a distant cousin, Frank VanMeter, owned and trained that year's Kentucky Derby winner, His Eminence.

With a full brush of dark hair, a trim build, and a barrel chest, VanMeter was a polished-looking Bluegrass gentry almost. He was a veterinarian primarily but boarded mares on his farm and dabbled in breeding and selling Thoroughbreds. In fact, that is how he met Littleprincessemma's owner, Ahmed Zayat — or Mr. Z as VanMeter called him. He had sold him a horse, one that Zayat thought he outfoxed the veterinarian on, getting him for a mere $150,000. He named the colt after VanMeter's sales company at the time, Eaton's Gift. Mr. Z often needled him about the bargain colt, especially after the colt won a couple of Grade 1 sprint races as a three-year-old. However, VanMeter knew better than most that no one gets one over on someone else in the horse business for long. In 2006, when Zayat introduced himself as a major player in horse racing with the $4.6 million purchase of a colt at the Keeneland September Sale, VanMeter raised an eyebrow and

30

thought what every other horse trader did: "He's jumped in with some money and made a big splash." By 2008, Zayat Stables had won nearly $6.9 million, leading all American Thoroughbred owners in earnings, and the next year, he matched that total, highlighted by Pioneerof the Nile's second-place finish in the Derby. He also started throwing big money around at auctions — spending $24.5 million on seventy-seven horses in 2009. That's when Van-Meter (and everyone else in the business) raised the other eyebrow.

"We've seen these guys come and go," said VanMeter.

Yes, they had. There is no better adage than "the best way to become a millionaire in the horse business is to start as a billionaire." NFL franchise owners Eugene Klein (San Diego Chargers) and Robert McNair (Houston Texans), software billionaire Satish Sanan, entertainers like rapper MC Hammer, and scores of Wall Street tycoons had dropped fortunes in the sport before abandoning it altogether with a lot less in their coffers. Now all VanMeter and everyone else in the business had to do was follow the newspaper headlines or look in his "Past Due" file to set an over/under line on when Zayat was going to leave the business for good.

All that winning and buying was costly. While Zayat Stables was borrowing money and bringing home trophies, it was also losing more than $52 million, according to bankruptcy records, all while Zayat was paying himself a salary of $650,000 and withdrawing $2 million from stable accounts. Beyond the $34-plus million due Fifth Third Bank, his creditors' list read like a who's who of the Thoroughbred industry — he owed $3 million to Keeneland, the auction company; hundreds of thousands to breeding farms owned by the ruler of Dubai, Sheikh Mohammed bin Rashid al-Maktoum, and Canadian industrialist Frank Stronach; and tens of thousands to trainers, veterinarians, and even horse transportation vendors. Zayat owed VanMeter and Stockplace nearly $30,000 and Eaton Sales another $50,000.

VanMeter knew Mr. Z was a slow payer, which was preferable to a no-payer, of which there were plenty scattered across the Bluegrass. This was a handshake rather than contract business and sometimes all there was to cling to was a twisted and unwarranted trust that a horseman's better angels would make him honor a deal. Sure, Mr. Z was going to pay him when he got a little ahead. Besides, VanMeter liked Mr. Z's company, his childlike exuberance that turned excursions to the racetrack into life-and-death passion plays when the emotive Egyptian touted his betting selections like they had been passed down from on high and then turned every stretch run into a struggle for his soul. Mr. Z cackled and screamed. He worked up a sweat running to the betting windows. Victories were celebrated with moist bear hugs and tough beats with wails of grief.

"He's a very passionate guy, and so emotional," said VanMeter.

Now it was his duty — no, his oath — to forget about Littleprincessemma's complicated owner and focus on getting the mare's baby safely out of her uterus and onto this earth. It was Groundhog Day, and that morning Punxsutawney Phil had awoken to see his shadow, signaling that six more weeks of winter were in store. It was a mild night in the Bluegrass in what so far had been a warm and wet winter. VanMeter made the short walk to his farm's "maternity ward." About 90 percent of all foals were born at night, between 11:00 p.m. and 3:00 a.m. mostly, a statistical anomaly attributed to Mother Nature. Long before there were breeding farms, mares dropped their foals when predators were asleep. It gave them time to get them to their feet, nurse them, and have them ready to run like hell if necessary.

VanMeter knew that horses did not need his help to bring new life to earth, but there was so much money at stake that breeders felt obliged to have eyes on their investments around the clock. Mostly, however, VanMeter couldn't beat back the flutter in his heart when the foals hit the ground.

"It's like the heavens open up and deliver a little piece of magic," he said. "It's the best part of what I do."

He had about forty mares in the fields, and it was still early in the foaling season. He had been down to the Stork Barn for two previous births, but the pace was about to pick up. It took somewhere between 343 and 365 days for a foal to gestate in the womb. Some of the mares were beginning to wax, their teats producing a white crystal substance that was seemingly weaved from fine salt. Overnight, a yellow teardrop often forms at the tip of the teat, stopping it from leaking.

Earlier in the day, VanMeter noticed Littleprincessemma's teardrops were turning white, indicating she was coming to the end. He had poked his finger into her tail muscles and felt the squishy, jelly-like pillow that signaled her vulva was lengthening. VanMeter was fond of the mare. She was a striking chestnut with the presence of a girl who knew that she was more than just pretty. She was a confident sort. He didn't anticipate any problem, as this was her third go round in the foaling barn and she had been walking in circles for the last two hours as the contractions began. Except for the sweat glistening on her coat, she appeared poised and oblivious to the convulsions going on inside her. VanMeter had heard mares groan and bite walls to express the excruciating pain that can accompany delivering big-shouldered foals.

Now Littleprincessemma was lying on her side in stall 15 — in the center of the barn. No one had to help her get there. As soon as the placenta bubbled with its thick goo, followed by a small hoof, Littleprincessemma folded herself into the hay like a queen taking her throne. In an instant, the second hoof poked through. Mother Nature's hand at work again, making the foal aerodynamic to scoot through the opening. A small, wet nose shot through and gulped for its first breath. At 11:15 p.m., the foal squirted out as if hurtling down a water slide. He was wriggling there, slippery as a seal. VanMeter toweled the baby off himself.

It was a colt, a sturdy one.

No drama — just a nice, good-sized, and strong horse, he thought.

Littleprincessemma gave her baby a lick, then another. It didn't take long for him to find his legs, scaffolding up at first unsteadily and then standing atop the hay like he had been staked there. He was quick to take to his mama's nursing as well, feeding greedily. There was no way of telling whether he'd be a great racehorse, but VanMeter knew he'd be able to run like hell in the morning if it was necessary.

The odds were very strong that somewhere in a pasture here in the Bluegrass was the future winner of the 2015 Kentucky Derby. In the 138 prior runnings of America's signature race, Kentucky-bred Thoroughbreds had already captured 105 of them. The odds were even more prohibitive that the winner three years from now was going to be a colt, as the boys have won all but three Derbies. The three fillies that managed to actually win the battle of the sexes did it long ago: Regret in 1915, Genuine Risk in 1980, and Winning Colors in 1988.

There have been all sorts of theories and folklore offered about why the Commonwealth of Kentucky is the cradle of fast

Thoroughbreds. There's the right place, right time argument — that rich New Yorkers, Virginians, and Marylanders had no choice but to come south in the late 1800s and early 1900s as their home states were cracking down on gambling and deemed betting on a horse race to be one of society's great corrupters. It didn't hurt that Colonel Matt Winn's race, the Kentucky Derby, was gaining more notoriety every year since being run at Churchill Downs in Louisville, Kentucky, beginning in 1875. Even better, Winn had found a way to cut the bookmakers out completely by offering pari-mutuel betting, which eliminated fixed-odds betting. By putting all bets in a pool and calculating winning payoffs by the total amount, the racetrack could take a commission, which helped fund the purses of races and paid local and state taxes.

Horses, of course, were here long before the well heeled from the Northeast decided they needed big farms to breed their Thoroughbreds and a safe innovative way to bet on them. The story goes that soon after Daniel Boone settled in Kentucky, he declared that "every man needs a wife, a horse, and a gun," which perhaps is the basis for a Bluegrass proverb that a "good horse never stumbles and a good wife never grumbles." It was Boone who introduced a bill to improve the breed of horses at the territories' first legislative assembly in 1775. The Virginians who followed Boone here were experienced breeders, wealthy landowners and among America's first true horse people. They imported from England descendants of the Darley Arabian, the Godolphin Arabian, and Byerly Turk stallions from which all Thoroughbreds descend. By 1800, in fact, 92 percent of Kentuckians owned a horse, and the average owner had 3.2 horses, according to tax rolls.

Then there was the bluegrass itself with its thin blades whose origins trace back to the Black Sea and are woven deep into the sod by a roots system that regenerates itself and paints a vivid tapestry on the land. In the spring, blue-purplish buds rolled over it like a royal carpet and gave Kentucky's horse country a postcard quality that linked its past to the present. "When God made the picturesque valleys of Southwest Virginia, He was just practicing for the Bluegrass country," a turn-of-the-century circuit judge once wrote. It was the limestone beneath the ground, however — in places 25,000 feet thick — that was most mythologized by the hardboots. It meant iceberg concentrations of calcium and phosphorous oozing vitamins and minerals, transforming 120-pound foals into 600-pound yearlings and, finally, half-ton racehorses with steel in their bones and wings on their feet.

Mostly Kentucky's success as an incubator for these stunning, ethereal creatures was because of people like Frances Relihan. She was one of the thousands who believed in her soul that Thoroughbred racing was truly the sport of kings. They were the unseen hands, shovels, and rakes that were whirling eighteen hours a day, seven days a week, foaling horses, helping them wean from their mamas, feeling their legs and putting thermometers in their bottoms. They fed them, treated them, cared for and loved them. You rarely saw them in the winner's circle after a race. They knew little about Cristal champagne, private jets, or the Mercedes-Maybach. The owners of the horses they cared for, who knew such luxuries, barely knew the names of the people entrusted with their assets. It was not an occupation for a narcissist, an action junkie, or even an extrovert. Your days creeped along and you were mostly alone as you relied on a skill set that required a bit of mechanical know-how (tractors break down) and a lot of grit (the manure doesn't sweep itself up). You also had to be half horse — how else would you know a slight hip roll on a weanling might mean a bruise on a back foot, or a whisper of a rattle in the chest might be the beginning strains of a respiratory infection?

As she patrolled the grounds of the Vinery, Frances Relihan wore the uniform of her tribe — rubber muck boots, a fleece zipped up to the neck, and a barn jacket. She eyed the mares for any sign of disturbances, a rheumy eye, swishing tail, and then let her gaze fall hard on the babies that followed them. She smiled at the playful ones that zigzagged in the mares' wake, chasing each other like kids do as they walk home from school. She watched more intently the docile babies that lumbered in their mothers' shadows. What could she do to relieve their stress?

This was all Frances Relihan ever wanted to do when she was a little girl growing up in Listowel, Ireland, a rustic hamlet along the River Feale in County Kerry. It proudly wore its title as the "Literary Capital of Ireland" and annually celebrated the achievements of its poets, playwrights, and writers such as Bryan MacMahon, Brendan Kennelly, and John B. Keane with Ireland's largest literary festival. Keane, one of its most famous denizens, had returned the favor in a poem:

> Beautiful Listowel, serenaded night and day
>   by the gentle waters of the River Feale,
> Listowel where it is easier to write than not
>   to write,
> Where first love never dies, and the tall
>   streets hide the loveliness,
> The heartbreak and the moods, great and
>   small,
> Of all the gentle souls of a great and good
>   community.
> Sweet, incomparable hometown that
>   shaped and made me.

It was another Listowel institution, however, that had shaped and made Frances Relihan: the Listowel Races, a weeklong gathering whose origins trace back to the 1800s, when it was initially held nine miles north of her village in Ballyeigh, Ballybunion. It started as a rough-and-tumble affair, featuring a closing day faction fight between clans where hundreds, sometimes thousands, engaged in a mass brawl. A death, or two, or a dozen were guaranteed and the maimings were de rigueur as the combatants brandished stones, knuckle dusters, and homemade pistols all in the name of instilling courage and a love for a good fight into the next generation. It wasn't until the festival moved to Listowel in 1858 that it became a kinder, gentler celebration with the horse races as its centerpiece. What once was a destination for farmers and small towners to blow off steam and lose some money had transformed over the generations into a low-key but chic and highly anticipated week of quality racing.

As a little girl, Frances could not wait for the start of the harvest races over at "the Island," as the locals called it, because you could cross a bridge over the River Feale to where the mile-and-a-quarter course was laid out like magic carpet on undulating farmland. The races were reason enough for school to shut down and for Frances to trade the sport horses on her family's dairy farm for the magical athletes that — for a week per year — haunted the 147 stalls, like old souls in a familiar resting place. They turned Frances's tiny corner of Ireland into Brigadoon. In the mornings, hundreds of horses sprang to life, crossing the grounds, their hooves beating out a rhythm on the soft grass and sounding like a symphony of sleepy heads gratefully hitting their pillows one after another. Steam poured from the necks of horses bobbing and ducking during their baths as bubbles wafted from their lips as their "lads" lovingly soaped and bathed them.

In the afternoons as the races neared, the empty spaces were filled in with men in smart suits and women sporting hats, one more fanciful than the next. The bookies dotted the apron atop makeshift stairs, a smudged chalkboard getting erased and redrawn with the latest odds for each horse in the upcoming field. It was a carnival rolled into a cathedral with all awaiting an act of God handed down from on high, and that's what Frances witnessed as the horses galloped around the track, disappearing into unseen valleys and then emerging to fly into the air and extend their front legs like Superman and clear impossibly high hurdles. This is what Frances wanted to do with her life — she wanted to help horses like those before her reach levels of full flight that gave horse lovers like herself goose bumps.

That is exactly what she had done. She worked in whatever yard would have her as she pursued a degree in Equine Science at the University of Limerick. She then took a turn in horse sales at Mellon Stud, learning to turn out yearling horses into their Sunday best to attract a big price from bidders at sales held by Goffs, Ireland's preeminent auction house since 1866. Her next stop was Newmarket, Suffolk, sixty-five miles north of London and widely regarded as the Bethlehem of Thoroughbred racing as well its global center. Horses have lined up against each other there since 1174, and it was King James I (who reigned from 1603–1625) who built a palace there and established racing as a royal pastime that continues to this day. In 1967, Queen Elizabeth II opened a breeding center called the National Stud and remains a frequent visitor to watch her horses train. The people-to-horse ratio is 5 to 1, as the town has a population of 15,000, largely to take care of the 3,000 racehorses.

The Aga Khan, the rulers of Dubai, and the princes of Saudi Arabia are among the top-end breeders and owners who ready their top-flight horses for the European races in England, Ireland, France, Germany, and Italy. It was among the gallops and training trails here that Frances watched Sir Michael Stoute, John Gosden, and Saeed bin Suroor care for and nurture some of the most expensive horses in the world. It was like watching Shakespeare direct one of his plays at Stratford-upon-Avon.

Still Frances wanted to learn more. So it

was off to the Bluegrass state, where scores of "lads" (they were predominately men) from the European circuits before her had gone and found a home. Frances did, too.

"One year turned into five years, and then ten," she said with a lilting brogue.

Now it was fifteen years, most of them here at the Vinery as first the farm manager before becoming the farm's assistant general manager. Frances, thirty-six, was pretty and blond — there was nothing about her that suggested "farm" or "manager." However, when you saw her dirty-faced, toting a medical box or her elbows deep into a mare's abdomen boots pressing into her rump as she helped a foal along, there was no mistaking the fact that she was to the horse farm born. She was totally in charge of the more than 400 acres of rolling hills, veined with limestone and dark plank fences. With its plantation-style big house, spired barns, and groaning weathervanes, it was not lost on Frances that she had landed in a far different world from her humble Listowel. Those limestone fences? They were laid centuries ago by stonemasons from her native country and are recognized as work of masters now, but back then Irish were a rung below the black slaves — "white niggers" the Kentucky colonels called them

— and had to settle for the backbreaking work of laborers.

Not anymore. A young Irish horsewoman was in command of every inch of bluegrass here and was valued, even revered, for her dedication and skills bringing racehorses to the track. It was rewarding for Frances to hear Rick Porter, owner of the mare Havre de Grace, the 2011 Horse of the Year, tell people that she was the reason he sent his horses to the Vinery.

"I have never had a trainer not compliment the condition of the horse when they receive it after Frances," he told top horsemen, always bringing a blush to her cheeks.

That was not why Frances climbed out of bed at three in the morning to check on a baby or sleep alongside a mare all night. She was rewarded when her hands climbed the legs of a yearling checking for heat and not finding any or having her neck unexpectedly nuzzled while rubbing a belly warm. It was the whinny of a hungry mare at feeding time or the barely audible crunch of hay on a late night. She loved those old stone walls too, and would sit atop them and watch the fresh fillies and colts dart in and out of the bluegrass as if trying to figure out what exactly to do with those vibrating legs.

Frances knew she had been blessed as well to have a hand — no, two hands and a bursting heart — in developing wonderful racehorses like Havre de Grace and the gorgeous gray mare Joyful Victory, a Grade 1 winner who raced at ten different tracks. There was the Arkansas Derby winner Archarcharch and the Louisiana Derby champ Friesen Fire. Even better, Frances knew there was no place better in horse racing than being at the center of the industry where hope springs eternal and where horses were simply horses and their owners' dreams were a long way from being dashed. Each and every one of the approximately 23,500 colts and fillies born in 2012 was a potential Kentucky Derby or Kentucky Oaks winner, a future Horse of the Year, or, God willing, a Triple Crown champion.

The secret was no secret at all but an edict for Frances and her ilk: You treated each and every horse like the gifts that they are and the champs they could become.

In fact, she had a good feeling now about a colt in Barn 9 that liked to spend his summer days in the field on the corner of Spurr Road and Yarnallton Pike. He had arrived in June from Tom VanMeter's Stockplace Farm to begin his initial lessons on becoming a racehorse and had gravitated to what was the playground for some of the farm's most promising athletes.

The previous summer it was where a Tapit colt grazed and chased a Pioneerof the Nile colt around. Tapit was an extraordinarily bred horse and already among the most successful sires in the world. He stood at Gainesway Farm for $125,000 and had a handful of classy babies at the Vinery now. The jury was still out on Pioneerof the Nile. Frances was certain, however, that was about to change with this colt out of Littleprincessemma that continued to catch her eye. At first glance, he was exceptional only because he lacked any "chrome," as the white markings on the feet or face are known. He looked like he had been dipped whole in a vat of mahogany paint except for his black mane and tail. She knew his father well. Pioneerof the Nile was a mainstay of the Vinery, and she had seen a good many of his foals. As important as bloodlines are to creating a quality racehorse, Frances believed that, much like people, certain body types work together. She was beginning to see the type of mare that physically worked well with the stallion.

"He is a big, rangy horse with a classic physique. He displays an exceptionally athletic walk to him and covers a lot of ground," she said. "Littleprincessemma is compact, ripped even, and has a powerful hind end with good bone and substance. It is a great physical cross. He is long but strong."

Even as a foal and weanling, Frances saw how easily he moved, his head high, folding and unfolding himself with exquisite balance. His stride had range and scope and he had a lovely sloping shoulder and great body angles. There was nothing out of place on him, especially when he was in flight. The colt shared a field with nine mares and their foals, and when playtime broke out, he looked like a bullet train among steam engines — he was that efficient and aerodynamic. It was the joy he exuded, however, that took Frances's breath away. One evening on her daily run, she spied him all alone darting back and forth. Suddenly, he bucked and spun, bucked and spun, and then got into a full sprint so quickly that it was as if he had been shot from a cannon.

It stopped Frances in her tracks. "Did I just see that?" she asked herself.

As blessed physically as the colt was, his mind was even more impressive. Of all the mares and stallions on the farm, Pioneerof the Nile and Littleprincessemma were among the most even keel. Despite his precoital quirks, Pioneerof the Nile was a gentle giant who enjoyed the company of people. Littleprincessemma was even more of a softie but still managed to become something of a Queen Bee among the broodmares. It was no secret Thoroughbreds were high-strung animals, and it was in the hands of people like Frances on farms like this that get them into a routine so they can take the necessary steps to becoming a professional racehorse. At this stage, it was not much different from raising a baby. They were turned out at night and brought in for the days where they were exercised, bathed, and groomed. Their biorhythms were heeded and the human interaction done on schedule and in small doses. They got their shots and were dewormed. There are sponges and combs pulled over their coats and through their manes. They must be taught how to stand still for a farrier and to hold each foot up to be trimmed. Sometimes it looked like beauty school, but most of the time it was a nursery.

Weaning the foals from their mothers was a critical step in their development and often was fraught with anxiety for both babies and the people like Frances who cared for them. At birth, the foals depend on their mothers for all of their nutrition and the mamas respond by producing thirty pounds of nutrient-rich milk a day for the first two months. Then, feed tubs are introduced filled with sweet feed and vitamin and mineral supplements. At four months of age, a foal will weigh on average 400 to 450 pounds, and it is then they need to be weaned so managed feeding can allow for moderate and steady growth — up to two and a half to three pounds a day — putting them in top condition for weanling and yearling sales. The Littleprincessemma colt was in the middle of the weight range and the program Frances designed for the Vinery let the foals stay a little longer with their mothers.

It wasn't until late June that she started separating the mares, one at time, from their foals. Frances took a mother out every three days or so, watching intently as the baby figured out his mom was gone, but there were still some mares in the field along with all their buddies. Some of them fell to pieces, getting stressed and agitated and finding all kinds of harm: from a nail sticking out of a fence post or twisting an ankle on some uneven terrain. They simply lost their composure and that's when bad things happened. Frances was eager to see how the Littleprincessemma colt handled the separation. On the day she turned him out without his mother, he was confused for a spell but remained coolheaded, then took to playing with his field mates with his usual enthusiasm.

In a few days, Frances was certain this was a special colt after he walked into the barn, cleaned out his feed bucket, and laid down in his stall for a nap.

She had been around too long to project a blanket of roses being draped on him in the winner's circle of Churchill Downs on the first Saturday of May 2015. Frances Relihan did do something she rarely did and placed a phone call to Ahmed Zayat. She didn't know him well.

"I don't do this often," she told him, "but the Littleprincessemma colt has been a standout here and I wish you luck with him. There's something special about him."

CHAPTER THREE:
THE "GET-OUT" HORSE

August 6, 2013

It was fitting that Ahmed Zayat had his true coming out party as one of horse racing's major players in Saratoga Springs, New York, a town that has long made Thoroughbred lovers weak in the knees and has elicited poetry from some of the great sportswriters of our time. Joe H. Palmer, a Lexington-bred former English professor who wrote the nationally syndicated racing column "Views of the Turf" for the *New York Herald Tribune,* wrote that "he was no noted lover of the horse, but of a way of life of which the horse was once, and in a few favored places still is, a symbol — a way of charm, and ease and grace and leisure." The great Red Smith, a Pulitzer Prize winner for the *New York Times,* put the town's hold on New Yorkers more succinctly: "You drive north for about 175 miles, turn left on Union Avenue and go back 100 years." The heart of the town, of course, was the 350-acre Saratoga Race Course, which was veined by white fences and tangled with shade trees that hid barns immaculate enough to look like an equine Ritz-Carlton. From late July through Labor Day, the Spa, as horseplayers called it, was the center of the horse racing universe.

From before dawn until 10:00 a.m., horses stopped traffic on Union Avenue as they clip-clopped back and forth from their barns to their workouts on the racetrack. It was founded in 1863 by John "Old Smoke" Morrissey, a gambler, casino owner, boxing champion, and future U.S. Congressman. It has been devoted to racehorses for more than 150 years and has been the genial host of gamblers since the days of Diamond Jim Brady. It is where the horse Harry Bassett, representing the South, beat Longfellow, representing the North, in the 1872 Saratoga Cup; where Man o' War experienced his lone defeat in twenty-one starts to a horse fittingly named Upset in the 1919 Sanford Stakes; and where 1930 Triple Crown champion Gallant Fox was beaten by a 100-to-1 long shot named Jim Dandy in the Travers Stakes. It is quite simply the Vatican of American horse racing and where the best bred and most expensive horses usually take their baby steps in their two-year-old year on the road to the Triple Crown.

In the summer of 2007, Zayat was in Saratoga with one of those precocious horses and a whale of a tale to tell about how the colt came by his name. Now, the Spa is no stranger to characters, and over its illustrious history it has been visited by all sorts of them from the muck-raking journalist Nellie Bly to the late Augustine Williams, a retired carpenter from nearby Albany and part owner of 2003 Kentucky Derby winner Funny Cide. While Bly wanted to shut down a town that she considered strictly a sinners' city, Gus, as he was known, reveled in its vices and was a fixture in the local watering holes, where he passed out a business card with his photograph and title, "Professional Italian."

Beyond the communion with the horses, Saratoga was the kind of place where your body, soul, and bank account took a beating in the name of a good time.

It's hard to surprise people there, but one morning the sight of Rabbi Israel Rubin leading a group of students from the Maimonides Hebrew Day School in Albany along the backside of the racetrack on their way to Barn 70 drew second, third, and fourth looks. It was an unusual field trip, conceded the rabbi, but he explained that they had come to see a horse that, like his school, was named for Moses Maimonides. Rubin thought long and hard before arranging to take his students to the track. He did not attend horse races or gamble and worried that the expedition might be considered sacrilegious by his colleagues and parents within his community. Ultimately he decided this was an opportunity for a teaching moment about Maimonides, who lived more than 800 years ago and is considered among the greatest Jewish philosophers. He was the chief rabbi of Cairo and the physician to the sultan of Egypt.

"He blended religious study and intellect with worldly manners to heal the sick and guide the healthy," Rubin said. "He was respected and honored by both Jews and Arabs. This is especially relevant now in our life and times."

Zayat had chosen to name the colt that he bought for $4.6 million for exactly that reason. At the time, no one in Thoroughbred circles knew much about Maimonides's owner, not even the colt's trainer, Bob Baffert, other than he was new to the game and spending lots of money. The year before, 2006, Zayat's horses won forty-one races, including a handful of stakes, and he employed a variety of trainers. Baffert passed on his cell phone number and said he believed Zayat had an interesting story to tell. He was in California at the time, and by phone, Zayat explained how he had grown up Muslim in a suburb of Cairo and was waiting for the right colt to name Maimonides.

"He was a very special man who was highly regarded by all people, regardless of faith," he said of the philosopher. "What has happened with September 11, Iraq and what's going on in the region is contrary to the way I grew up. If this horse is going to be a superstar, I want an appropriate name. I want to say something with the tool I have, which is a horse. I want it to be pro-peace and about loving your neighbor."

When Zayat tried to register the name Maimonides with the Jockey Club, however, he discovered that it had been reserved for more than nine years by Earle I. Mack, a New York real estate investor and a former ambassador to Finland. In 1997, Mack, then the chairman of the board for the Benjamin N. Cardozo School of Law at Yeshiva University in New York City, was instrumental in bringing King Juan Carlos I of Spain to New York to accept the school's Democracy Award. Mack had been moved by the king's remarks about how much Spain's culture had lost when the country expelled its Jews in 1492 as part of the Inquisition. The king mentioned Maimonides, who was born in Córdoba, Spain, in 1135 and who, with his family, was forced out of the country while Spain was ruled by Muslims.

"I was just waiting for a horse good enough to deserve the name," Mack said.

Mack had owned and bred horses for more than forty years and knew that Zayat's colt, a son of Vindication, was bred to be special. Each also understood the other's good intentions. Zayat donated $100,000 to Cardozo to commemorate the king's visit there and to promote tolerance. Mack released his claim to the name Maimonides. Now Maimonides, on the strength of an eleven-and-a-half-length victory in his one and only race, was one of the favorites to win the Hopeful Stakes, one of the most important races for two-year-olds.

"He had the right horse and the right motives," Mack said. "We are all after the same thing: to touch people across cultures."

Horse racing is an unpredictable business, and a thoughtfully named horse hardly guarantees future fame and fortune, but this was a nice story, right?

It was until the day it appeared in the *New York Times* and the phone calls and e-mails began pouring in from members of a synagogue in Teaneck, New Jersey, saying that Zayat was, in fact, an observant Orthodox Jew. It was the first time, but no way near the last, that Ahmed Zayat would offer his version of a conflicting story and continue to make headlines in horse racing.

By August 2013, Ahmed Zayat, age fifty-one, was no longer unknown in the world of horse racing, which was not necessarily a good thing. In a sport long populated with outsize characters, he had already become a gargantuan one by combining an old-fashioned lust for betting with a new-age mastery of social media. Zayat is a small man with delicate features and a country club wardrobe that is at odds with a nervous energy that makes him vibrate like a ten-year-old boy confined to a classroom. He made no secret that he bet on horses with both hands — up to $200,000 a week — and craved the adrenaline rush that comes when a six-figure first-place check or wager hung in the balance. Zayat was an exuberant talker and racegoer who bantered with fans on Twitter and held contests for them to name his horses. At the racetrack, the Zayat family moved en masse, more often than not in frenetic fashion. His wife, Joanne, was always on his arm with his four children — Ashley, Justin, Benjamin, and Emma — trailing behind. Theirs was a close family, perhaps because they had spent so much time apart when Ahmed was pursuing his fortune in Egypt. Since entering the business, Zayat had earned a reputation as a combative personality who drove hard bargains and was not beyond withholding payments.

Zayat was loud and often profane. He frequently scaled a range of emotions in a single conversation: from tears to red-faced anger to spewing expletives from a frothing mouth.

"I am Middle Eastern — I have a hot temper," he often offered by way of explanation.

He grew up in Maadi, a suburb of Cairo, Egypt, the son of Alaa Zayat, who taught medicine at Cairo University and was the physician to President Anwar Sadat. The Zayats were a prominent family in Egypt — his grandfather, Ahmed Hassan al-Zayat, was a leading intellectual who founded *Al-Risala,* a well-known literary magazine. His grandfather was a self-made man who studied at Al-Azhar University before taking up legal studies in Cairo and Paris. Before founding *Al-Risala* in 1933, al-Zayat taught Arabic literature in Baghdad as well as the American University in Cairo.

Ahmed Zayat got on his first horse at an upscale riding club near his home and learned to ride show jumpers well enough (he says) to capture two national championships in the under-twelve and under-fourteen divisions. When he was eighteen, Zayat moved first to Boston, then to New York to pursue an undergraduate degree from Yeshiva University and eventually a master's degree in public health administration from Boston University. Until the spring of 2013, Zayat also claimed that he had earned a master's degree from Harvard, a fact that had appeared in his biography on websites for his company and for entities that he has been affiliated with, including the National Thoroughbred Racing Association. When a New Jersey paper reported that Harvard had no record of Zayat, however, his lawyer, Joseph Vann, told them that "unfortunately, early in his career there was misinformation reported about Zayat's education" that was erroneously repeated by other outlets.

Whether Zayat was actually Muslim or Jewish was another complicated facet of his life. Most Jews left Egypt in the 1950s, when its ruler, Gamal Abdel Nasser, made it a less hospitable country to them, but some affluent Jews stayed. Zayat alternately had identified as each, even though he gave amply to Jewish causes and was known as Ephraim in the modern Orthodox neighborhood of West Englewood in Teaneck, New Jersey.

What was not in dispute was that Zayat's horse trading was financed by his proceeds from the sale of Al Ahram Beverages Company, the formerly state-held beer company in Egypt that he had privatized. In 1997, the beer company was one of more than 300 state-owned companies that the government had been hoping to sell as Egypt tried to move toward capitalism. It took his family connections as well as some inventive negotiating and a high-flying stock offering on the London Stock Exchange for Zayat to get control of the company. The government wanted nearly $200 million in exchange for a 75 percent stake in the company because the main plant sat on some of Cairo's most valuable real estate. Zayat proposed that the government keep the land but lease it to him for five years while he built a $50 million state-of-the-art brewery in the desert on the outskirts of Cairo.

It took him eighteen months and twenty-two negotiating sessions, but he got the deal for $70 million, less than a third of the government's asking price.

Then Zayat had to take the idea of selling beer to Muslims to international investors in an effort to raise $70 million. It was not even good beer — dilapidated equipment pumped a foamy brew into dirty green bottles, often along with insects, twigs, and clumps of dirt. Its flagship brand varied from one batch to another, and a common joke was that it could power heavy machinery if there was no diesel fuel available. He lined up a public offering of global depository receipts in London and picked off investors from Europe and the United States.

"Half the people in the government are still asking, 'If he did it, couldn't we have done it?'" said Daniel C. Kurtzer, the American ambassador to Egypt at the time.

Zayat paid his bankers and lawyers $10 million and came away with $25 million in instant profit for himself and a handful of American backers. After all the financial wizardry, Zayat and his backers wound up with a 12 percent stake in the company.

Zayat brought in consultants from Carlsberg, the Danish brewer, and began producing first-rate beer. He hired a director of marketing from PepsiCo who launched blanket television advertising, an army of sales representatives, and a fleet of trucks to provide home delivery — all new tactics here. Within two years, sales revenue jumped 60 percent and profits rose nearly 30 percent, to $26 million. He then came up with the idea to export nonalcoholic beer to Saudi Arabia and other Middle Eastern, African, and Asian countries, particularly places like Nigeria and Indonesia with big Muslim populations.

In 2003, Zayat sold the company to Heineken for $280 million and stayed on until 2004 running it. He no longer needed to work and no longer wanted to. Every weekend for eight years, Zayat flew home to his family in Teaneck to observe the Sabbath and then returned on Sunday to Cairo. He had already missed too many of his children's milestone events.

"I didn't want to live on a plane anymore," he said.

Zayat was not the retiring type. He needed action and the challenge of building something more than he needed money. He remembered a night spent at the Meadowlands Racetrack in East Rutherford, New Jersey, when he attended a birthday party at Pegasus, the trackside restaurant. It was the birthday of Lenny Jelinsky, a financial planner with Shearson Lehman, and among the guests were Lenny's two teenage sons, Michael and Jeff.

"That was the first time ever that I have been to a racetrack," Zayat said. "I knew nothing about horses from the sense of betting, except riding horses as a kid."

He was having fun listening to Lenny and his boys talk horses, getting a thrill as he followed their betting tips with a few dollars of his own.

"The kid had a photographic memory, he told me, and he loved horses," Zayat said of Michael Jelinsky. "He was talking to me about horses."

Lenny Jelinsky thought it would be a good thing if Zayat served as a mentor for his two sons. He did, informally, checking in on them on some of the weekends that he was home.

"I kind of took a liking particularly to Michael," Zayat said of the younger son. "He was a high school star athlete. The kid was a basketball wizard."

Eventually, he heard the Jelinsky brothers had moved to Las Vegas to become professional gamblers and that Michael had taken his gift for breaking down and remembering vital information about horses and become one of the biggest horseplayers in Sin City. So it was only natural for Zayat to consult almost daily with Michael on trainers to use, tracks to run at, and the foundation of building a stable. Mostly, however, the two spoke about gambling.

"We used to call sometimes on a daily basis, talk about the race . . . 'How do you like the field? How do you like the card?' " Zayat recalled. "It's two people who love horse racing just talking about their passion."

By 2008, Zayat Stables had won nearly $6.9 million, leading all American Thoroughbred owners in earnings. The next year, he matched that total, and Pioneerof the Nile finished second in the Kentucky Derby. Zayat was also among the most active buyers at horse auctions, paying $24.5 million for 77 horses in 2009, according to BloodHorse.com. As his stable ballooned to 250 horses, Zayat both wowed and wore on people. He fired Bob Baffert, who had just been inducted into the National Museum of Racing's Hall of Fame in Saratoga Springs. He moved horses from one trainer's barn to another on what appeared to be a whim.

"I'm kind of a compulsive guy," Zayat said. "I can't do things halfway. If I'm in,

I'm totally in. I can't just have two or three horses. Honestly, I'm very competitive in nature like all of these beautiful equine athletes, and I want to be number one."

One morning on the backside of Del Mar, the track Bing Crosby founded near San Diego, Zayat got into a shouting match with its chief executive officer Joe Harper. They had always been on friendly terms. Zayat had a suite at the racetrack and had requested (and received) a souped-up automatic wagering machine that could process more and bigger bets than the standard betting terminal. Now Zayat was upset with the new synthetic surface the track had installed in the hope of making it safer for the horses — instead Zayat thought the synthetic was inconsistent and made his horses slower. Dissatisfied with Harper's response, Zayat took the twenty-five horses that he had on the racetrack and shipped them east to race at Saratoga.

Zayat's zeal to win spilled into public view before the 2009 Preakness Stakes, when he said in a television interview that he was considering helping the owner of that year's Kentucky Derby winner, Mine That Bird, keep the filly Rachel Alexandra out of the race. Pioneerof the Nile had finished second in the Derby, and both owners would improve their chances to win by entering inferior but eligible horses to fill up the Preakness gate. Instead, other owners persuaded them to abandon the plan, and Rachel Alexandra became the first filly to win the second leg of the Triple Crown in eighty-five years.

Zayat's bankruptcy illuminated his prodigious gambling habits and raised questions about some of his associations. It unearthed a previous personal bankruptcy under the name Ephraim David Zayat. It showed that he was paying himself a $650,000 salary and had withdrawn more than $2 million from stable accounts before the bankruptcy filing. In his name, the stable also paid $1.2 million to New Jersey Account Wagering, $350,000 to the Las Vegas Sands, $150,000 to the Palms Casino and Resort, and $100,000 to NHPlay.com (an account wagering platform for horse racing). Zayat said that he filed for Chapter 11 reorganization as a legal defense against a bank that had reneged on its promises to his stable. He was unapologetic about his gambling, too. Zayat said he bet a lot because he could afford it.

"I like gambling on horses," he said. "Everybody has a different wallet size."

Sometimes he claimed to bet to generate

cash flow for the stable.

"It's called hedging," he said.

Among the money he says he was owed was $155,000 he lent to Michael Jelinsky and $450,000 he lent to Jeffrey Jelinsky. In May of 2008, the Jelinsky brothers, his former protégés and sometimes advisors, pleaded guilty to illegal bookmaking in Las Vegas. In the federal plea agreement, the brothers said they had operated an illegal gambling business out of Nevada. Michael Jelinsky was sentenced to fifteen months in prison and Jeffrey to twenty-one months; together they forfeited nearly $5 million seized by authorities.

The Jelinskys, according to the plea agreement, accepted wagers from bettors across the nation. They would then either hold the bets themselves or hedge their risk by placing them through offshore accounts or at the sportsbooks at the Palms and Poker Palace casinos in Las Vegas. Among the money confiscated by federal authorities from casino safe-deposit boxes and banking accounts held by the Jelinskys was $1.5 million found in accounts of the International Racing Group (IRG), a Netherlands Antilles-based betting shop that caters to high rollers. In January 2005, IRG was named in an indictment brought by the

Justice Department. Fourteen people, including three alleged associates of New York organized crime families, pleaded guilty to running an illegal gambling operation.

Zayat maintained that the $605,000 the Jelinskys owed him was not from wagering. He said he had lent money to them because one brother needed the money, as he was going through a divorce and the other was having financial problems.

"I was trying to help them out," Zayat said.

None of it played well in the Bluegrass, especially when farms like Tom VanMeter's Stockplace and Taylor Made Farm were getting slow-paid and then no-paid before finally refusing to do business with Zayat altogether. There were trainers who quit training his horses after being stiffed on their bills — among them the nation's most successful trainer, Todd Pletcher. There were vendors who demanded cash up front from Zayat Stables — the most prominent being Keeneland, the prestigious auction company where anyone and everyone in horse racing had to do some business.

Shortly after a horse Zayat owned finished second by two and three-quarter lengths in the 2011 Kentucky Derby, the colt's trainer, Steve Asmussen, stretched his arms out wide to both sides when he passed Baffert one day.

"I came that close to getting paid," Asmussen said, eliciting a knowing laugh from Baffert, who had taken to calling a Zayat colt in his barn Prayer for Payment rather than his name Prayer for Relief.

Sometimes his gambling brought unintended scrutiny. A suit filed by the owners of Freehold Raceway against the New Jersey Sports and Exposition Authority claimed that Zayat was improperly granted credit in the state's online betting system. New Jersey law prohibits betting more money than is in the account, but court papers showed he was allowed not to pay $286,000 for several months as a courtesy because he was betting $200,000 a week and had put more than $9 million in play through its pools. The court filings also show that one check for $100,000 from Zayat to the sports authority was returned for insufficient funds and that he had stopped payment on another check for the same amount.

"I was a client betting legally and proud to support the pools of New Jersey in the state that I live," he said. "I was getting VIP treatment and I appreciated it."

It was this ability to put lipstick on whatever pig he produced by either denying his transgressions or blaming someone else or shouting someone down or simply choosing to forget the trouble that he had caused people that kept Zayat in the semi-good graces of an industry that sometimes he beat, and more often than not evaded.

Asmussen still trained for him. Baffert welcomed his horses back to his barn. Two summers after Zayat had taken his horses and headed east, Harper ran into Zayat at Del Mar.

"Joe, it never happened, it never happened," Zayat told him.

Zayat could be as charming as he was outrageous and as passionate about the sport as he was cold-blooded in his business practices. For Harper, some of it was explained by Zayat's Egyptian temperament. Harper had lived in Zayat's country as a young man and had many friends from there. His sister had married an Egyptian.

"They have a certain passion," Harper said. "The first day I was in Cairo, we were driving, and there were two men on the street screaming at each other. I asked the Egyptian driver what they were arguing about, and he said, 'They're not fighting. They're just talking.' "

Mostly, putting up with the emotional Egyptian was good for business.

"He's a real treat for a racetrack, because he loves to bet, and he bets pretty good," Harper said. "We want to make him as comfortable as possible."

It also wasn't like the horse business was comprised of a heavenly body of celestial angels. It has long been a rough game where chicanery was not only institutionalized but also celebrated. As far back as 1969, a horse trader in Kentucky with a sense of humor and wishing for secrecy signed a sales ticket in the name of Neil Armstrong, the astronaut who was still in space and returning to earth from his walk on the moon. The bigger the sales like this one, the eighty-seventh annual Fasig-Tipton Saratoga Selected Yearling Sale, the bigger potential for chicanery. The Saratoga Sale was a tony gathering, usually in the first week of August, of horse aficionados and jet setters who over the years have bought iconic horses, from Man o' War to Raise a Native to Danzig. Zayat was here to sell Hip No. 85, the Pioneerof the Nile colt out of Littleprincessemma, and there were plenty of potential buyers drifting barn to barn at the sales grounds eyeballing colts with the same intensity with which jewelers scrutinize diamonds. Instead of cut, color, and clarity, however, they were looking for conformation, balance, and fluid movement. Before them were one-year-old horses that had feasted on the finest feed, taken untold protein supplements, and exercised until their muscles were rippling. Their coats had been combed incessantly, and in some cases rubbed with corn oil to bring out the sheen of a champion.

Buyers needed to worry what nips and tucks these young Thoroughbreds had undergone that were undetectable to the eye of the keenest horsemen.

What were they missing? Was an invasive surgery — perhaps a periosteal elevation — performed to straighten a colt's ankle? How much of a filly's puffed-up chest and powerful hind quarters was steroid-induced rather than genetic? Which yearling might have undergone electrostimulation to make its throat look larger and cleaner? There was a fine line between showmanship and fraud. They clutched catalogues detailing the yearling's pedigree and scoured a repository of X-rays and medical records.

They worked in squadrons with systems of their own devising. Mike Repole, co-founder of Glacéau, which was bought by Coca-Cola for $4.1 billion, employed a three-man team to spend his money. J. J. Crupi, a bear of a man, judged the horse. Eddie Rosen, a lawyer by trade, was the pedigree guy. Dr. Randy Brandon was the veterinarian who made sure that the horse Crupi was enamored with — the one with the regal bloodlines Rosen vouched for — was a healthy yearling worth the hundreds of thousands Repole might spend on him.

Bill Mack and Bob Baker, real estate titans, let their Hall of Fame trainer D. Wayne Lukas pick their horses — he had won four Kentucky Derbies, after all. Others relied on bloodstock agents like John Moynihan, who blends the skills of both a horseman and pedigree sleuth with the polish of a salesman who can persuade billionaires that they-got-the-horse-right here, one certain to be a Kentucky Derby winner and money machine as a stallion. There is no surefire prescription for identifying the next LeBron James from what essentially is a group of seventh graders. Still, they get paid handsomely for trying — usually 5 percent of the purchase price. All were looking for one thing: a horse with an exquisite blend of balance, structure, intelligence, and athleticism. They can ogle the horses all they want, read up about them, and watch them stand and walk a bit, but they can't take them out for a run.

There are no lemon laws when it comes to buying racehorses, and legal disputes over horse sales gone sour do happen. Horsemen who value their reputations have policed the line between proper disclosure and high-stakes swindling.

Nearly everyone who has persevered in the racing business seems to have been stuck with a horse that was not quite as advertised. Charlotte Weber, whose family founded the Campbell Soup Company and who is an owner and breeder, once took an expensive yearling home to her farm in Ocala, Florida, only to discover he had a broken leg. Without a money-back guarantee, Weber could only acknowledge the flaw by naming the horse Fissure.

Sometimes, alterations aside, you get lucky. In 1996, Baffert bought a colt for the bargain-basement price of $17,000 because he looked athletic.

"Does he have cancer?" asked Baffert's friend and the new owner of the colt, Mike Pegram.

Only later did they discover that the colt had undergone a transphyseal bridge, or what is known as a "screw and wire," to straighten a knee. Two years later, that colt, Real Quiet, went on to capture the Kentucky Derby and Preakness Stakes in 1998, and his Triple Crown bid was thwarted by only a nose in the Belmont Stakes.

It was a client of Moynihan's, the late Jess Jackson of Kendall-Jackson wine fame, who did the most to clean up the horse-trading industry a bit by putting some safeguards in place. There always have been whispers of false bidders who conspire with agents to run up the prices of horses as they pass through the sales ring. Rumors circulate of back-room deals between sellers and the agents for wealthy newcomers to the sport: They agree on a price, say $250,000, entice the buyer to pay $300,000, then split the difference. Jackson filed a lawsuit, saying that what one horse trader calls commission to an agent for help in selling a horse is actually a bribe or a kickback. He lobbied for legislation in Kentucky that prohibits a practice known as dual agency, in which an agent receives money from the buyer and the seller in a horse trade.

Breeders and consignors have acknowledged that agents of buyers had approached them, seeking to inflate prices on their horses.

"When you tell them no, you understand that they are never coming back to buy one of your horses," said Arthur Hancock III, whose Stone Farm has produced three

Derby winners. "Honest sellers can't compete with those who cheat. I'm a fourth-generation horseman, and I'm ashamed that a winemaker had to clean up our sport."

It is a combination of hubris, deep passion for the sport, and the expense and embarrassment of litigation that has kept many new owners out of the courtroom and, eventually, run them out of the business. Satish Sanan, a computer magnate, who built a farm and racing operation, Padua Stables, in Florida, became a reformer after an admittedly rough start in the business in the late 1990s. He had invested more than $150 million in the sport.

"Most of us have come from other fields where we've done well and think we won't make the same mistakes the guy before us did," said Sanan, who left the horse business in 2012. "But we all do make those mistakes. Some just take their lumps and go away."

Zayat was determined not to be taken advantage of or be chased from the sport. He had reached the top levels of the game extraordinarily quick but at a deep cost. He had cut his racing and breeding operation in half and was still paying the bank and his creditors. Horses carrying Zayat's distinctive blue and gold silks splattered with Zs included twelve Grade 1 winners and five Eclipse Award finalists. In the past six years, three of his horses had finished second in the Kentucky Derby, first Pioneerof the Nile, followed by Nehro in 2011 and Bodemeister the next year. He had come close, agonizingly close, to winning the race that everyone in the sport most wants to conquer. He had the bank breathing down his neck and knew there only was one way out for Zayat Stables.

"I got to sell horses," he said.

It is, indeed, the golden rule of horse racing: take the suitcase full of cash today because the talented horse you love now may, God forbid, twist an ankle or suffer something worse tomorrow. Frances Relihan was not the only horse person who had fallen hard for the Littleprincessemma colt; the crew at Taylor Made Farm, where the bay was transferred the previous January, marveled at how the weanling was filling out.

For Frances, it was heartbreaking to see horse vans descend upon her farm and take away the mares and stallions, along with their babies. Simon had put the Vinery up for sale and now Frances's life's work was somebody else's. She was especially bummed to see the Littleprincessemma colt be driven off to Taylor Made. The farm was owned and run by four brothers — all third-generation horsemen — who had earned a reputation for operating a first-class operation specializing in high-quality horses. She knew the colt was in excellent hands but brushed and caressed him a little longer than she had some of the others. Frances cried when the Littleprincessemma colt was led into the van and driven off. She knew she was not likely to see another one like him and she told the Taylors so.

Mark Taylor, who took care of marketing and public sales, understood immediately. The colt came in with a large group of better bred peers — sons and daughters of Tapit and Giant's Causeway — but the bay moved among them with a confidence that said they were going to spend the rest of their careers chasing him.

Taylor called it the "It factor" — the colt had something that no one could put a finger on . . . at least not yet.

John Hall, the farm's yearling manager, recognized the colt as an "old soul" because he projected a been-there-done-that aura. The yearling was so cool and unflappable that Hall felt he must have been a top-class racehorse in a previous life. It was the colt's walk, however, that moved Taylor the most.

"You know when horses kind of unhinge their shoulder and just really flow when they walk?" he said. "It was a walk that the more you looked at him, the more you loved him."

So when the Taylors told Zayat that the Littleprincessemma colt was the best yearling on their farm and was likely to fetch a big price, all agreed that the Saratoga Sale was their target. Zayat looked at the amount of money he needed against what he thought the colt would bring and put a $1 million price tag on the colt. He decided not to take a penny less. Zayat would buy the colt back if he had to, just write a check to himself and consider the 5 percent commission he had to pay Fasig-Tipton as the cost of doing business.

It was a plan, a pretty good one, until the colt banged himself up in the weeks before the sale and two members of Zayat's horse-picking team sowed some seeds of doubt in the owner.

There were some among the team that believed $1 million was overly ambitious. He was a good-looking colt, but the first crop from Pioneerof the Nile was just now hitting the racetrack, and there weren't many of them yet because it was early in their two-year-old careers. The sire was a decent racehorse with a nice enough pedigree, but there were scores of stallions that fit that profile at this stage of their career and were now standing for $2,500 to $5,000 in the hinterlands of California and Florida, Pennsylvania and New York. Buyers weren't going to go deep in their pockets without a proven track record. The sensible price point was $250,000 or perhaps $300,000, but then some bad luck visited the colt and left a blemish.

No one is sure when or how exactly, but the colt got a scrape on the back of his front ankle that was starting to swell. He could have gotten his foot caught in an opening in his stall or banged it in the trailer or just stepped on himself. Suddenly, however, Hip No. 85, as he was listed in the catalogue, was drawing attention for all the wrong reasons. This large, lovely bay yearling had a swelling the size of maybe two marbles below his fetlock, or ankle. He wasn't lame. He didn't limp. The Taylors' veterinarians shrugged it off and said it would vanish by the following week. Still, his potential sales price continued to drop each time prospective buyers watched him walk amid the barns and spotted the imperfection.

"It was just like a pimple on a kid's face on prom night," Taylor told Zayat. "It's unfortunate it happened, but it'll be gone by next week. Prom pictures might get screwed up, but that's kind of the way it is at a horse sale."

Whether Hip No. 85 was nicked up or not, Jeff Seder and Patti Miller believed — *no, knew* — that this colt was not only the best horse in the sale, but also potentially one of the best horses they had seen at a horse auction in many years. They were the principals of EQB (Equine Biomechanics and Exercise Physiology), a Pennsylvania-based bloodstock agency that was as unusual as its name, mainly because of its reliance on science and an ever-evolving database. This database was maintained by Seder, a Harvard-educated MBA, attorney, entrepreneur, and business-turnaround-artist who had spent much of the last forty years trying to convince horse owners that he wasn't a crazy voodoo doctor. Seder was a free spirit but a disciplined one, who was interested in the impact of genes and organs and design on athletic performance of horses as well as humans. In the early 1980s, he had worked with the U.S. Olympic Sports Medicine Committee on ways to identify, nurture, and build better bobsledders, shot putters, and figure skaters. He was an excitable sort who talked in riddles and often lectured with the verve of a favorite professor.

"Pedigree is really a set of variables used to predict the probability of what you'll get before the horse is born," he said, laying out the foundation of his core belief. "After the horse is a physical specimen standing in front of you, there are more reliable measures. The fact that something may have been unlikely in a horse because of its pedigree should not overrule the observation of an individual who has that quality anyway."

To that end, Seder measured horses' hearts, spleens, throats, and airways often with instruments that he invented and subsequently patented. He employed a high-speed, high-definition camera that clicked off up to 500 pictures per second. He kept precise measurements ranging from stride lengths, stance times, limb segment velocities, center of gravity deviations, and step lengths. Seder wanted to know how a horse interfaces with the track and what happens to its gait as it goes faster. He sought out the best minds at the best medical, engineering, and biomechanics universities and collected his data and built his models to the most rigorous academic standards as well as contributed to scientific veterinary journals.

EQB was not just about collecting wall-to-wall data but putting it into the proper context and interpreting it precisely. Much has been made, for example, of the large heart the great Secretariat possessed. The legend goes that Dr. Thomas Swerczek, head pathologist at the University of Kentucky, estimated it at twenty-two pounds or nearly twice the normal size found in racehorses. Seder was less interested in the size of the heart. His data included 2-D echo ultrasound scans of many heart variables and digitized slow motion videos of racing speed workouts of real racehorses at major racetracks around the world. His database took decades to build and covered more than 50,000 horses and every detail of every race they ran.

"So the heart measurement has to be looked at tightly in the context of a huge database so you only compare it to other horses of the same sex who are also similar within thirty days of chronological age and within a tight weight and height comparison as well," Seder said.

It was Miller, however, who brought two attributes that Seder needed help with: horsemanship and a human touch. She grew up around horses, riding pony races and fox hunting throughout the Mid-Atlantic region, graduating to steeplechase racing and eventually becoming one of the nation's first professional female jockeys. She learned the racetrack in prominent barns on both the East and West Coast before starting her own public stable and becoming a leading trainer at Delaware Park. While Seder started with measurements and spreadsheets, Miller could recognize a runner with her eyes and hands. She also was more plainspoken and patient with EQB's clients and delivered their assessments with a gentler touch.

In short, they complemented each other, and in Zayat they had a client who believed in their system. There's a Middle Eastern proverb that says the horse created by a committee is a camel and with EQB on the payroll and in charge of selecting breeding stock as well as sales horses, Zayat Stables was finding itself in the winner's circle of Grade 1 races and in the stallion barns of top breeding farms with horses like Eskendereya and Pioneerof the Nile.

Like Seder, Miller thought the Little-princessemma colt was hands down the best-looking prospect among the 150 horses on the sales grounds. She knew the colt's pedigree well, as she and Seder had picked out Littleprincessemma. Miller, too, was awed by his physical aura. Hip No. 85 earned the high marks on her physical checklist of physical attributes from walk to balance, intelligence to conformation. Miller agreed with Seder as well that the colt's cardiovascular scans were "literally as good as it gets." She was not concerned by the blemish on the colt's ankle, but she knew it was dropping the price on the colt.

"It was something you might get if you got a little paper cut, or a scratch from a rose or something," she said.

Miller called Zayat on the eve of the sale and told him how impressed she was with his homebred. She told him that she had seen horses fall out of favor at sales before and it usually turned out for the best. In 2004, at the Mid-Atlantic two-year-old-in-training sale, a well-bred and well-put-together colt had an allergic reaction to the ointment that the sales company put on a small cut, prompting his ankle to swell up to the size of a cantaloupe. His price fell to $75,000 and a group of Philadelphia businessmen new to the trade snatched him up. The following year the colt, named Afleet Alex, went on to win eight of his twelve races, including the Preakness and Belmont Stakes, and earned more than $2.7 million.

"This is the kind of horse we try to buy, so why are we selling it?" she asked him.

Seder urged him to hang on to the Little-princessemma colt.

"Sell your house; don't sell this horse," he told him. "This is your get-out horse."

On Tuesday, the last of the two-day sale, Hip No. 85 was led into the sales ring looking as regal as the tuxedoed groom at the end of his shank. He stood still with ears pricked high and head turned as if he were posing for a sculptor. He circled once, twice as the auctioneers sang in the singsong melody of money to a crowd that wasn't listening — or at least bidding. They couldn't get past Hip No. 85's flawed ankle or Pioneerof the Nile's lack of credentials. Zayat listened on his phone from Disneyland, where he was on a trip with his family. There were some ringers — or plants — who signaled interest solely to get the bidding started, but there was no one out there who really wanted the colt. It didn't take long for the auctioneer's cadence to lose steam, much like a bag of microwave popcorn loses its pop when the kernels are cooked. Zayat told another sales agent to buy back the colt at $300,000, far below what he had hoped for.

By the end of the evening, a total of 137

horses would bring in more than $31.8 million to the Saratoga Sale. The sales topper was a Dynaformer filly that fetched more than $1.2 million. The Littleprincessemma colt remained with Zayat. Seder and Miller could not have been happier.

CHAPTER FOUR:
GET HIM OUT OF HERE

March 23, 2014

The McKathan brothers knew their horses. They might as well have been foaled themselves in a stall, seeing how they spent the better part of their lives with runners in their backyards. Their father, J.B., or Luke trained quarter horses at the long-gone Seminole Downs in Central Florida before deciding to chase bigger purses at racetracks from Florida to California. A quarter horse was an American breed that excelled at sprinting short distances, usually in races of a quarter mile or less. He eventually switched to Thoroughbreds and did all right on the grits-and-hard-toast tracks of West Virginia and later Tampa Bay Downs. Luke McKathan eventually returned to Florida and became a pinhooker, buying horses as weanlings or yearlings, raising and training them himself, then selling them at auction or privately long before they hit the racetrack. More often than not, he did this at a profit. If horses were automobiles, Luke McKathan had earned the reputation as an ace mechanic who could take apart and put back together a fast machine in the course of a weekend. No one was surprised that his sons, J.B. Jr. and Kevin, ended their formal education after high school to go into the family business. They had already been home-schooled by a master in the only subject they truly cared about. They had learned their lessons well enough to strike out on their own in their mid-twenties, owning and operating a 200-acre training, boarding, and breaking center in Citra, Florida, near Ocala.

While Central Kentucky had its bluegrass and history dating back to before the Revolutionary War, Central Florida was an upstart Thoroughbred incubator, the vision of a post–World War II highway builder named Carl Rose. He believed horses would thrive in the region's eternal sunshine and would build strong bones from eating the calcium- and phosphorus-enriched grass and water that seeped through the more than 70,000 acres of lush farmland. In 1957, Needles became the first Florida-bred horse to win the Kentucky Derby. Twenty-one years later, in 1978, another colt by the name of Affirmed, born and bred on Harbor View Farm, swept America's three classic races to become the eleventh Triple Crown champ. The wait has been on for another one ever since.

This was as good a place as any for the McKathan brothers to put their name on the gate of a farm and training center and they did just that in 1988. They worked the horse sales and backside of racetracks to solicit clients. They leaned heavily on the friends their father had made in the horse business. Like Luke McKathan, there was nothing they could not do with a horse. They prepped them for sales, getting them fit and buffed up. They rehabilitated injured racehorses, transforming their shedrow into a hospital. They got yearlings ready for the racetrack, putting first a saddle, then the weight of a rider on them, giving them the first taste of their new career on a five-eighths-of-a-mile training track. The breaking and training of horses kept the place afloat, but the real money was in the pinhooking and bloodstock agent work. It was what vaulted you into the circle of deep-pocketed owners who could afford to roll the dice on six-figure-plus horses. Before you landed a real big money owner, however, first you had to find someone as hungry as yourself.

In the early 1990s, the McKathans found their soul mate in a California-based trainer named Bob Baffert, who was trying to transition from the quarter horses to the Thoroughbreds like their father had decades ago. Baffert sported pressed jeans, snap-button shirts, and a cowboy hat that sat atop a full head of snow-white hair. He was in his late thirties, not much older than the McKathans, and traveled with not exactly an entourage, but a good-time crew of small-time (by Thoroughbred standards) owners. He didn't have any rich patrons, either — or at least not yet. His main client, Mike Pegram, was a former college-bookie-turned-McDonald's-franchise mogul. It was Pegram, after a spontaneous trip to Las Vegas, who had persuaded him to graduate from quarter horses to the more lucrative Thoroughbred circuit. Such sage advice should be heeded from a man you just watched sign a voucher for $50,000 from a croupier, as Pegram had, especially when come morning you would be sharing a Jacuzzi with him and two young women with your cowboy hat and boots on as Baffert did. In the McKathans, Baffert recognized hands-on horsemen whom he appreciated for their youth and hustle. They had met in Lexington, Kentucky, at the Keeneland September Sale after J.B. became irritated that Baffert had outbid them on nearly every horse the brothers had tried to buy.

"If you just leave, I'll upgrade your ticket to first class," said J.B. McKathan.

"I'm already flying first class, buddy," Baffert said.

It was the beginning of a warm and lucrative friendship. Baffert sent them his babies to break. He already knew they had a similar eye for horses as he did, putting a premium on the way it moved and looked rather than fixating on a horse's pedigree or flaws. The McKathans were his forward guard. He sent them to sales to weed out the unaffordable or not-good-enough and relied on the half-dozen or so horses they put on a list for him that fit his taste and budget. Baffert and the McKathans had done pretty well together, but all were still looking for their breakout horse.

In April of 1996, Baffert was at Churchill Downs in Louisville, Kentucky, preparing a gelding named Cavonnier for the Kentucky Derby. It was Baffert's first starter in America's greatest race, and he was anxious because Cavonnier had just won the Santa Anita Derby and definitely had a shot to capture the blanket of roses. He was hardly an overnight success. It had taken him twelve lean years as a quarter horse trainer to surpass $1 million in earnings. In fact, he almost quit at one point after his father, Bill, took a horse away from him to train himself. Since switching over to Thoroughbreds, his barn climbed steadily up the national trainer standings. The nearly $3 million his stable earned the previous year was solid, but he had yet to achieve national prominence as a top-tier trainer. Being at the Derby for the first time with a contender like Cavonnier helped, but he needed to keep coming back.

So he was looking to buy a horse for a client at the Ocala two-year-old-in-training sale, one that would return him to the hallowed ground beneath Churchill's twin spires. J.B. McKathan had one in mind, a gray son of Silver Buck. McKathan had watched him work a quarter mile before the sale and was impressed. His front legs were turned out a bit, but at $80,000 the colt was within Baffert's price range. He sent a video of the colt to the trainer in Louisville, but one, two, three days went by without a word. When he finally got to it, Baffert told the McKathans to buy the gray colt privately and then promised them a $5,000 fee. They ran into a problem almost immediately. Baffert's client did not want the horse. J.B. and Baffert thought about keeping the horse themselves, but neither of them felt financially secure enough to take that kind of risk. The trainer, however, had one big spending owner in his barn, Bob Lewis, who owned one of the nation's largest Budweiser distributorships.

There were two problems, though. Baffert was Lewis's second-string trainer and lately he hadn't been winning any races for the owner. D. Wayne Lukas got to spend the big money for Lewis and his wife Beverly's stable. The owner had already put Baffert on notice with the two phrases that precede a van arriving at the stable to spirit a horse to a rival trainer: "You are winning for other people but not me. We've had no luck together." A phone call was about to change all that. Baffert picked up the phone and told Lewis that he was stuck with what he believed was a pretty nice horse. His name was Silver Charm. Would Lewis be willing to buy him for $85,000? When Silver Charm ran off with the Derby and Preakness before getting caught at the wire by a head in the Belmont Stakes, it looked like a bargain. By the time Silver Charm was retired, he had won the Eclipse Award, the sport's year-end honor, as the 1997 Champion Three-Year-Old Colt, and eleven stakes — including one of the richest, the Dubai World Cup. He had banked $6,944,369. It would be a while before someone would take away a horse from Baffert or turn his back on the McKathans, especially when the following year the $17,000 screw-and-wire job Real Quiet, another of their joint ventures, came within a nostril of winning the Belmont Stakes and sweeping the Triple Crown.

Over the years, the McKathans helped pick out three other champions for Baffert and his clients, including the Mike Pegram–owned Silverbulletday and sprinter Midnight Lute and the Stonerside Stable filly Chilukki. Dozens of stakes runners, among them thirty Grade 1 winners, had taken their first steps on the racetrack beneath the sun in Central Florida at their farm.

Neither J.B., now forty-nine, nor Kevin, forty-seven, had seen a horse as talented as the one that they were about to unveil on a steamy March morning. This son of Pioneerof the Nile had given both the brothers goose bumps ever since arriving from Saratoga along with more than a dozen other horses from Zayat Stables. They had worked with a number of the sire's young horses in all shapes and sizes but had recognized they

97

all shared a common trait: desire. They all wanted to win whether playing out in the field or carrying a rider around the training track. When the brothers first got a look at the big, rugged bay colt, J.B. turned to Kevin and asked, "How did this guy get through the ring without anyone buying him?"

With 125 horses on their farm, it was easy for one brown one to blur into another even for the most astute professional horseman. Inevitably, however, a handful of horses make an impression simply by the way they carry themselves, especially in the early weeks and months when not much is asked of them. Teaching a horse to race is a painstaking step-by-step process. They must learn how to accept a bridle or a saddle and girth. They are skittish, anxious, or just plain slow to figure out what to do. The Pioneerof the Nile colt was another story altogether. When they put the tack on him, the big bay stood upright like a medieval knight await-ing his armor from his valet. When he walked the shedrow, he high stepped and looked as if he was ready to bolt out the door and sail clear into the fields. The first time a rider "belly upped" or lay on his back to give him the sensation of weight, he looked bored. With a rider on his back for the first time, he responded to his cues like he had done it all before.

"His mind was just so far advanced than anything I had ever seen," said Kevin McKathan. "It was like he was in a hurry to learn his lessons. It was clear early he was the best horse on the farm."

The first time the McKathans let the colt sample what an open gallop felt like, it was at once breathtaking and terrifying. He burst into a stride that skipped over the ground like a hovercraft. He went way too fast and way too far. When the rider finally pulled him up, J.B. McKathan told him, "If you let that horse run again, I'm going to break your arm."

Soon, the McKathan brothers realized that it was no one's fault that this long, tall, powerful colt possessed something horse-men dream about and can no way teach: speed, freaky speed. In fact, the first time the brothers put him on the track and asked the rider to push a button or two, he just ran off from the other horses. He had so much natural ability that the brothers did everything in their power not to tax the colt. He was still growing, still getting fit, and they were afraid he would get hurt. None of his riders were allowed to use a whip on him. J.B. changed bits — the small piece of equipment put in a horse's mouth to help a rider communicate with him — repeatedly looking for a safe and effective way to slow him down.

"It was speed! Speed! Speed! Speed!" said Kevin McKathan. "He had plenty of it."

On the morning of March 23, 2014, it was time for the McKathans to let some folks, namely Ahmed Zayat and some of his trainers, see exactly how fast this colt was. They were staging a breeze show for Zayat Stable two-year-olds, an annual rite of spring, where the owner could size up his next group of contenders and place them with the trainer and circuit that best fit their talents. Zayat ran his horses everywhere — from Florida to New York and from Kentucky to California. Even post-bankruptcy, he had a lot of them. Mr. Z was a slow-payer, and sometimes a no-payer, and farms and small businesses like the McKathans paid for it. The horse business is tough, and the McKathans always were hustling to make ends meet. Still, everyone doing business with him agreed on three things: "He plays the game hard," said Kevin McKathan. "He buys good horses to give himself every opportunity. It's fun to be a part of."

The McKathans could not have asked for a more perfect setting to premier a magical horse. The pine oaks that canopied their farm had trapped the mist low to the ground and transformed the farm into an enchanted stage worthy of the wizard Merlin. The sun dappled the horses and training track with beams of light as birds sang noisily. The McKathans treated events like these as an open house — the farm was manicured to postcard-quality perfection, and the horses looked like they were ready for a model's runway. As soon as they started, timed workouts would put all of the brothers' horsemanship skills on display. Spirits were high among the contingent on the clockers' stand. The Kentucky-based trainer Dale Romans and his partner Tammy Fox were there, as was the Delaware-based Anthony Dutrow. All were giving Justin Zayat the third degree about dating. Justin was a junior at New York University and easing his way into the stable as its racing manager.

There were a couple dozen people on the clockers' stand, the small gazebo-style house with a wraparound porch on the rail near the center of the track. The stock of Zayat Stables did not disappoint as one well-bred horse after another took its turn blazing either a quarter or three-eighths of a mile around the track. There were colts and fillies from Eskendereya and Zensational and

Maimonides and Pioneerof the Nile, each bounding around the track more impressive than the last one. The McKathans were saving the best for last, though: The Pioneerof the Nile colt out of Littleprincessemma was going to send people home with something to think about. There was no bigger fan of the colt on the farm than Chris Alexander, the brothers' farm manager. He told anyone who would listen that this unraced two-year-old was the best horse he had ever been around in his life. He decided to put Susan Montanye on the colt's back for the breeze, despite the fact that she had never been on him. She was lighter than his regular riders, and even though the colt was hard to handle, Alexander believed he would relax under her light touch.

On the clockers' stand, racetrackers have a talent for carrying on multiple raucous conversations while clicking a stopwatch but still meticulously following the flight of the horse around the racetrack. It's a hand-eye-mouth coordination necessary to make four hours on your feet each day clocking hundreds of horses seem like a breakfast meeting rather than hard labor. There was no pause in conversation or lowering of their voice when Montanye galloped the colt by the stand the first time. He had his neck bowed and head hanging low and rocked back and forth in a lullaby rhythm, looking every bit like a child's rocking horse. Montanye let him lift his head a bit heading into the turn, and the power was apparent immediately. He was barrel-chested and sturdy, almost like one of those horses from an old Hollywood Western that thundered toward the sunset and certain glory. It got awful quiet, however, when she shook her reins ever so slightly, backed into a crouch, and just took off like a drag-racing car.

"J.B., tell me the time, please," asked Mr. Z.

"Eleven and three," J.B. McKathan replied, confirming the colt was moving fast, 11.60 seconds for the first eighth of a mile.

"Holy shit!" Mr. Z said.

"That'll do," offered someone else reverently.

No one spoke as the colt hugged the rail and then rolled around the turn in perfect synchronicity — smooth, effortless without a single wasted motion.

"Twenty-two-point-one," called out J.B.

By then, nobody needed a time to understand what they were watching — a fast, beautifully put together machine.

"Holy shit!" Mr. Z repeated.

"That's what I'm talking about," said J.B.

"Thirty-six and three."

"Holy shit," said Mr. Z.

"I'm scared of this horse," said J.B. "Figure out who you want to send him to and get him out of here."

Montanye came by the stand and smiled when she saw every gaze fixed on her mount. Every one of their jaws dropped. She had just sat on the colt. She had not asked him to do anything.

"That was him," she said.

J.B. McKathan wanted to put a fine point on what they had all just witnessed.

"He can fucking go, man," he said. "You just don't see horses work like that."

"Dale, I want that one," said Tammy Fox.

"Who's getting him?" someone asked.

"It has to be a trainer in attendance," said Romans to laughter. "You can't send him to Baffert. He didn't show up."

Everyone knew that was exactly where he was going, though.

"What's his name?" someone else asked.

"American Pharoah," said Justin Zayat.

CHAPTER FIVE:
A LONG SUMMER

August 9, 2014

Bob Baffert's hair was still snowy white and his eyes still watered beneath his ever-present shades. It is a hell of a thing that a horse trainer is allergic to horses. At sixty-one, the cowboy hat and western shirts were long gone and had been replaced by crisply starched button-downs and fleece vests during the morning training hours and tailored blazers for the clubhouse on big race days. His mouth now moved faster than his legs. Then again, it always had.

It was August at Del Mar, which was the equivalent of saying it was Happy Hour in Heaven. The seaside track that Bing Crosby founded north of San Diego, "where the turf meets the surf," as only he could croon, was in full swing; this meant the grandstand and clubhouse were filled with good-looking people — many of them young, all of them decked out, some slightly buzzed, but all here to drink in one of the finest places to watch horses run fast. If Saratoga was where horse lovers went to worship, Del Mar was the place they came to throw a beach party. It was the premier meet of California racing, and Baffert had summered here for nearly fifteen years. It was where he raised the curtain and debuted his most promising two-year-olds, especially the colts that he was counting on to get him to the Kentucky Derby. He had won the Del Mar Futurity, the track's biggest race for two-year-olds, eleven times in the past eighteen years. Some went on to become future Classic winners like Silver Charm (1996) and Lookin At Lucky (2010 Preakness); others like Flame Thrower (2000) and Icecoldbeeratreds (2002) were never heard from again. There was nothing "been there, done that" about how Baffert approached the fourth race on the card this afternoon, a six-furlong sprint for maidens, or horses that had yet to win, worth $75,000.

He was excited about the bay colt named American Pharoah that had just ambled into the paddock. The colt was a flawless specimen, except for a short, thinning, ratty tail. He arrived in Baffert's barn that way and the only explanation offered was that one of his equine buddies must have chewed it off at the McKathans' farm. It didn't matter. This was going to be his Del Mar Futurity winner and, he hoped, so much more. Still, Baffert was trying not to get too excited. He understood better than most how fragile these Thoroughbreds were and how unforgiving horse racing could be. Silver Charm, Real Quiet, and War Emblem in 2002 all had pulled into Belmont Park with a chance to sweep the Triple Crown and make history. Silver Charm got caught by a head, Real Quiet a nose, and War Emblem stumbled out of the gate and lost all chance. In 2001, the most talented horse he had ever trained, Point Given, saw his bid for history end before it ever began. At a height of 17 hands and a weight of 1,285 pounds, the colt was a beast and dwarfed his rivals, going off as the odds-on favorite to win the 2001 Derby. Instead, he bumped into a horse coming out of the starting gate, forcing his jockey, Gary Stevens, to chase a wicked fast pace from far outside and finished a devastating fifth behind the closer Monarchos in the second fastest time in Derby history. Only Secretariat's was faster. Point Given went on to win the Preakness, Belmont, Haskell, and Travers Stakes — four consecutive Grade 1, $1 million races — before a strained tendon was discovered in his left foreleg and he was retired. The colt won nine of thirteen starts and accumulated $3,968,500 in prize money. He was named Horse of the Year, but Baffert knew that Point Given would never be considered a truly great racehorse because of his Derby loss.

"It's a sacred race," he often said.

He was right. It was the race that defined horse racing in America. It brought more than 150,000 to Churchill Downs, attracted millions more to watch on television, and pushed more money through the betting windows than any other single American race. It was the one day that mattered most in American horse racing, followed by the Belmont Stakes when a Triple Crown was on the line and the Preakness, which decided if the Derby winner was going to arrive in New York with a chance for immortality. Baffert knew better than most that it was the Triple Crown races or bust if you ever wanted to get the best horses and be considered among the greatest trainers in history. Winning the Derby, the Preakness, and almost the Belmont Stakes with Silver Charm had transformed him from a former quarter horse trainer into a guy rich men (and, yes, they are predominately men) wanted to meet, wanted to follow around at horse sales where they let him spend several million dollars of their money. He almost swept the series again the following year with Real Quiet. He was famous. Baffert was the most recognizable horse trainer in the world. He had an awful lot to do with it. He courted the media like a long-ignored politician and charmed them with his stream-of-consciousness musings. Sometimes what he said was funny, other times inappropriate, but all of it made him popular among casual fans of a majestic sport trying to regain its foothold on a larger audience.

On the backsides and in the owners' boxes of American racetracks, however, Baffert stirred resentment and suspicion. Horse racing is an insular world inhabited by hyper-competitive rich people possessing massive egos who want the limelight for themselves. In 2002, when he brought War Emblem to New York for his third attempt to win the Triple Crown, the trainer's popularity was waning. Baffert had bought War Emblem three weeks before the Kentucky Derby on behalf of Prince Ahmed bin Salman of Saudi Arabia. With the tragedy of the September 11 terrorist attacks on the World Trade Center still fresh, the thought of a colt owned by a Saudi prince and conditioned by a flaky former quarter-horse trainer taking down horse racing's most sacred feat was too much to bear. As one of Baffert's friends, Julian (Buck) Wheat, said, the thought of it was "blasphemy" among old line owners and breeders.

"You're walking on hallowed grounds and to have some jack leg quarter-horse trainer win the Derby and now on the doorstep of history, well, that isn't done," said Wheat, the longtime director of horseman's relations at Churchill Downs.

Baffert was forty-nine at the time and understood his precarious place within the industry. He tried to filter his remarks and temper his combativeness, but he resented those who whispered behind his back about his credentials and black bag magic. His father, Bill, had introduced him to horses growing up on a farm in Nogales, Arizona, a town of 20,000 near the Mexican border. The Chief, as his father was known, plowed a dirt track into a hay field and that was where ten-year-old Bob started each morning before school on top of a horse. Bill Baffert had built his ranch from scratch and raised his six kids there. They had cattle and young Bob sold the eggs of the chickens he raised for extra money. Bill was chairman of the county board of supervisors. His mother, Ellie, was a teacher at the local elementary school, where she eventually became the principal and a friendly but strict influence on a generation of Nogales children.

The Bafferts were by no definition race-trackers, but the Chief bought some cheap quarter horses and trained them to race in unsanctioned races at an airstrip at a neighboring ranch or at local bush tracks like the Santa Cruz County Fair and Rodeo Association in Sonoita. Racing quarter horses is a pastime in the Southwest, much like building race cars in your garage or playing softball beer leagues is in other parts of the country.

Baffert got proficient enough to become a second-rate jockey (by his own admission) and won his fair share of match races and cheap purses at third-rate tracks. His hobby terrified the Chief and his mother, Ellie. She forbade him to race while Bill either looked the other way or prayed hard nothing would happen when he was at the races with his son.

Baffert went to the University of Arizona, where he graduated with a degree in animal sciences and a minor from its racetrack management program. He then took out a trainer's license and did his time running for peanuts at remote tracks, such as Rillito

Park near Tuscon. He never took a job as an assistant trainer, so anything he learned at the racetrack was through trial and error, mostly error. Baffert's focus and ambition made up for his lack of experience, and his first big break came in Arizona after some local trainers got caught doping horses and asked him to run their stables until they returned from suspension. It helped that Baffert was a glib, fun-loving kid, and they liked and trusted him. When he had more and better horses, he started winning more and better races. What bothered him the most about the fire he was taking from owners and other trainers was the disrespect it showed for his discipline and horsemanship.

"I broke them, rode them, wrapped them, and slept with them since I was a boy," he said.

Not long after their trip to Las Vegas, Mike Pegram gave Baffert $300,000 and told him to buy some Thoroughbreds for him. In 1975, Pegram bought his first McDonald's with 100 percent financing from a banker in his hometown of Princeton, Indiana. He understood what made the trainer special — and potentially great. The first time Baffert tried to claim a horse — or buy one that was running in a race — he forgot to write its name down on the slip and lost the chance to buy it. He tried again with the help of Bob Baedeker, who at the time published a tip sheet his family sold at the racetrack and promised winners. Baedeker found a horse called Presidents Summit, so Baffert claimed him. The first morning he took him out to train at Santa Anita Park, he did not have an exercise rider. At the snack bar, Baffert recognized Gary Stevens, one of the best jockeys in the nation, and asked him if he would ride him. He did not know that Stevens had an agent and that it was a breach of racetrack etiquette to not ask him first. Stevens agreed, but when he asked Baffert how he would like to train him, Baffert was stumped. He had never trained a Thoroughbred and did not know what to do — but he learned. He also remembered those who had believed in him.

When Baffert came up with his first good horse, he gave Pegram a piece of him free of charge: Thirty Slews won the $1 million Breeders' Cup Sprint in 1992. He picked out Real Quiet for him on the cheap — $17,000 — and the colt ran off to more than $3.2 million in purses. The champion filly Silverbulletday cost $155,000 and earned more than $2.8 million in purses.

"First of all, I liked the guy," said Pegram.

"Second, he had ambition and a tremendous eye for spotting a talented horse. No one else needs to like the guy, but you have to respect his horsemanship. Next to selling hamburgers, giving the money to Bob was the smartest investment I ever made."

Baffert's flair for self-promotion, however, was wearing on people as well. He put the Preakness trophy on his head as he has done after each of his victories in Baltimore and donned a psychedelic Austin Powers get-up for a television segment. He coauthored an autobiography and talked about everything from his use of hallucinogenic drugs as a bell-bottomed teenager to the one-year suspension California horse racing officials gave him for a positive drug test on one of his horses while he was a college student and part-time trainer. He wrote that he did it — partly out of ignorance, partly out of desperation to win. Baffert too often spoke before he thought and insulted his fellow trainers and the jockeys that he hired. At a press conference, he suggested that Jenine Sahadi, an accomplished female trainer, needed help from her husband or jockey. She told him he lacked class, left the podium, and then beat him with her colt, The Deputy, in the 2000 Santa Anita Derby. In the winner's circle of the Haskell Invitational, he told Hall of Fame rider Gary Stevens, a friend, that his poor ride had nearly gotten Point Given beat. Stevens yelled back at him and both stormed out of the winner's circle.

He even goaded Bob Lewis, one of his most loyal owners, into an embarrassing public episode. Two years after Silver Charm, Lewis returned to the Belmont with a second chance at capturing the Triple Crown with Charismatic, a colt trained by his first string trainer, D. Wayne Lukas. When Baffert decided to enter the filly Silverbulletday in the Belmont, Lukas thought Baffert was trying to steal the spotlight and the two trainers traded increasingly dismissive statements about the merits of each other's horses. Lewis got angry and publicly offered Baffert and Pegram a $200,000 bet that Charismatic would finish ahead of the filly. Eventually, the bet was rescinded and apologies exchanged. Nobody benefitted: Charismatic sustained a career-ending injury in the stretch and finished third and Silverbulletday was overmatched and finished a well-beaten seventh.

Baffert got into another bitter public dispute with one of his wealthiest owners, Aaron Jones, an Oregon timber baron. It was bad enough that Jones pulled his horses from Baffert's stable, but he insulted the trainer when he refused to deliver a promised breeding season for Forestry, a colt Baffert ran to four stakes victories. When horses go to stallion duty, breeding seasons are often given to trainers as a sort of tip that subsequently can become a lucrative annuity. Lukas, for example, received a Storm Cat season that he sold each year. In his prime, Storm Cat commanded $500,000 a breeding. Instead of giving Forestry's season directly to Baffert, Jones put it in the name of Baffert's wife, Sherry, who he was divorcing at the time, and his four children.

Baffert considered it a slap at his integrity.

As 2002 began, even Baffert was tiring of his own drama. He had completed his divorce and planned a new marriage, but now was struggling to find a Derby horse. One by one, the most promising three-year-olds in his barn were either injured or proved to be not good enough. Baffert resigned himself to missing his first trip to the famous race on the first Saturday in May since 1996. Then he watched War Emblem romp in the Illinois Derby on television. The Prince, a member of the royal family, saw it on television from Saudi Arabia too. The trainer started working the phones and discovered the colt had been for sale since December. War Emblem won twice as a two-year-old but showed that he had chips in both front ankles and a knee — information that was discovered by a potential buyer. It didn't matter to Baffert or the prince: They wanted another shot at the Derby. In a matter of days, Salman owned 90 percent of the colt for $900,000 and War Emblem was in Baffert's barn.

He led every step of the way on the first Saturday of May to win at odds of 20 to 1, giving Baffert his third Derby victory. War Emblem prevailed impressively in the Preakness, and when his jockey, Victor Espinoza, popped a baseball cap promoting an Internet betting service onto his head in the winner's circle after the Preakness, Baffert snatched it from his head and threw it into the crowd at Pimlico Race Course. He told him that this was no time to think about picking up some endorsement cash.

"These are the classics, man," Baffert said. "This is not about you or me; it's about a horse making history. It's sacred. Most people don't remember the trainer or jockey or owner of Secretariat or Affirmed. I have to look most of them up. This is about the horse."

As soon as the gates popped open for the 134th Belmont Stakes, it was clear that neither owner, trainer, jockey, nor colt would wind up anywhere near the winner's circle. War Emblem nearly scraped his knees after stumbling at the start as Espinoza's head curled over the colt's ears and from there the mile-and-a-half trip that was supposed to end in the record books only got worse. Jockey and colt bounced off Magic Weisner on their outside and then angled toward the rail with a hurried dash between horses into the first turn, the skittish sprint up the backstretch to assert the dominance shown in the Derby and the Preakness. Finally there was exhaustion and retreat around the far turn as one, two, three, and finally seven horses blew by War Emblem. What had been a throaty roar from a record crowd of 103,222 gave way to muffled murmurs as Sarava, a 70-to-1 shot, ran down Medaglia d'Oro to become the biggest long shot to win the Belmont. War Emblem was beaten by more than nineteen lengths.

"It was lost at the start," Baffert said. "If I was on the walkie-talkie, I would have told Victor to pull him up. I didn't want him to go a mile and a half like that."

If someone would have told Baffert as he was driving out of the parking lot that night that it would be twelve years until another truly exceptional colt graced his barn, he would not have believed them. Over the past five years, he had won three Derbies, four Preaknesses, and a Belmont — or more than half of the American Classics. His barn was full of million-dollar colts and he had owners like Bob Lewis and Prince Salman willing to buy him more. The fates turn cruelly and quickly in horse racing, though. Six weeks after War Emblem stumbled at Belmont, Prince Ahmed bin Salman, just forty-three, died, supposedly of a heart attack suffered sometime after abdominal surgery in Riyadh. A year later, several news organizations named bin Salman as one of several financiers — along with two other princes — of al-Qaeda. All three had died within a week of one another: one in a car accident, another was found dead in the desert and authorities said he had died of "thirst." In 2006, Bob Lewis was gone as well at the age of eighty-one after first his kidney, then his heart failed. Mike Pegram was still a client, but he scaled back his operation as he entered into the casino business in Nevada.

It wasn't like Baffert had completely disappeared. He remained among the top ten nationally in earnings in all but two of those years and won seven Breeders' Cup races over that span. Baffert, however, did not have a horse hit the board again in any of the Triple Crown races until 2009, when Pioneerof the Nile finished second in the Derby. The following year, the Pegram-owned Lookin At Lucky won the Preakness, skipped the Belmont Stakes, captured the Haskell, and was voted Outstanding Three-Year-Old Colt and was given an Eclipse Award. No one was crying for Baffert. He was fifth on the all-time earnings list among trainers with more than $210 million in purses, and he had a feeling the Triple Crown blues were about to lift, mostly because of the colt standing before him now, American Pharoah, and the owner who gave him to him, Ahmed Zayat.

The notorious Mr. Z, as he was aften called, had fired him a few years earlier and stiffed him on his training bill during his bankruptcy and a couple times since. They were starting to have some luck together, though. The McKathans had raved about the colt as soon as he hit their farm, and next to him, he believed the brothers had some of the best eyes for horseflesh in the business. Even though Baffert was a no-show that morning for the colt's breeze, he knew the horse was coming to his barn. He was Zayat Stables' first-string trainer, and even though he had been wandering in the

Triple Crown desert for a spell, his record still spoke for itself.

As the colt walked in circles around the paddock, Baffert started to tingle. American Pharoah had been with him for five months and had not missed a single day of training, which was unusual for a young horse. Most were accident prone or spiked fevers or caught colds as they moved from the country to the city, from the serenity of farm life to the hustle of the racetrack. American Pharoah had turned in eleven timed workouts, or breezes, each time reluctantly bouncing off the track as if he were a barely winded NBA star being benched after warm-ups. Baffert was notoriously demanding of his horses, even his two-year-olds. He worked them hard, fast, and consistently because he could. He was the A-Team trainer for his owners, and if he didn't believe the horse was sound or talented enough, they were banished from his barn and designated to the B Team. He suffered his share of casualties on the Triple Crown road, another knock leveled against him by his critics. Baffert's whole program was designed to identify Triple Crown horses, build their fitness so they'd be able to endure the grueling series, and, hopefully, make some history. Lord knew that three times he had come *this close* to doing just that.

American Pharoah's last work at Los Alamitos at the end of June was a scary-fast five furlongs in 1:00.60 — two-year-olds should not be that fleet and Baffert knew accomplished trainers shouldn't be letting them go that fast. So Baffert gave him three weeks of galloping before letting him loose at Del Mar for another five-eighths of a mile. American Pharoah went even faster — 1:00.20. What was most remarkable was that the colt did it breaking from a starting gate for the first time in his life. Baffert had recognized a bit of his old man, Pioneerof the Nile, in the colt. Both had a big, long stride with a springing motion as if they were running on a trampoline. American Pharoah already had shown far more acceleration. Every time Baffert worked him, he went back and took a look at the pedigree. He believed the turn of foot was traced to Pioneerof the Nile's sire, Empire Maker, and his dam, Star of Goshen.

"It comes from his mother," he decided. "She was a freaky filly, really, really fast."

The paddock was getting crowded as owners, rival trainers, clockers, touts, and media types — racetrackers all — wanted to get a look at the colt that Baffert was so high on.

American Pharoah was no secret among this community. Everyone was talking about the colt in Southern California, about his speed and efficiency of motion, about how the great Baffert had already proclaimed him the best two-year-old to ever come through his barn.

"The easy part is training a horse; the hard part is finding a good one," he said. "I know how to do it. There's no maybe in me. I either see it or I don't."

Baffert saw it in American Pharoah. Now everyone else wanted to see it for themselves. That, however, turned into a problem. The colt appeared to be spooked by the noise, bothered by all the commotion. He fought the groom on the other end of the shank. Baffert could tell he was agitated. American Pharoah worked up a sweat. Suddenly, Martin Garcia appeared at Baffert's side. He was Baffert's first call jockey and had the mount on American Pharoah. Garcia didn't like what he was seeing, either. He got a leg up from Baffert on a clearly stressed out American Pharoah and didn't recognize the colt. In the morning breezes, Garcia was used to hopping on a Ferrari, not the broken down pickup truck down to its last coils he was on now. As American Pharoah joined the eight other horses in the race for the post parade, the colt was unnerved by the crowd, his rivals, and their riders. He skittered sideways, high-stepped, reared, and kicked. He tried to run off from the outrider. Still, American Pharoah remained the favorite on the tote board at the prohibitive odds of 2 to 5. Maybe this was part of the best-two-year-old-Baffert-had-ever-trained's act? After all, this was the first time at the racetrack in the afternoon for American Pharoah. He would pull it together, wouldn't he? When Baffert saw the antics continue during the warm-up, he hoped Garcia could calm the colt down. It wasn't happening. Garcia had no control over American Pharoah. He felt like the parent standing outside of school trying to coax an inconsolable child through its doors as everyone else looked on feeling sorry for him.

Garcia whispered to the colt. He whistled. He smooched to American Pharoah. Nothing. He wrestled with him and jerked on the reins. It made his behavior worse. He just wanted American Pharoah in the gate and the race to be over. When the gates finally opened, American Pharoah simply ran off on his own, leaving Garcia to hang on as the colt went head-to-head with a colt named Om on the rail and Scorpious in between them. He certainly was fast — the half-mile went in 45 seconds. While Om continued to fly, Scorpious backed up. Garcia tried desperately to keep American Pharoah moving forward and got within a head. Baffert was praying his colt was out of gas: He knew they were going too fast, and an extended effort might cook him and set his training back weeks. He got his wish as three horses rolled by American Pharoah and the colt finished a soundly beaten fifth — nine and a quarter lengths behind Om.

Jill Baffert nudged her husband.

"That's one of your best two-year-olds?" she asked.

He nodded.

"It's going to be a long summer," she said.

CHAPTER SIX:
BLINKERS ON; BLINKERS OFF

August 2014, Del Mar Thoroughbred Club

Bob Baffert was certain that he could get American Pharoah back on track, but he was worried about how he was going to fare if the colt was not as capable as he thought of winning the Kentucky Derby and taking a run at a Triple Crown. He was too old to become a completely changed man, but he wanted a fresh start on what he knew was his third and final act. Much had happened over the dozen years since his last good horse. He had gotten divorced from his wife, Sherry, and married Jill Moss, a Louisville morning television anchor twenty years his junior. They had a son, Bode, who was now nine and named after the Olympic skier Bode Miller, a family friend. Then there were the three stents in the left side of his heart, courtesy of a lousy diet, stress, and a fraught trip to the Mideast.

We all come to our own mortality our own

126

way, in our own time. Baffert took his first steps toward his on March 26, 2012, in a hotel room in Dubai. He had arrived the day before feeling awful. He was tired, sick to his stomach, and wrung out from a long flight from Los Angeles. He made himself check on his horses — The Factor was running in the $2 million Golden Shaheen and Game On Dude was running the $10 million Dubai World Cup, the richest race in the world. Upon his return to the hotel, he canceled dinner reservations out and ate at the hotel with Jill and Bode. He awoke in the middle of the night and felt even worse. Jill got her laptop out and started Googling his symptoms and turned ashen when she thought she discovered what was going on: "You're having a heart attack," she told him.

Fortunately, Dubai is among the most modern of Arab Emirates, and its ruler, Sheikh Mohammed bin Rashid al-Maktoum, probably spends more money than anyone in the world on Thoroughbreds and was a friend of the Bafferts. They called for an ambulance and Sheikh Mo, as he's known, sent his cardiologist. In future tellings, the cardiologist would be known as "Dr. Armani" because he was the best dressed doctor Baffert had ever seen, and his first question upon seeing Sheikh Mo was, "How do you say 'this guy is fucked' in your language?" Baffert, however, was truly terrified. The angioplasty revealed two clogged arteries, including one completely blocked. The "widow maker" is what Jill had read on her computer about her husband's symptoms, and now they were hearing it from doctors. He started babbling to Jill a stream-of-thought last will. What to keep. What to sell. What seasons he had to what horses. To call his owners and reassure them their horses would be fine. Jill wasn't listening. While Baffert was being wheeled into surgery in a hospital far from home, hearing the concerned chatter of doctors in a language he didn't understand, he got angry.

"Is this really how it's going to end?" he asked himself.

So in went the stents, and hours later a groggy Baffert awoke to Jill and Dr. Armani at his side. The well-dressed doctor told Baffert how fortunate he was. If he had waited another hour, another five minutes, he might now be dead.

Mr. Z was among the first people to get a hold of him after surgery. Did his trainer need anything? Should he send a plane? The owner had already endeared himself to the Baffert family. He kept trying to name a horse after Bode as he did for his own kids, but Bob was intensely superstitious and thought it would be bad luck and ordered him not to do so. When Mr. Z sent him a son of Belmont Stakes winner Empire Maker, the colt had a name Zayat no longer wanted because he had been named for a long-departed racing manager. Offhandedly, Baffert said that around the barn they would just call the colt Bodemeister, his son's nickname, until he got a real one. Not long after, papers from the Jockey Club arrived that officially declared the colt Bodemeister. Baffert was forgiving of Zayat's sleight of hand; the colt had won two of his first three races, including the Grade 2 San Felipe Stakes. He was potentially his Derby horse.

Baffert was released from the hospital in time for the Dubai races a week later. He was a shadow of himself and neither The Factor, who finished sixth, nor Game On Dude, who was ninth, ran very well. Much later, when cameras were rolling and tape recorders turned on, and Baffert was in stand-up mode, that evening at the track in Dubai would be turned into another laugh line.

"Hey, I know you guys are disappointed," Baffert said he told his owners, "but I'm just happy I was here to see your horses run bad."

Maybe Baffert should have seen it coming. He had high cholesterol but did not consistently take the statins that were prescribed to him. He preferred chicken fried steaks to broiled chicken, fried eggs to egg whites, and the treadmill and elliptical machines in his home were used as clothes racks rather than as a way to walk off pounds, stress, or to strengthen his heart. There also was a history of heart disease on his mother's side of the family.

Fortunately it was easy for Baffert to get a handle on his diet and spend at least forty-five minutes a day on the treadmill. He lost twenty pounds and his cholesterol came down. As a self-professed control freak in an occupation that requires seven-days-a-week-around-the-clock attention, truly slowing down for Baffert was like trying to throttle back American Pharoah in his racing debut. Ever since they were married in 2002, Jill Baffert had been fighting a mostly losing battle of getting her husband to live in the moment. Over the years, much had been made about Baffert's penchant for sleeping late and not arriving at his barn before dawn as most of his peers did. He encouraged his slacker image. Jill Baffert

130

knew better.

"Everybody thinks he just blows in here late," she said, "but he's consumed twenty-four-seven with his horses. He's at the barns all morning, the track in the afternoon, and if we're home the races are always on the satellite and the phone is always ringing. He needed to find some peace with his place in the world."

With good horses especially, Jill understood her husband was always looking forward, planning for the next couple of races, coming up with contingency plans so if a horse spiked a fever and missed one day or a week of training, there were other options. They never went on a honeymoon or did anything else where horses were not involved.

"We would never take a vacation because we could go somewhere physically, but Bob's mind would never go," she said. "He would always be at work."

Jill was a South Carolina native who looked like the television personality she once was: blond, warm, and quick to offer a smile. Besides being his wife, Jill was Baffert's top lieutenant, the barn's communication advisor, and his staunchest defender. Jill told him when he was being an asshole, and she went after rival trainers and owners who she thought were treating her husband poorly. She was the first to tell him that he was out of line with his criticism of Gary Stevens's ride of Point Given at the Haskell and told him to apologize.

Jill also was quick to light into anyone she thought was doing the Bafferts dirty. In the days before the 2012 Pacific Classic, she got into a profanity-laden shouting match with Mark Verge, then the CEO of Santa Anita Park, after he and some other investors bought a contender named Richard's Kid and moved him out of her husband's barn. Verge was the best friend of trainer Doug O'Neill, an upstart who was challenging Baffert's position as the West Coast's top trainer, and he was as loquacious and often as inappropriate as Baffert was when he burst in on the scene.

After the heart attack, Jill stepped up her efforts to slow her husband down and make him take care of himself. She didn't care if he watched race replays on the treadmill as long as he put his miles in. She pushed him to scale back his operation and delegate more responsibilities to a staff that mostly had been with him for decades. He kept a string of 70 horses now rather than the 120 he once had. His top assistant, Jimmy Barnes, did most of the traveling with the barn's big horses. He was the one now who went to New York or Kentucky for a big race weeks early and put the contenders through their paces until Baffert arrived a day or two before post time. Jill scheduled the vacations now herself and made her husband go on them. She got him to skip an afternoon or two at the racetrack to spend more time with Bode.

That part wasn't hard at all for Baffert. He adored his son, and he and Jill took Bode with them everywhere. Baffert worked on his Pinewood Derby car with him for the Boy Scouts, got to school events and games early, and stayed late. Bode was in the paddock before the race and the winner's circle afterward. Baffert exposed him to every aspect of being a horse trainer and often told him not to follow in his old man's footsteps. Baffert knew he was getting an opportunity to learn from his mistakes. To claw his way to the top of first the quarter horse and then the Thoroughbred industry had meant late nights, early mornings, and long trips away.

By his own admission, he had been a largely absentee father for his sons Taylor, Canyon, and Forest and his daughter Savannah. He would listen to them tell him about basketball and baseball games that he had missed and his stomach would churn and he would feel awful, but he also knew how hard he had worked to get to the top level. Between those missed connections and the divorce from Sherry, there was some tension with the older kids.

"There are a lot of trainers out there who are happily married and have time to spend with their children, but most of them cannot compete at the level we're competing at," he said. "To stay at the top, you cannot let up for a second."

Baffert was trying to do his best to let up enough to be a good father as well as remain healthy. He had lost his mother, Ellie, in 2011, and the Chief the following year. He was a grown man and still missed them deeply. It had been a wake-up call to become more present in all of his children's lives.

"Lost my first hero and mentor today. There's a new cowboy in Heaven," Baffert tweeted on the day Bill died. "R.I.P. Chief. I miss you already."

Another decision he had made recently to preserve his physical and mental health was to stop participating in or reading social media such as Twitter and Facebook. Seeing what others are saying about you in real time and anonymously is not a good thing for a control freak, especially one who could be as thin-skinned as Baffert. Among turf writers and mainstream sports reporters, the trainer had enjoyed mostly favorable coverage as he ascended in the sport. In fact, in 2009, Baffert was voted into the National Museum of Racing's Hall of Fame by a landslide on his first year of eligibility. Most everyone liked him. He was always available and possessed a motor mouth that spit out as many non sequiturs as jokes but always filled up a notebook. Even when he wasn't "on," Baffert was a pleasant guy to be around and tried to engage you on a human level. There were some difficult conversations over the years involving the overuse of drugs in the sport and the lack of consistent rules, regulations, or transparency that had pushed horse racing closer to boxing when it came to the perception of lawlessness. Times were changing and the general public was more concerned about how horses were treated away from the racetrack and what kind of harm was being done to them on it. It took the death of the filly Eight Belles, who had to be euthanized on the track after breaking both her front ankles after finishing second in the 2008 Kentucky Derby, to get the attention of everyone from Congress to animal rights activists. Though no drugs or anything else untoward showed up in Eight Belles's autopsy, Rick Dutrow, the trainer of the winning Big Brown, made them a focus when he admitted that he treated his colt with the steroid Winstrol.

Dutrow was not alone and everyone on the racetrack and around the sport knew so. Just as Major League baseball had its steroid era, so did horse racing, and at a Congressional hearing later that year, owners such as Jess Jackson acknowledged that Curlin, twice Horse of the Year, had been given steroids for some of his campaign. Steroids were subsequently outlawed but the pursuit of finding an edge through chemistry to win races continues to be woven in the fabric of horse racing. Baffert didn't like talking about it, nor anyone writing about it, especially the incidents where he was sanctioned for drug violations. He refused to make his veterinarian records public when asked and rebuffed the tough questions by saying that they were only intended to hurt the sport.

In 2012, the *New York Times* published a series of stories that found that twenty-four horses a week died on American racetracks and that the industry continued to put animal and rider at risk. A computer analysis of data from more than 150,000 races, along with injury reports, drug test results, and interviews, showed an industry still mired in a culture of drugs and lax regulation and a fatal breakdown rate that remained far worse than in most racing jurisdictions of the world. There was plenty of blame to go around, but it was clear the new economics of racing were making an always-dangerous game even more so. Faced with a steep loss of customers, racetracks have increasingly added casino gambling to their operations, resulting in higher purses but also providing an incentive for trainers to race unfit horses. In 2012, at Aqueduct Racetrack in Queens, the number of dead and injured horses had risen sharply since a casino opened there the previous year. Laboratories are unable to detect the newest performance-enhancing drugs, while trainers experimented with anything that might give them an edge, including chemicals that bulk up pigs and cattle before slaughter, cobra venom, Viagra, blood-doping agents, stimulants, and cancer drugs.

Legal therapeutic drugs — pain medicine in particular — pose the greatest risk to horse and rider. In England, where breakdown rates are half of what they are in the

United States, horses may not race on *any* drugs and the rules are aggressively enforced. At higher levels, pain medicine can mask injury, rendering prerace examinations less effective. If a horse cannot feel an existing injury, it may run harder than it otherwise would, putting extra stress on the injury. As many as 90 percent of horses that break down had preexisting injuries, according to California researchers who studied necropsies of horses that died at the state's racetracks. The spotlight on the sport became even more unflattering that spring when a colt named I'll Have Another won the Kentucky Derby and then the Preakness Stakes. He was trained by Baffert's West Coast rival, Doug O'Neill, who began the Triple Crown with more than a dozen drug violations in four states, among them three instances where one of his horses appeared to receive a "milkshake," a concoction of baking soda, sugar, and electrolytes delivered through a tube down a horse's nose to combat fatigue. In between the Preakness and I'll Have Another's bid to sweep the Triple Crown, O'Neill was suspended for forty-five days in California for exceeding the allowable limit for total carbon dioxide in one of his horses. Elevated carbon dioxide levels indicates a horse was given a "milkshake." The suspension would start in July, after O'Neill saddled I'll Have Another in the Belmont Stakes. New York regulators responded with strict security and surveillance measures on all trainers competing in the race, including housing their horses in secured barns beginning three days before the race. They had specific requirements for O'Neill solely. Neither he nor his veterinarian could treat the colt without a board investigator present. All treatments and feed had to be discussed and logged with the investigator. All vet records had to be turned over daily to regulators.

The saga of O'Neill and I'll Have Another took one final and unpredictable turn: On the eve of the Belmont, the colt was scratched from the race because of a sore tendon in his left foreleg. It was a minor injury, the equine equivalent of a sprained ankle, but O'Neill and his owner concluded it would have compromised I'll Have Another's chances and decided against risking additional injury. He was retired immediately.

"It's far from tragic," O'Neill said, "but it's extremely disappointing."

Both New York State officials and O'Neill moved quickly to try to eliminate any suspicion surrounding the decision. The New York State Racing and Wagering Board said that all entrants in the Belmont Stakes were tested for prohibited substances and that all the tests came back negative. O'Neill blamed only bad luck.

"It's just a freakish thing," he said.

Between the public's increased desire that horses be humanely cared for, drugs prohibited, and the ability of the Internet to shrink the world, Baffert and other high-profile trainers were under increased scrutiny. The backsides of racetracks are fiercely competitive and a rumor or real incident can ripple from groom to exercise rider to barn foreman to trainer to owner in the course of a morning. There is a great deal of jealousy, which is perhaps natural when you have anywhere from 50 to 150 trainers knocking heads against one another day in and day out. Familiarity breeds contempt and words get twisted and lies told. Up until a decade ago, each circuit — New York, Kentucky, and California — was its own small town and the damage didn't travel much beyond the racetrack gates. Turf writers knew things as did gamblers and racetrackers, but they preferred to use it to their own advantage, like dropping a lot of money on a horse with an unpublished workout or betting against a sore prohibitive favorite. Now workout times are tweeted out moments after the final click of a stopwatch and suspicions can be raised in an instant from California to New York, and alliances are formed between people who may not even know each other's real names.

Bob and Jill Baffert are nothing if not modern and each opened social media accounts like many do to communicate better with friends and business associates. It also opened them up to hearing the unflattering things that were said about them in Santa Anita Park's track kitchen or the bar rooms ringing Del Mar. It's not pleasant and most ignore the ugliest sentiments and dismiss them as isolated. Baffert found himself in a social media firestorm in the last week of 2012, however, when a former stakes-caliber racehorse he trained named Tweebster had to be put down after suffering multiple fractures in his left front leg in a cheap claiming race at Santa Anita.

Not many horses from the Baffert barn ran in $12,500 claiming races, especially ones that had finished third in the Native Diver Handicap, a Grade 3 race, and competed in stakes races as recently as three months before, as Tweebster had. Even rarer was to see a horse trained by Baffert have only two timed workouts in the two months since its last race. Baffert decided to issue a statement through Santa Anita that said he dropped Tweebster into the bottom ranks of racing in the hopes of getting the horse a "confidence booster" in an easy race. He acknowledged the criticism on Twitter and other social media that pointed out gaps in Tweebster's workout schedule and his precipitous drop as telltale signs of a lame horse.

"I understand a severe drop in class can indicate a horse is unsound, but I assure you that was not the case with Tweebster," Baffert said.

He said that Tweebster was thoroughly examined by the state veterinarian that morning and found to be perfectly sound going into the race. He did not respond to a request to share Tweebster's veterinary records, to detail his medication history, or to explain the gap in the horse's workout patterns.

"The death of any horse on the racetrack is hard to accept," Baffert said. "When that horse is one who you saw and took care of every day, the pain is physically gut-wrenching. While I realize some people are going to think what they want, I want to express my feelings and deepest regret over the loss of a horse for whom I had a great deal of affection."

Baffert went viral again four months later when word came that the California Horse Racing Board (CHRB) was investigating the sudden deaths of seven horses he trained over a span of sixteen months. Thoroughbreds rarely die suddenly: A 2010 study in the *Equine Veterinary Journal* found that sudden death occurred in 9 percent of fatalities in California. In four of the Baffert-trained horses, cardiac or heart problems were the cause; two died of internal bleeding, and another had a massive abdominal/thoracic cavity hemorrhage, according to the necropsies. He cooperated with investigators but hired a crisis management firm to help him navigate the negative press.

In November, the horse racing board issued a final report that Baffert had been giving every horse in his barn a thyroid hormone without ever checking to see if any of them had a thyroid problem. The drug thyroxine was so routinely prescribed in the Baffert barn that it was dispensed for one of the horses a week after the horse had died. Baffert acknowledged directing his veterinarians to use thyroxine on all his horses, which is in conflict with the policy of the American Association of Equine Practitioners, the industry's most influential veterinary group, which says treatments "should be based upon a specific diagnosis and administered in the context of a valid and transparent owner-trainer-veterinarian relationship." Baffert told the investigators that he thought the medication would help "build up" his horses. This came as a surprise because the drug is generally associated with weight loss. He said he quit using the drug after the seventh horse died. At least one study indicated that the drug can cause "cardiac alterations" in horses. In summarizing his report to the board, CHRB's equine medical director, Dr. Rick Arthur, said he had no conclusive explanation of how seven horses belonging to one trainer dropped dead during a sixteen-month period.

"Statistically, it is extremely abnormal," Arthur said. "We couldn't find anything. It doesn't change the fact that we don't have an answer. It does say there is something wrong here."

The board, however, ultimately found no evidence that any rules or regulations had been violated, which said plenty about how loosely regulated the sport is and how a wide array of questionable tactics would be considered permissible. After the report's release, Baffert claimed vindication: "I'm gratified that CHRB completed its investigation and found there was no wrongdoing," he wrote on his Twitter account.

It took an unfortunate experience with a small-time grifter for Baffert to swear off social media altogether and to look inward for how the rest of his career was going to evolve. Jonathan Pippin, a twenty-seven-year-old Ohio man, was able to convince Bob and Jill Baffert that there was a conspiracy among racing officials and media members to tarnish the trainer's reputation. He was a career con man who sold shares of horses he didn't own to unsuspecting victims at some of the cheapest racetracks in the nation. He made his way west and somehow gained the confidence of the Bafferts, managing to get an invitation to their home on the weekend of the Santa Anita Handicap, one of the West Coast's premier races.

"How Pippin traveled from a world of bottom-level claimers at Thistledown and Mountaineer Park to the Santa Anita Handicap winner's circle alongside Game On Dude and American racing's most famous trainer is a tale of deceit, opportunism, and unmitigated gall," wrote Ray Paulick, who broke the story for the online Paulick Report.com. "It's a bewildering story of social media gone wrong, fake e-mail accounts, online bullying, secretly recorded tapes and voice changing machines."

It was, indeed, a remarkable tale of how Pippin dummied up e-mails allegedly from media members saying they were out to get Baffert, created Twitter accounts to harass any perceived critics, and posing as a lawyer, contacted some people at their homes. Pippin employed a voice changing machine and called reporters, claiming to have hours of recordings from the Baffert barn. It took a while, but Baffert started to suspect Pippin was not who he said he was and hired a private investigator and an attorney. In the widely read August 11, 2014, Paulick Report.com story, Pippin laid out how he gained the trainer's and his wife's trust and tried to make money off them. Baffert has refused to address it directly, but he did indicate that he was embarrassed by the episode.

He needed to appreciate the opportunity the arrival of American Pharoah had presented to him. Baffert could win his fourth Kentucky Derby. He could be the trainer of the twelfth Triple Crown champion and the first since Affirmed thirty-seven years ago. To do so, he needed to put blinkers on, to focus on the horse, his family, and his barn. No distractions.

Baffert was worried about American Pharoah's poor performance in his debut at Del Mar. For all the colt's talent, he was a slow, sometimes stubborn learner, and often hard to handle. He earned the nickname *pendejo* around the barn which, in Spanish, translated into something like "idiot." Baffert recognized that he was a well-built horse who wanted to go fast — a good thing on the racetrack but not around the barn. So he decided to write the debut off as a bad day at school for a young horse. American Pharoah had been rank in the paddock and just run off. Baffert thought he should have schooled him more, walked him over there to the paddock on an afternoon of a race, and let him get used to the sights and sounds of race day. He'd do more of that beginning now. Baffert had fit American Pharoah with blinkers, or cups on his eyes, believing if he took away the colt's peripheral vision he would focus on what he was doing and relax easier. He also wore a shadow roll on the bridge of his nose to keep him from seeing the shadows below him on the ground. Nine days after his debut, the colt returned to the track for a breeze without blinkers and cotton stuffed in his ears. The latter was an old quarter horse trick that Baffert had employed previously on a handful of highly strung Thoroughbreds. American Pharoah ripped off a powerful four furlongs in 48 seconds like he was strolling in his sleep.

Baffert thought American Pharoah was too good for another maiden race for non-winners. Instead, he circled the Del Mar Futurity for American Pharoah's next race. He rarely tossed a maiden into a high-quality stakes race, especially one that had finished a well-beaten fifth the only time he had ever run, but Baffert felt good about it.

Now all he needed was to find a new rider for American Pharoah. Martin Garcia had neither a winning nor a fun experience with the colt. Both colt and rider needed a change.

CHAPTER SEVEN:
A ROCKET SHIP!

September 3, 2014

It already had been an eventful closing day at Del Mar for Victor Espinoza. He was sitting in the gate atop a two-year-old named Visitation, awaiting the bell for the Oak Tree Juvenile, when the colt next to him by the name of Increase launched his rider, Fernando Perez, into the air and started swirling and kicking like a bucking bull and startling the other horses. Espinoza's mount was banged against the stall; two other colts broke through the gate and ran off. All three were scratched, including Visitation, sending Espinoza back to the jockey's room with his tack in hand and a smile as bright as a lighthouse beaming from a face as cracked and weathered as an old saddle. Nothing much ever got under Espinoza's skin, and in a race an hour later he was looking forward to climbing on the back of a colt trained by Bob Baffert named American

Pharoah in the $300,000 Grade 1 Del Mar Futurity.

Espinoza didn't know much about the colt. He had only picked up the mount a couple of days ago after the field of nine was entered and Baffert found himself without a rider. Espinoza knew he was not Baffert's first choice to ride the colt, or even his second or third. He had not done much business with the trainer recently. Martin Garcia was the barn's first-call rider, but he was on another Baffert horse, Holiday Camp. Gary Stevens, a close friend of Baffert's, was getting a knee replacement and was unavailable. Rafael Bejarano and Mike Smith, two jockeys Baffert liked to use, were already on other horses for the Del Mar Futurity. Baffert was out of options and Espinoza didn't have any.

His agent, Brian Beach, had been working the trainer Mark Casse about getting Espinoza on his horse Skyway, who had just won the Best Pal Stakes and whose rider Stewart Elliott was out with an injury. Casse chose Corey Nakatani instead.

"You still open?" Baffert asked Beach in the Del Mar racing office shortly before entries to the Futurity were taken. "I'm thinking of running a horse who is sort of a problem child."

Baffert had been thinking of War Emblem, who had been hands down the most hateful horse he had ever been around: "He was mean, didn't want anyone around him, savage." The colt could run, however, and Espinoza somehow got along with him.

"Sure," replied Beach.

Beach flashed back to a July morning, leaning against the rail with Baffert taking in the sea air when a big bay colt blew by.

"This is my best two-year-old," Baffert had told him.

The previous month in his debut, however, American Pharoah looked merely ordinary when he finished a well-beaten fifth behind two horses that ran past him and were entered today in the Futurity — the runner-up Iron Fist and fourth-place finisher Calculator. The winner, Om, however, had to miss the race with a minor injury, perhaps a result of going too fast too early in his career. Two-year-olds were still growing. Baffert also had told Espinoza that American Pharoah had left his race in the paddock but that he had had ample schooling in the paddock since and was becoming a quiet horse. The trainer also showed him the cotton that he was going to put into the colt's ears and gave him a single, confident instruction: "Let him run."

On the puzzling, if not negative, side, was the fact that American Pharoah was a winless horse trying the deepest water of his infant career and Baffert was not even at the racetrack. He had gotten a jump on getaway day and headed to Los Angeles with Jill and Bode to move back into his home. It wasn't exactly the show of support for what you have proclaimed to be the best two-year-old you ever had in your barn. Maybe Baffert didn't expect to get his photo taken in the winner's circle after the race. It had been a quiet meet for Baffert, with his barn winning only twelve races. For the first time in many summers, he was out of contention for winning the meet's training title.

Espinoza, however, refused to read too much into the conflicting evidence. In fact, he was in the midst of a remarkable mid-career rejuvenation; he was embracing the role fate played in it and was choosing whimsy over worry to stay happy. The previous year, Espinoza didn't have a Futurity mount but felt compelled to stay and watch the race because there was a colt in the field named California Chrome. One morning earlier in the Del Mar meet, Espinoza had been working a horse on the racetrack when he saw a flash of white blow by him. He saw the ivory face, a blaze the width of his snout, and the matching socks — the "chrome" that figured in its name. The colt's narrow frame and playfulness left little doubt he was a two-year-old. When the colt got to running, however, Espinoza was transfixed. He hit the ground softly, as if he were skipping on talcum powder. Espinoza asked around and found that the horse's name was California Chrome. He didn't usually study the Daily Racing Form or pore over video in preparation for races. He rode on instinct, a rider who let the horse tell him how he should be ridden, but Espinoza did go and watch replays of California Chrome's previous races and liked the way he fought.

"I fell crazy for that horse," he said. "I told Brian that someday I'd like to ride him."

He watched intently as the colt lined up against ten of the best two-year-olds in California. Nearing the far turn of the seven-furlong race, California Chrome hurtled forward as if sprung from a slingshot. His rider, Alberto Delgado, decided to split horses in the stretch, but the colt took an accidental whip to his face from the jockey of a rival, stopping his momentum. They finished two lengths behind the winner, in sixth place. Espinoza was even more impressed — most horses would have quit running after a whip to the face.

Two months later, the colt's trainer, Art Sherman, called Beach and asked him if Espinoza was available to ride in the King Glorious Stakes. Sherman, seventy-seven, was beyond the twilight of his career. He cherished his naptime and confessed to spending too much time with morning television. Sherman also was at the opposite end of the spectrum as Bob Baffert, training twenty-five to forty horses at a time for middle-class owners trying, but mostly failing, to break even as they experienced some thrills and had some laughs hoping for a home-run horse. In California Chrome, Sherman had found his and did not want to screw it up. He had ridden Espinoza at Golden Gate Fields in Northern California when the jockey was first starting out twenty years ago. He was looking for a "steady rider" for California Chrome, one who would get out of the way of the best horse Sherman ever had in his barn.

Beach remembered his conversation with Espinoza about the fast colt with "all that white." He said absolutely. California Chrome won the next six races with Espinoza in the irons, including the Derby and the Preakness. Just three months earlier, Espinoza had hustled Sherman's California Chrome out of the starting gate for the 146th running of the Belmont Stakes for his second crack at sweeping the Triple Crown. He swung his colt into the stretch with a shot, but Chrome was out of gas and fought hard to finish fourth. Instead of bringing home horse racing's twelfth Triple Crown champion, Espinoza and California Chrome joined twelve other would-be champions who could not get to the finish line first in the Belmont Stakes.

Espinoza slipped off California Chrome that evening with a smile and gave the colt a long nuzzle. As soon as he came out of the gate, Espinoza knew he didn't have the same colt beneath him that had emphatically run off with the Derby and Preakness. Horse and rider were in unfamiliar territory — behind and inside other horses with dirt spraying the colt's chest. Espinoza knew California Chrome preferred launching just off the flank of horses from the outside. Worse than that, however, he sensed a dangerous rival by the name of Tonalist, who was floating ahead of him on cruise control. Beneath him, Espinoza felt something he had never felt from California Chrome in his six previous starts: not enough horse.

"He was empty," Espinoza said.

As they pursued Tonalist, Espinoza tried to rouse California Chrome by swinging to the outside. For an instant, it looked as if that had done the trick. His colt found a rocket boost that sent him into orbit around the front-runners as he headed into the final turn. Tonalist, however, was gobbling up ground like a John Deere combine at harvest time, and his rider, Joel Rosario, felt a rumble beneath him, one that he liked a lot. He knew that he was going to win. Behind him, Espinoza knew that his magical run was not going to end in the history books. It was going to be interrupted atop a noble but dog-tired horse.

"He's one of the best horses I've ever ridden," said Espinoza afterward, disappointed but still smiling and at peace. He and his colt had discovered again what eleven others before them had in the previous thirty-six years: Winning the Triple Crown is really, really hard. "It's tough for California Chrome to come back in three weeks and run a mile and a half."

Espinoza, however, was a different rider, a different man than he had been twelve years earlier when he and War Emblem staggered out of the gate, the colt scraping his knees and subsequently finishing nineteen lengths behind the 70-to-1 long shot Sarava. Then, Espinoza struggled with his English and was being pushed and pulled by the pressure of the Triple Crown and the demands of a tough boss in Bob Baffert. He never felt as alone as he did when he galloped War Emblem back to the front of the grandstand and was met by an angry, rather than heartbroken, silence coming from the more than 102,000 who had come there hoping to see something — at least a gallant try. Instead, the stumble at the gate had plummeted the crowd's spirits. Then for the next 2:29.71 it took the field to circle the track with Espinoza and War Emblem trailing far, far behind, people seethed. What they were watching was just a horse race, one that could have been the fifth on any Wednesday at Aqueduct, that grind house of a track seventeen miles east of here, but definitely unfitting for a Triple Crown race.

Espinoza made his way back to the jockey's room looking like a condemned man, pushing his way through the jubilant winner's circle, playing back how the race had unfolded. Did he do all he could? New York tracks are tough and the railbirds were screaming and cussing at him as he made his way to the breezeway that led to the jockeys' room. Once inside there, none of his fellow riders even looked at him. They all knew there was nothing to say. Gary Stevens had been crushed when he had lost here with Silver Charm. He started toward Espinoza, but thought better of it when he saw how dark and shell-shocked the rider looked.

"It was like somebody had died," he said.

When his valet handed Espinoza an envelope, he was at first confused. It was a check for $85, the guaranteed saddle fee all riders receive for getting their horses around the track. His stomach turned; the previous five weeks had taken far more than that out of his hide: "I thought that was my shot, and worse, I didn't even want another one."

Espinoza lost more than a horse race that evening. He had lost his heart for riding. Espinoza grew up on a family farm north of Mexico with goals rather than dreams. He was the youngest of twelve children, and it took all of them to make ends meet. Espinoza was barely fourteen when he lifted an older brother's driver's license and got a job behind the wheel of a Greyhound-style bus that was overflowing with people like him working whatever jobs they could find in the bigger towns and cities and needed a way to get there. His brother, Jose, had moved to Cancun and found work on a farm where quarter horses were trained. When Victor was fifteen, he joined his older brother. At eighteen, Jose was now the head trainer and needed help. They worked long hours, but the brothers learned how to keep a horse healthy. Victor had saved his money and was attending jockey's school. Soon he was riding Thoroughbreds at Mexico City's premier track, Hipódromo de las Américas, even though he remained terrified of being on a horse's back. He felt like he had no other choice.

"I wasn't born to be a jockey," Espinoza said. "I didn't always want to be a jockey. I just wanted to survive and have a better life."

He came to Northern California as a seventeen-year-old and picked up a few dollars and some valuable experience galloping horses in the morning. He talked a handful of trainers into letting him ride in the races in the afternoon and demonstrated enough talent to attract an agent and to enter the racetrack world as an apprentice jockey. It was an entry-level position that offered trainers the opportunity to ride a jockey anywhere from five to ten pounds lighter than his rivals, which can mean the difference between a third-place and first-place check. It also gave them an eager and free-of-charge exercise rider in the mornings. For a bug boy, as they are called, it put Espinoza in the proximity of seasoned horsemen and experienced riders. It was in Art Sherman's interest to teach Espinoza how to read a horse and how to report back what it had done well and what it needed to work on.

It was vital as well for Russell Baze, North America's winningest rider, to pass on the tools and etiquette of a dangerous trade. It is an interesting dynamic inside a jockeys' room where, on one hand, no one wants to help a kid so much that he beats you, but on the other hand, you need to teach him how to ride safely and professionally because the lives of every jockey inside depend on it. It also is not easy losing race after race under the watchful eyes of colleagues and competitors in a room that is part claustrophobic frat house and part tense waiting room to the winner's circle.

"You got to leave the last race in the room," said Espinoza.

Espinoza, the reluctant jockey, learned early that if he was going to achieve his goals and have a better life, he needed to get stronger. One afternoon in a cheap race easily 20,000 mounts ago, he was atop a horse that he could not control. Espinoza held on for dear life and then was angry at himself for being so terrified. The next day he joined a gym and went about sculpting a body where his thighs and arms looked pulled through with cable.

"I needed to be able to dominate a horse," he said. "To make him do what I wanted."

At 112 pounds, Espinoza was a natural lightweight who preferred five-mile runs in the San Gabriel Mountains that sprayed a rouge halo around his home, the weight room, and eating when and whatever he wanted. He was able to bench press his body weight thirty-eight times and pop off endless pull-ups as if he were on a spring. Most riders are forced into the sauna and the flipping toilets that are standard issue for jockey rooms everywhere so they could sweat and throw up and shrink their natural 130-pound frames into the 118-pound package they needed to ride. It is a process that transforms the most mild-mannered riders into cranky and ill-tempered competitors.

"He doesn't drink, and he's not a partier," Beach said. "He's light and a good finisher. He gives an honest appraisal of the horse after he gets off. No sugarcoating it — you know where you stand with Victor. The guys who constantly fight their weight are snarly and grumpy. That life wears on them. Victor is one of the few who's always happy."

Espinoza's loss aboard War Emblem in the Belmont continued to haunt him. He kept his head down and continued to grind out a living at the top of the national jockey standings, averaging more than 200 victories and more than $12 million in purses over the next five years by being what Art Sherman had wanted for California Chrome: a steady hand.

In 2010, as his thirty-eighth birthday approached, Espinoza took an honest appraisal of himself. He was receiving fewer mounts and winning less often. His annual earnings were half of what they had been. He was in a slump and decided it was his own fault. He was tired and bored.

"I wasn't hungry and I wasn't having any fun," he said. "I was thinking of retiring."

Espinoza also was beginning a personal relationship, one that made him consider abandoning his bachelor ways. Stephanie Kunkel was thirteen years younger than Espinoza and did not know much about horse racing or his career. Espinoza liked it that way. They would get in his Lamborghini and just drive the coast or pull into a shopping center to indulge his inner mall rat, buying a new suit, some Salvatore Ferragamo shoes, or a piece to set on the bureau in his bedroom. Stephanie was blond and eight inches taller than Victor and he was falling in love. They were nearly a year into the relationship when she found out he had won a Kentucky Derby and Preakness Stakes and was aboard one of those horses who had gone to the Belmont Stakes with a shot at sweeping the series.

"Have you ever thought about doing it again?" she asked him.

Espinoza explained to her that winning a single Derby was hard enough and that the odds were long that he would find a horse with the ability to win another one, let alone capture the Preakness and return to New York with a Triple Crown hanging in the balance. The conversation stuck with him, though.

"Now that I'm happy away from the track," he told himself, "why can't I be happier on it?"

There was no reason. Espinoza decided to look forward to the mornings when he would get on horses and try to drum up new business instead of dreading them. He chose to enjoy his time aboard the creatures who had taken him from a farm in Mexico to a big house at the foot of the San Gabriel Mountains and another on the beach near Del Mar.

"I became more joyful," he said, accompanied by a burst of laughter.

In fact, Espinoza laughed a lot. He smiled even more and looked the same way in the winner's circle as he did walking alongside a trainer after a race explaining why his horse finished up the track. He was carefree.

Espinoza decided to win another Derby for his girlfriend, to win another one for himself. Now all he needed was the right horse. One year passed, then another, and another, and America's most famous race went off without him.

Then last summer in Del Mar, California Chrome came along.

Then California Chrome lost in the Belmont.

At forty-two years old, with twelve years of racing under his belt, Espinoza understood that it was okay. He had done all he could to get the horse to the finish line first.

"It's an animal," Espinoza says. "He wakes up every day like you and I, but he decides, 'I don't want to run.' Or he's in a bad mood, or he's tired. I've learned to remember that they are animals and I can't always control them."

He had learned something else far more

important away from the racetrack a decade earlier when a friend, a wealthy one, took him to a hospital in Los Angeles for cancer patients. Like Espinoza, his friend was a private man who had come from nothing and made a very comfortable life for him and his family. One day, they were having lunch and the friend felt Espinoza's sadness, a feeling that the rider was feeling sorry for himself. Afterward, he took Espinoza on an unannounced trip to the pediatric floor at City of Hope Hospital. They walked in and Espinoza immediately had his breath taken away by the sight of toddlers, four- and five-year-olds, with sunken cheeks, without their hair, and moving as if they were in slow motion. Still, the kids smiled at him and laughed with each other. Espinoza lasted about five minutes inside. He returned to the car and waited. He did something else that he could never remember doing as an adult.

"I cried," he said.

Soon after, Espinoza started donating 10 percent of his earnings to the hospital. He did it through his corporation and bookkeeper and sometimes sent it weekly, sometimes monthly or even quarterly. The money arrived in odd amounts wholly dictated by whether he was riding well and winning or not riding very well. He still couldn't actually visit the children; even the thought of it broke him in pieces.

"Sometimes I forget to pay my bills, but I never forget about City of Hope," he said.

No one would have ever known about his ties to the hospital if he had not lost his composure at a press conference immediately after winning his second Kentucky Derby aboard California Chrome. Steve Coburn, one of the colt's co-owners and breeder, brought up the death of his sister, Brenda, and how divine intervention was at work.

"The colt was born on my sister Brenda's birthday," he said. "She died of cancer at age thirty-six. It will be thirty-six years this year since there was a Triple Crown winner."

Espinoza, sitting next to him, turned and looked at Coburn. His shoulders started to shake, and then he began to sob, and out tumbled the story of his connection to the children of City of Hope and how his share of earnings — roughly $100,000 — was bound for the hospital. Now Coburn was consoling Espinoza.

"Here we are, worrying about whether we can win a race and stressing about all the decisions we have to make," Espinoza said, "and then you see these kids, and they're happy."

Espinoza had no choice but to choose joy over worry and to believe that California Chrome had carried him to the brink of glory because he had willed a chance to ride him. No wonder he chose to ignore the fact that he was the third or fourth choice to ride American Pharoah in the Del Mar Futurity. Espinoza didn't need Baffert to be here. He and the colt would figure out if they were meant for each other.

In the paddock, Espinoza glanced at the tote board and saw that Skyway, the Mark Casse colt his agent could not get him on, was the favorite. American Pharoah was taking some money as well, though, and was the second choice at 3 to 1 despite his poor debut. Baffert had called earlier in the morning and told him, "Whatever you do, put him on the lead."

Espinoza liked the looks of his colt. He stood tall and was balanced. He was cool and composed today, the cotton peeking out of his ears was doing its job. Head-to-toe bays were rare and the jockey thought it was almost as startling as the white flashes of California Chrome. Espinoza asked Baffert's assistant Jimmy Barnes about American Pharoah's sawed off tail.

"That's the way he came to us," Barnes said. "He'll swat at a fly and come up short, but it doesn't seem to make any difference in the way he runs."

American Pharoah had drawn the Number 1 hole and would be breaking from the rail, which was often tricky for young horses at today's distance of seven furlongs. It was a long run up the chute until the field actually hit the main track. Before giving Espinoza a leg up on American Pharoah, Barnes reminded him that the "rail was golden today."

"Just break and bounce out of there," he said.

Espinoza let American Pharoah tell him how he wanted to warm up. He had about ten minutes or so to make a new friend of the colt, and just like first dates, he thought that being a good listener made for a better impression. American Pharoah was well within himself as they loosened up, and Espinoza thought the colt carried his power lightly. They were first to load into the starting gate, and American Pharoah remained poised as the other eight horses banged their way into their posts. When the field was still enough, the gates clanged and the race was on. American Pharoah was caught flat-footed and was slow to get out, so Espinoza shook up his reins, gently asking him to run on. He felt the colt accelerate beneath him and within two strides he was in the bit. It was like tapping the accelerator of a sports car and being surprised by how quickly and powerfully it showed its colors. Espinoza made the lead before they hit the quarter pole and was a length ahead of the other Baffert horse, Holiday Camp, at the half-mile mark. He could feel that American Pharoah possessed a high cruising speed, a characteristic of a nice horse. As they rounded the far turn, Espinoza knew that he and American Pharoah were going to end up in the winner's circle. They were two lengths ahead as they hit the quarter pole and Espinoza so far was just along for the ride. It was time to give the colt an education. He crossed his reins and felt American Pharoah's stride start to lengthen. He had his whip in his left hand and thumped the colt twice on the saddle cloth, and then twice more. Yep, there was another gear. In mid-stretch, Espinoza brandished the whip once more but just waved it in front of his eyes. The colt was flying. As they hit the wire, four and three-quarter lengths in front, Espinoza ever so slightly pumped his right arm.

"American Pharoah, son of Pioneerof the

Nile, has absolutely annihilated them today in the Del Mar Futurity," he heard track announcer Trevor Denham say.

He knew they went fast, but when he saw the final time of 1:21.48, he was surprised by how fast. It was the second-fastest running of the race at the seven-furlong distance. It was Espinoza's third Futurity victory and a record twelfth for Baffert. In the sixty-seven runnings of the race, American Pharoah was only the second maiden to win the Del Mar Futurity and the last since Go West Young Man won in 1977. All in all, it was a satisfying finish to the Del Mar meet. After the race, Espinoza was subdued in his appraisal of American Pharoah.

"He looks like a nice horse and he feels like one," he told reporters. "He could be a good one."

On his way home, however, Espinoza was pumped up. For the second year in a row, he had landed on a big, fast colt. Espinoza knew American Pharoah was potentially another life-changing horse. Fate again had interceded.

He had run into Baffert shortly after riding California Chrome to victory in the Derby and now remembered their brief conversation.

"Congratulations, Victor," Baffert said.

"That was amazing."

"Thanks, Bob," Espinoza said.

"Next year," said Baffert, pointing at the jockey, "you and me."

Espinoza usually waited until the following morning to speak with Beach, but today he could not wait and called him from his car.

"Man, that's a rocket ship!" Espinoza told his agent. "This is our Derby horse right here if we keep the mount."

CHAPTER EIGHT:
TWO TURNS?

September 27, 2014, Santa Anita Park

Despite its global reach, despite the hundreds of races run simultaneously daily, horse racing is a very small world and the community that bets on it is even more compact. News of American Pharoah's performance in the Del Mar Futurity ignited the first spark of Kentucky Derby fever, a malady that usually is dormant throughout the fall as the two-year-olds get a race or two to hint at what's to come. It was not just felt in the Bob Baffert barn. The speed figures American Pharoah put up were too huge to go unnoticed. The Beyer Speed Figure, for example, was a numerical representation of a horse's performance, based on the final time and the inherent speed over the track on which the race was run. The 101 Beyer Speed Figure American Pharoah had earned was the top figure of the year for a two-year-old and was among the strongest numbers in history for a juvenile this early in a career. It also validated the big figure Om earned the previous month when he beat American Pharoah, Calculator, and Iron Fist. In fact, those two horses had finished second and third in the Futurity, and as Baffert expected, Om suffered for going so fast, injuring a leg and getting sidelined for the year.

In the Blue Grass, Frances Relihan experienced a rush as if she owned American Pharoah herself. Much had changed since the little colt had left the farm. It was under new ownership for one. The previous year the Thoroughbred breeding arm of one of Chile's largest conglomerates — Don Alberto Corp — paid $13.82 million for the property. It operated a 500-acre farm in Los Ángeles, Chile, which was home to about 180 mares, and the Solari family who owned it were certainly horse people. They had retained Frances and then went on a shopping spree, spending millions on royally bred mares in Kentucky and England, including ten that were bred to Frankel, who was unbeaten in fourteen races in Europe and now stood at stud in Suffolk, England. They were shipped to Kentucky and were among the first Frankel foals born on Southern Hemisphere time. It meant juggling two foaling seasons.

Still, she had time to track the development of the Littleprincessemma colt that she just knew was destined for something special. She had spoken with the Taylors when the colt was still in Kentucky and was pleased to know that they were as impressed with him as well. He was harder to follow while in Florida at the McKathans, but she had heard how he was the star of the Zayat Stables showcase. Now that American Pharoah had a name and a home in Bob Baffert's barn, it was easy to track his progress online through the Jockey Club's portfolio services, and she eagerly awaited the e-mail alerts that came after each of his workouts.

Frances had to reconcile the stout times American Pharoah was turning in with the pint-sized athlete she had helped wean and watched grow into a graceful athlete. There were thirteen of them now, each better than the last. Her heart sank a little when she watched American Pharoah's debut; he certainly did not look like the cool customer she had known as a youngster. She chalked it up to a learning experience. When she saw the colt in the Futurity, however, it was as if beholding yesterday's kindergartener turn into today's high school graduate.

Frances had American Pharoah ending this race in the winner's circle after the first quarter mile. Her heart filled with wonder as the colt seemed to shift through his gears as if he were on a Formula 1 racetrack.

"So in command," she said. "Just beautiful."

In Las Vegas, Johnny Avello walked out to the floor of his sportsbook to watch the horse he had been hearing so much about run in the Del Mar Futurity. Avello was the executive director of race and sports operations at Wynn Las Vegas, where point spreads and fast horses were spoken with the same intensity with which farmers discuss the weather. He is a Don in one of this town's most respected fraternities, the brotherhood of bookies. He's a wizard, a Wizard of Odds. He has predicted the winners of Super Bowls and World Series as well as Miss America Pageants and the Westminster Kennel Club Dog Show. Earlier in the year, he correctly selected the winner of twenty-two of the twenty-four Oscar categories. He singled out seven *Dancing with the Stars* winners before they ever rhumbaed or anything else onstage.

It was his passion for racehorses, however, that had given him those opportunities and had transformed a plush corner of one of the city's finest casinos into his own comfortable speakeasy, one with a giant odds board winking in red and wall-to-wall televisions blinking sporting events. Avello grew up in Poughkeepsie, New York. He was a bookie at fifteen years old and a regular at New York racetracks from Saratoga to Yonkers Raceway. As soon as he finished high school, he enrolled in a gaming school and learned how to deal everything from blackjack to baccarat and how to work the stick in craps and rake the chips at the roulette wheel. He arrived in Las Vegas in 1979 and established himself as a polished, versatile casino hand at the long-gone Hotel Nevada. Seventeen years later, Avello returned home in a sense, crossing the Strip to the Las Vegas Hilton and an entry-level job writing tickets at its sportsbook. He paid attention to his math. He got comfortable trusting his gut. He learned to dole out premium customer service. Mostly, Avello listened — to his customers, to his horse owner friends, to anyone who had a sliver of information that might be useful in correctly anticipating an outcome.

"I've been around the entire portfolio for quite a bit," he said of his vocation, "and have learned what a gambler does and his habits."

Avello was preparing his Kentucky Derby Futures Bets board, assigning odds to hundreds of horses, many of them who had yet to actually run in a race but were pointed to run in America's greatest race. It didn't bring a whole lot of money into the sportsbook. Avello did it as a courtesy to his horse-playing customers and friends, as well as to tip his hat to the pastime that he loved most and that had made him the man he was today. Horses were in his blood, and each summer of his life he made the pilgrimage to Saratoga Springs, New York, to watch races in a place, and in a fashion, befitting the Sport of Kings. Like everyone who was in the least bit devoted to the sport, Avello badly wanted to see another Triple Crown champion but doubted that he ever would.

As he watched American Pharoah zip down the lane, however, he had an inkling — a welcome one — that he might be wrong. It was too early to post a proposition bet on the Triple Crown, but Avello thought he may have just seen the future Kentucky Derby champ. Twelve days later, eight months prior to the first Saturday in May, American Pharoah opened as the 40-to-1 favorite to wear the blanket of roses at the Wynn Las Vegas.

Bob Baffert's primary base was Santa

Anita Park, 320 acres of perfect Hollywood backdrop about forty miles northeast of Los Angeles. The track was rimmed by the San Gabriel Mountains that were almost always bathed in sunshine and that made you long for an old-fashioned Western movie. Mornings were especially spectacular as flight after flight of horses took to the track for gallops and breezes amid fresh mountain air. At the corner of the grandstand, near the stretch, was Clockers' Corner, which was always bustling with trainers and flack-jacketed jockeys who sipped coffee alongside touts in crumpled clothes with the *Daily Racing Form* beneath their arm and the most tanned, healthy-looking men and women that you can find this side of a magazine fashion shoot. By far, it was the best-looking morning racetrack crowd in the nation. Many of them were horse owners or jockey agents and other industry types. They started each workday here on the apron trading gossip as they sipped lattes and picked at omelets from the only racetrack kitchen whose daily fare resembled haute cuisine.

This was Baffert's front porch and water-cooler, where he skinned and grinned with jockeys like Gary Stevens but always with an eye on his horses on the track. American

Pharoah had come out of the Futurity better than ever. He was thumping his nose against the feed tub, digging out every oat. He was pointed toward another Grade 1 race six days from now, the FrontRunner, right here at his home track. American Pharoah was going to try the one-mile-and-sixteen distance, which meant he had to go two turns for the first time. No matter how primed for endurance a pedigree might suggest, Baffert believed that you could not be certain if you had a horse suited for the classic distances until he proved that he could navigate two turns. To do so took more than speed and agility; it took a sharp mind to heed the cues of a jockey to avoid hazards or get out of trouble when you find it. Some horses could not harness their speed and burned themselves on the backstretch; others grew bored and lost focus.

Baffert always held his breath when he sent a promising colt or filly out for their first route race. It was where flaws were exposed and hopes dashed. The trainer did not expect American Pharoah to disappoint him. Beside the paddock meltdown in his debut, the colt so far had been a perfect pupil. The only flaw American Pharoah had displayed was nature's, not his, and that may not have been a flaw at all. First at Del

Mar, now here at Santa Anita, the racetrack horse identifier had reported American Pharoah to the Jockey Club as a ridgling, meaning that one of his testicles had failed to descend at puberty. In normal colts, they dropped from the abdomen down the inguinal canal to the scrotum. In ridglings, they either remained in the abdominal cavity or fell partially down the inguinal canal. American Pharoah was sent through the Fasig-Tipton Sale in Saratoga as a colt, and no one in the Baffert barn found any signs that he was anything other than that. It was an uncommon condition widely thought to be handed down through genetics. Several horses in the Seattle Slew line were ridglings, most famously A.P. Indy. His undescended testicle was removed and, after capturing the Belmont Stakes and Breeders' Cup Classic, he was voted the Horse of the Year in 1992.

It did not handicap him in the breeding shed, either. When he was retired in 2011 at the age of twenty-two, A.P. Indy had sired more than 135 stakes winners, including champions Mineshaft and Bernardini.

Whether he had one testicle or two, American Pharoah had Baffert and his staff as upbeat as they had been in years. The trainer was once more the center of attention at Clockers' Corner and was enjoying it. Earlier that morning, the colt had sizzled five-eighths of a mile in 59.60 in his last breeze before the race.

"He has that extra something that all the good ones have," Baffert said.

Baffert had put an old hand, jockey Joe Steiner, on the colt for the breeze. Steiner was a gifted horseman whose opinions were valued after workouts in the morning more than his talents as a jockey were in the afternoon. He had been one of Baffert's go-to exercise riders in the late 1990s when the trainer was dominating the Triple Crown races and owners were clamoring to put expensive horses in his barn.

"Have you worked a horse like this in a while?" asked Baffert.

"It reminds me of the old days," Steiner said.

The FrontRunner used to be called the Norfolk Stakes and was the race the West Coast–based two-year-olds used as a tune-up for the Breeders' Cup Juvenile, a $2 million race to be held five weeks from now at Santa Anita Park. A relaxed American Pharoah ambled into the paddock like he was stepping beneath the shade of a weeping willow to lie down for a nap. He looked every bit the 1-to-2 favorite that bettors had made him off the blowout at Del Mar. The skittish colt of two months ago was now as grounded and steady as a Clydesdale.

Espinoza hopped on his back, pointed him toward the tunnel, and just like that, the duo went back at work. The rider knew American Pharoah was a cinch to win this heat, as the colt had beaten a couple of these in the Futurity with Espinoza primarily acting like a passenger. There were seven other colts edging into the gate, and the main threat — Calculator — was outside of him in the Number 8 hole. In the Futurity, the gray had mounted a late run to finish a distant second. Espinoza suspected his rider, Elvis Trujillo, would be a lot closer today. Next to him in the Number 4 post, Martin Garcia was aboard another Baffert-trained colt, Lord Nelson, who had defeated Calculator back in his debut in July but had not raced since.

It was in races like these that Espinoza not only earned his money but also demonstrated to trainers that he fit with their horse. He wanted to win another Derby, too. He needed to continue to build trust with American Pharoah. He needed to continue the colt's education as a racehorse.

American Pharoah broke perfectly and dragged him to the lead through a quarter mile of 23 seconds before Espinoza gently relaxed and slowed him down. He wanted American Pharoah to hear other horses alongside him, to feel their breath and the dirt flying. He wanted the colt to have a taste of pressure without being intimidated. Skyway, the horse he couldn't get the mount on for the Futurity, pressed them from the outside through a moderate half mile of 1:11.4. American Pharoah heard him and felt him but never flinched, and Skyway disappeared behind him. Now Calculator glided up on the far turn, looking like he had plenty in the tank to tangle. He pulled even with American Pharoah's throatlatch at the quarter pole.

In the clubhouse, Baffert held his breath. He saw American Pharoah slinging around the far turn and asked himself, "Can he go two turns?"

Espinoza knew he could. He loosened his grip on the colt and scrubbed on his neck with both hands, coaxing a burst that vaulted them a length ahead of Calculator.

"I encouraged my horse a little," he said. "He's young, so I want to teach him that when he hits the stretch, it's time to go."

American Pharoah went. This time, Espinoza had the whip in his right hand and just waved it along his flank, letting him see it more than feel it. The colt's stride lengthened and they increased their lead by four lengths. Once more, track announcer Trevor Denman was roused: "Calculator is all heart, but this is a scintillating performance by American Pharoah."

By the final quarter mile, American Pharoah had run a withering 23.93-second split, with Espinoza back in passenger mode, dusting his rivals. He completed the mile and sixteenth in 1:41.95 and matched the 101 Beyer Speed Figure from Del Mar. One race earlier, two-time Breeders' Cup winner and champion filly Beholder covered the same ground in 1:42.19 to win the Grade 1 Zenyatta Stakes. Later in the day, the two-year-old filly Angela Renee was timed in at 1:43.45 for her victory in the Grade 1 Chandelier Stakes.

It was the performance Baffert was hoping for.

As Baffert walked Espinoza back to the jockeys' room, getting the download on his rider's trip, both men were smiling. The trainer had won this stakes race now seven times, but never with a horse like American Pharoah. In a quirk of history perhaps, not a single winner of the Norfolk — now

FrontRunner — had ever gone on to win the Derby. The trainer believed that he had the horse to end that drought.

"He moves really nice and is light on his feet," Espinoza told the trainer. "He's one of the best two-year-olds right now."

CHAPTER NINE:
BETTER LUCKY THAN SMART

October 2014

It had been a difficult five years for Ahmed Zayat on the racetrack as well as off of it. While Zayat put in the hard work of satisfying his creditors and downsizing his operation, his horses were being punished by the racing gods in biblical proportions. The walls of his stable's office in Hackensack, New Jersey, were filled with winner's circle photos, but many of them reminded Zayat that if he had found any luck at all recently it was mostly bad.

The momentum that Pioneerof the Nile was gaining as the sire of American Pharoah could not exorcise the heart pangs Zayat felt when he saw his photo hanging on the wall. He'd been Zayat's pride and joy at the time, a homebred that he believed could bring home the roses in Zayat's first try at the Derby in 2009. The colt looked like the winner in the stretch until a 50-to-1 shot named Mine That Bird, owned and trained by cowboys from New Mexico, rode the rail under a local journeymen jockey to a stunning from-last-to-first finish.

There on another wall was Eskendereya, who went to Louisville for the 2010 Derby as one of the strongest favorites in years off three straight victories, including an eight-and-a-half-length romp in the Fountain of Youth in Florida, followed by a runaway nine-and-three-quarter-length score in the Grade 1 Wood Memorial in New York. Seven days before the race, the colt's trainer saw some swelling in Eskendereya's left front and called in the veterinarians, who worked all night on bringing it down. He wasn't actually lame but his gait was off and his leg was puffed up from the ankle to the knee. He was scratched the following morning and retired with a soft tissue injury not long after the Derby.

"We sent him to two clinics for diagnostics and I wanted to send him to one more to get a third opinion, because I wasn't willing to give up," Zayat said, "but with a soft tissue injury, we pretty much knew he was done. The horse was sound as could be and had been training extremely well. Everything was ideal until it started going downhill when he went to Churchill."

He was a top stallion prospect, which would have been more of a consolation if Zayat did not have to sell a share of him to the wine baron Jess Jackson for $7 million that went straight to Fifth Third Bank under the bankruptcy agreement. The picture of Nehro doesn't begin to tell the story of the following year's Derby and how the colt got passed in the deep stretch and finished second to Animal Kingdom, a 20-to-1 long shot. It was tough enough that Nehro had already finished second by a neck in both the Louisiana Derby and Arkansas Derby before running at Churchill Downs. Now he had been edged by a horse with a turf pedigree and who had never run before on dirt, a first in the history of the Kentucky Derby.

In 2012, Zayat's horses found a couple of new ways to lose. Surely Bodemeister was the colt to snap the hard luck streak. How could the racing gods deny a colt named for the young son of his trainer, Bob Baffert, especially after the colt won the Arkansas Derby by nearly ten lengths? This time the racing gods really hit the Zayat camp with a hammer, allowing Bodemeister to blow a three-length lead at the eighth pole and get caught by I'll Have Another, who had started from the Number 19 hole, the only post in the 137 previous runnings that had never produced a Derby winner.

"That was the most crushing," Zayat said. "I saw Bode crying and Bob was upset. It was just terrible."

Two weeks later in Baltimore, Bodemeister blew another three-length lead at the eighth pole and was beaten by a neck by I'll Have Another. When Baffert sent Bodemeister back to the barn after the Preakness, Zayat ran a colt by the name of Paynter in the Belmont Stakes. He was a late-developing son of Awesome Again that Baffert believed had earned a shot at the Triple Crown race after leading every step of the way in a race at Pimlico on Preakness Day to win by more than five lengths. Baffert believed this was the colt to deflect the wrath of the racing gods. Baffert had a friend named Paynter who, he told Zayat, was one of the luckiest guys that he ever knew. If Zayat named the promising horse after his friend, Baffert was certain their fortunes would change for the better. Zayat agreed and as the field hit the stretch in the Belmont, it looked like the plan had worked and finally he was heading to the winner's circle of a Triple Crown race. Paynter had led every step of the way and had a length lead in the stretch. A late run from the colt

Union Rags caught him at the wire and Paynter lost by a neck.

In the span of four years, Zayat had finished second in the Kentucky Derby three times and lost the big favorite a week before the race the other year. Somehow, the hot-blooded Egyptian managed to stay Zen about this unfortunate turn of events.

"I feel we are very blessed to have the kind of horses that show up in these races," he said. "It hurts to watch the replays, but I am not sorry about any of it. It's a fantastic experience and it makes me want to go after it even more."

Miserable misfortune, however, was not finished yet with Zayat or his family. In July, Paynter returned east from Baffert's barn in Del Mar to run in the Haskell Stakes, a Grade 1 $1 million race for three-year-olds at Monmouth Park on the Jersey Shore. Zayat was unable to get away from his Del Mar summer home because his youngest daughter was sick. Baffert had obligations on the West Coast and could not make the trip either. Zayat decided that this was a good opportunity to reward his twenty-year-old son, Justin, for the work he had been doing on behalf of Zayat Stables. Justin was in school at New York University and still learning the horse racing game, but he had shown an aptitude for the business of the sport and shared his father's passion for horses.

It was not a heart-stopping race for once for the Zayats. Paynter was in control for the entire mile-and-eighth distance and won easily by more than three lengths. Ahmed had watched from California and called Justin immediately. He was proud of his horse, but he was also proud of his son and how grown up he looked leading Paynter into the winner's circle. Justin, too, was moved to near tears. He had never witnessed in person one of the Zayat Stables' horses win a big race. He was grateful for the opportunity and told his father so.

By all rights, there should have been a fade out on the Zayats' year of discontent, and father and son could get on with racing's second season with renewed hope for winning big races with Bodemeister and Paynter throughout the fall and leading into the 2012 Breeders' Cup World Championships.

Instead, two days later, Paynter spiked a fever, had a bout with diarrhea, and caught pneumonia and was hospitalized near the racetrack at Mid-Atlantic Equine Medical Center. He was given antibiotics and fluids and seemed to recover well enough to be taken to Belmont Park ten days later to start training for the Travers Stakes at the end of August in Saratoga. His stay there was brief before he was shipped to the Spa. Once Paynter arrived upstate, however, it was evident he was not in racing, or even training, shape to be ready for the Travers. He was scheduled to return to California but got sick again before his departure date. This time Paynter was taken to the Upstate Equine Medical Center in Schuylerville, New York, and was diagnosed with a more serious condition: He had colitis — inflammation of the colon.

Simultaneously, back at Del Mar, Bodemeister was retired to stud after injuring his shoulder during a routine gallop that unseated his rider. The beat was on again for the Zayats.

In New York, however, the medical saga of Paynter was just beginning and it would capture the attention of horse lovers everywhere, largely because of Justin Zayat's savvy with social media and Ahmed's operatic way of communicating his emotions in the 140-character-or-less Twittersphere. The poor colt could not catch a break. He developed blood clots, lost 300 pounds — or nearly a quarter of his body weight — and withstood aggressive medical treatment.

Under the hashtag #PowerUpPaynter, Ahmed and Justin put out daily updates on the colt's roller-coaster ride. He developed laminitis, an often-fatal inflammation of the hoof, in three of his feet and was fitted with casts on his lower legs to support them. His primary caregiver, Dr. Laura Javsicas, became his "angel" in Ahmed's Twitter dispatches. The grave days were given their due — three times the Zayats came close to putting the colt down. The dispatches went viral. The upbeat days were celebrated: *@jazz3162 @JustinZayat Paynter update: Been a super day today once again. Eating all day. Happy. Very bright. Playful! No fever. Feet totally normal.*

Soon, handmade posters and hundreds of get-well cards started arriving at the Upstate Equine Medical Center; some were from children but many were from adults. By October, Paynter required surgery and was sent to the University of Pennsylvania's School of Veterinary Medicine's New Bolton Center. It was where 2006 Kentucky Derby champion Barbaro had been treated and subsequently died after being pulled up in the opening yards of the Preakness with a fractured right hind leg.

When the New Bolton surgeons removed a fifteen-inch bacteria-filled growth from

Paynter's intestines and the colt was given a promising prognosis, the celebration of answered prayers under #PowerUpPaynter exploded. The colt's illness and recovery were not only voted in a landslide by fans as the National Thoroughbred Racing Association's moment of the year, but the occasion also cemented the Zayats as a new kind of horse owner: passionate about the sport, willing to promote it, and definitely of the people rather than above them. Even more remarkable, Paynter returned to the racetrack less than a year later. Although he finished second twice, he never won again, which no one ever would have known by the size of the crowds he attracted and the raucous reception that he received each race.

Finally, in the autumn of 2014, things were definitely looking up for Ahmed Zayat. Justin was growing nicely into his role as the stable's racing manager, allowing his father to focus on the business of breeding. Justin was earning the respect of the stable's array of trainers — among them two Hall of Famers who were counted among the best of all time, Baffert and seventy-nine-year-old D. Wayne Lukas. Justin knew what he didn't know and peppered them with questions about everything from training regimens to how to recognize what physical flaws in a horse could be overcome, and which could not. Justin also was the one who assigned the two-year-olds to the stable's various trainers. Best of all, Ahmed appreciated his son's effort to share his passion for the game with his peers. The sport needed to grow a younger fan base.

"This is my sports team," Justin Zayat said. "I want people to wear our stable hats like they wear their Yankees hats."

American Pharoah had come out of the FrontRunner in perfect condition and was continuing to dazzle Baffert and everyone in his barn. The colt was an absolute machine in the mornings and had already tossed off three breezes that are rarely seen from two-year-olds. American Pharoah was powerful as well as polished on the track. The Breeders' Cup Juvenile was approaching, and everyone around the colt was hardpressed to come up with a way of how he could lose. Usually it was Zayat who sounded like an over-excited ten-year-old when he spoke to his trainer by phone. Now, it was Baffert speaking buoyantly about American Pharoah, confident that the colt had yet to come anywhere close to running his best race.

"He's just a monster," he told the owner

one morning. "Sometimes I look at my stopwatch and wonder how he can do this."

Zayat just knew good fortune was on the horizon. Pioneerof the Nile was having a spectacular year as a stallion, topping the list of second-crop sires with progeny that earned nearly $3.5 million and had captured five graded stakes races. Just like first loves, horse people tend to remember their first big horse and Pioneerof the Nile was that and more to Zayat. He was the very first horse that he had bred himself. Sort of. Zayat bought his mother, Star of Goshen, privately when she was carrying the son of Empire Maker. He was born on May 5, 2006, on the eve of the Kentucky Derby. The foal nearly died a month later after being discovered in a field suffering from a severe bout of colic. He was small enough to be laid in the backseat of a car and rushed to a hospital, where emergency surgery untwisted his stomach to save his life. The episode was the inspiration for the first lesson Ahmed imparted to Justin about the horse business: "You need to be lucky more than smart," he said. "And always somebody has to be watching out for you."

In a perhaps prophetic preview of what was going to unfold six years later with American Pharoah, Zayat sent the colt through the sales ring — this time at the 2007 Keeneland September Yearling Sale. Like his son, the yearling barely drew any bidding interest, so Zayat bought him back for $270,000. The following year, the colt, now named Pioneerof the Nile, delivered Zayat Stables its very first Grade 1 victory in the CashCall Futurity. Worse than watching the colt come up short in the Derby was having to retire him after suffering a soft tissue injury the following summer while training for the fall season.

"Bob was one hundred percent convinced that he was going to win the Breeders' Cup Classic," he said. "That was his target right after the Derby."

Instead, Pioneerof the Nile was sent to the breeding shed and after a tentative start was now paying dividends in a variety of ways. He had runners in two of three legs of the Triple Crown, including his top earner for the year, the freakishly fast Social Inclusion. He had broken a track record at Gulfstream Park at a mile and a sixteenth and won by ten lengths; he then finished third in the Preakness behind California Chrome. Pioneerof the Nile was proving that he was versatile, producing winners on dirt, turf, and synthetic surfaces. He was delivering value: The average auction price of his yearlings was $400,000, or twenty times his current fee of $20,000. He was hitting these home runs with second- and third-tier mares. After another of his sons, Cairo Prince, won the Holy Bull Stakes, Sheikh Mo bought a share of the colt for Godolphin, the racing arm of his Thoroughbred operation. When Social Inclusion won an allowance race, his owners rejected $8 million offered for the horse. All this meant Pioneerof the Nile was putting out quality horses.

He was not getting blue hen mares — as the most royally bred and accomplished females are called — from French breeders such as the Wertheimers, who own Chanel, the perfume and fashion house, or the sheikhs of Dubai or the royal families of Saudi Arabia. Breeders are serious people, and when they propose a mare, they have done their homework and know the bloodlines back six to eight generations and what they are after in terms of offspring.

Pioneerof the Nile was still a new sire, and managing a stallion's book is a lot like being a Hollywood agent: in good times, you say no often; in bad times, you say yes to cut-rate prices. Neither Zayat, who controlled a significant portion of shares of Pioneerof the Nile, nor the stallion manager at the horse's home at WinStar Farm so far had the luxury of saying no.

That was about to change. His homebred American Pharoah had given his homebred Pioneerof the Nile his first Grade 1 progeny when he won the Del Mar Futurity and FrontRunner Stakes. Zayat and WinStar had already decided to triple the stud fee of Pioneerof the Nile to $60,000 for 2015. Not only would breeders pay it, but they would also offer better mares. Zayat was already reaping the benefits of his stallion's popularity. His creditors had to be paid in full by the end of the year, and Zayat was reallocating his assets. He claimed that Zayat Stables cost him $1 million a month to operate, which was a reasonable figure considering that the industry rule of thumb for keeping a racehorse in training is $50,000 a year while raising one is $20,000 or so annually. Zayat had a lot of horses on the racetrack as well as on the farms. He currently was offering some breeding shares — the right to breed annually — to Pioneerof the Nile and they were selling into the mid- to high six figures.

What was most exciting for Ahmed and Justin Zayat was the recognition they were getting as breeders for creating something potentially great: American Pharoah. The farms were already inquiring about his future stallion rights, and none had been more insistent than Coolmore America.

There are plenty of sharp, deep-pocketed breeding outfits in Central Kentucky — Lane's End, WinStar, Claiborne, and Calumet to name a few — but none carry as much mystery, command more respect, or strike as much fear among horsemen in the Bluegrass as Coolmore, the preeminent stallion station in the world with operations in Europe, America, and Australia and significant reach into the business of racing and breeding in five continents. In the Bluegrass, they are alternately referred to as "the Irish," "the Gangsters," and the "cleverest" horse operators in the world. Among its forty-plus stallions, they are in control of the best and most valuable horse semen in the world. Their stallion list reads like an all-star team plucked from the globe's most accomplished horses: Galileo and So You Think stand in Ireland, Giant's Causeway and Tale of the Cat in America, and Fastnet Rock in Australia.

In 1975, the original Coolmore partnership was struck when Britain's leading international owner, the bookie Robert Sangster; the trainer Dr. Vincent O'Brien; and stallion master (and future son-in-law)

John Magnier took over a 350-acre stud farm in Ireland. Back then, Kentucky was on top of the global market by purchasing Irish and English horses that the old country could not afford to keep. Coolmore reversed that model and became regulars at the Keeneland Sales, at first focusing on yearlings from the line of Northern Dancer, the 1964 Kentucky Derby and Preakness winner who was already proven as one of the most influential sires in Thoroughbred history. They hit the jackpot early when a colt named The Minstrel was among a group of yearlings that they paid a little over $1.7 million for and won the 1977 Epsom Derby. They bought Alleged for $175,000 and won France's biggest race, Prix de l'Arc de Triomphes, with him twice. Then Coolmore syndicated them and sold them back to American breeding farms: the Minstrel for $9 million and Alleged for $16 million, or $35 million and $60 million when adjusted for inflation.

It didn't take them long to spin off more partnerships and establish farms of their own in Kentucky and Australia with revenues from other sought-after sires they had in their barns, such as Sadler's Wells, Danehill, Southern Halo, Royal Academy, El Gran Senor, and Woodman. They were

201

blessed with another infusion of capital when another successful bookmaker, Michael Tabor, became a partner.

Sangster and company were among the first to get more bang for the buck by shipping their Irish-based stallions to Australia for the Southern Hemisphere breeding season. So instead of being limited to seventy-five or a hundred matings at home, Coolmore stallions could double that number, as well as the farm's fees, by going south in the month of August for breeding season that begins in September. Everyone agreed that they were smart. It was their swagger at the Keeneland Sales that pumped them up to mythical proportions, though, especially as they became involved in epic bidding battles with Sheikh Mohammed bin Rashid al-Maktoum and his family. It was like a Bloods vs. Crips rumble, except that the only weapons wielded were wits, bluffs, and bottomless bank accounts. The Coolmore crew moved as a pack with their "lads" and huddled in the back of the sales pavilion to launch their bids. Sheikh Mo also had a modus operandi, looking every bit of a stable groom in a white T-shirt, blue jeans, and a royal-blue satin jacket with Godolphin, the name of his racing stable, embroidered on it.

Both Coolmore and the sheikh have prompted each other into making expensive mistakes. In 1983, Sheikh Mo, trying to catch up with Coolmore, paid $10.2 million for a Northern Dancer colt that at the time was the most expensive horse sold at auction. He was given the name Snaafi Dancer but was so slow that he never made it to the racetrack. He was a bust as a stallion as well, exhibiting fertility problems and siring just four foals. In 2006, representatives of each camp went at it again over a Forestry colt that had blazed an eighth of a mile in 9.8 seconds at a Florida two-year-old-in-training sale. Coolmore won the battle, bidding $16 million, but definitely lost the war. They named him the Green Monkey and raced him three times, where his best finish was a third place. He was retired and stands in Florida for a fee of $5,000.

The gangster part of Coolmore's reputation came not only from the high theater they performed in tandem with Sheikh Mo, but also the code of silence they kept publicly and the ruthlessness they showed on deals. The Irish, it was often alleged, like to get one over on rival horse people, often entering presale agreements with a seller's representative for, say, $1 million, then bidding up the horse it already owned so an unsuspecting buyer purchases it for $2 million. They allegedly split the difference with the sales agent. It was the whispers of this underhanded practice that put an end to the Coolmore–Sheikh Mo bidding wars. Without coming out and saying so, the sheikh clearly was not sending any of his mares to Coolmore stallions or bidding on their yearlings or two-year-olds that showed up in the sales ring.

Now John Magnier and one of his top executives, Paul Shanahan, were trying to determine what it would take to secure the breeding rights of American Pharoah from Zayat Stables. Just as they pursued cornering the Northern Dance line forty years ago, Coolmore had been executing a game plan to lock up as many American two-year-old champions as they could as early as possible. Since 2009, it had bought four of them: Lookin At Lucky (2009), Uncle Mo (2010), Hansen (2011), and Shanghai Bobby (2012). The previous year the champion male was Shared Belief, a gelding, and thus had no future as a stallion. The others all stood at Ashford Stud, their American base in Versailles, Kentucky.

American Pharoah was thought to be the next in line. He was the favorite to win the Juvenile, which would seal the deal for

American Pharoah and make him a cinch to be named two-year-old champion. It was still early to lock up the juvenile horse's breeding rights, but it was no secret in the Bluegrass that Zayat was under financial pressure and needed cash to complete his bankruptcy. How much and how soon did he need it was what Coolmore, and other farms, were trying to figure out. The breeding business in the Bluegrass may be spread out over four counties, but it is the smallest of towns. Everyone talked and the numbers being passed over the fence post and in the feed shops were that Zayat needed $14 million by the end of the year.

On the fence-post wire, the word was that Coolmore had floated an offer of $10 million with immediate bonuses for a victory in the Juvenile as well as being named two-year-old champion, along with incentives for winning the Triple Crown races. It was a starting point, a reasonable one. No one expected Zayat to accept the first offer. He reveled in the back and forth of negotiations and believed that one of his greatest strengths was his tirelessness. When putting the Al Ahram deal together, Zayat once spoke for sixteen straight hours until everyone fell asleep in the room except for him and the person he was talking to. He told the story with relish, wanting you to know that making a deal to him was a form of combat and that he kept score in terms of what he was getting, not giving away. It didn't matter if you were a small farm owner or horse breeder. If Zayat was five months in arrears to you, he would give you two months now and call the bill settled. If you offered him $380,000 for a share of Pioneerof the Nile, he'd insist that he was not taking a nickel under $550,000.

Zayat was looking forward to the coming weeks. He had a Big Horse, a special one and now everyone knew it.

There are phone calls horse trainers dread and they come more often than they like, especially when you have a super-talented horse in the barn with great expectations that ride on its back. The previous morning, October 26, American Pharoah had turned in his final workout for the Breeders' Cup Juvenile, clicking off five-eighths of a mile in 1 minute flat, with his ears happily pointed forward, leading the way. The colt was one of the best workhorses that had ever passed through Baffert's barn. Where some might have found American Pharoah's dependability boring, the trainer thought it was absolutely thrilling. The colt was just perfectly engineered.

So whenever Baffert could drive through the gates of Santa Anita and park at his barn having not heard any bad news from Jimmy Barnes, his day was off to a good start. On Monday, October 27, the trainer was having one of those mornings. No calls meant no news, which meant all systems were a go for the Juvenile now six days away. At least they were until Baffert noticed a bobble in the colt's gait as he walked the shedrow. Something was off. He called in the veterinarians, who did their best to slip into Baffert's barn unnoticed. On the days before big races, the backside was crawling with reporters as well as the usual keen-eyed racetrackers, who made everyone else's business their own. The rumor mill was working overtime. The vets took X-rays and ultrasounds. Both came back negative.

The trainer called Zayat in New Jersey and told him where they were at with American Pharoah, which was pretty much nowhere.

"It's not soft tissue; it's not bone," he said.

Maybe the colt had a deep foot bruise? or maybe not. Maybe there was a hairline fracture? He hoped not. Zayat told him to give it a day and see if the vets could get American Pharoah better or at least figure out what was wrong.

The following morning, a glum Baffert drove through the gates of Santa Anita and pulled up to his barn. There was a racetrack saying attributed to the late Hall of Fame trainer Charlie Whittingham: "Horses are like strawberries and can go bad on you overnight." Baffert had quoted it often, usually with a microphone before him and a smile on his face. Sure, he had had plenty of horses come up lame before races. None would hurt worse than if he had to scratch American Pharoah from the Juvenile. Baffert did not have to watch the colt long. He was still off, and there was no sense in pushing him to the starting gate. He called Zayat and gave him the bad news.

The owner was devastated but understood.

"When he's that special and that good, you treat him as such," he told Baffert. "This horse was going to run away with that race."

While Zayat fired up his Twitter account and shared the grim news with his followers, Baffert faced a waiting media crush. The rumors of American Pharoah's imminent scratch from the Juvenile had ripped through the backside. His voice cracked as he told them that the colt was not going to run on Saturday.

"We all saw the way he was training," he said. "He's something special. I hadn't had a colt like this in a long time. It's a pretty tough pill to swallow. He's going to be okay, but it's just the timing — it's a killer. You get to the barn, and you want to vomit."

CHAPTER TEN:
HE'S READY

March 6, 2015

The closest Bob Baffert ever came to feeling what it was like to ride American Pharoah was when he spoke to Martin Garcia over the two-way radio on the mornings they breezed the colt. The wired exercise rider was Baffert's contribution to modern Thoroughbred training, a product of both his history as a jockey and his need for control. He pioneered the two-way radio for breezes because he liked to dictate his horses' workouts down to the fraction of a second. Through the magic of technology, he was able to slow a horse down or speed him up or change up the workout altogether. When a horse was moving well and looking too strong, Baffert would tell Garcia, or any of his other riders, to let it run another eighth of a mile. He often did it in Spanish, a language that he was fluent in thanks to his father, the Chief. Bill Baffert insisted that all his children speak the language the majority of their neighbors did on either side of the Mexican border. It was a good foundation for a budding horse trainer, as 90 percent of any racetrack backside in America was inhabited by Spanish speakers. There were more than forty in Baffert's employ, and with more than one hundred horses and more than one hundred different schedules, communication was the key to avoiding misunderstandings. The trainer did not get enough credit for his managerial skills. He found good people, put them in important jobs, and let them do their stuff.

One of those was Martin Garcia. If Baffert was to be successful at getting American Pharoah to the Kentucky Derby and beyond, his barn jockey would be owed a great deal of credit. It took a nuclear scan and a week of poking and prodding by veterinarians, but the colt had finally been diagnosed as suffering a high suspensory strain. In laymen's terms, American Pharoah had over-extended his left front knee. Usually it requires thirty days' rest, but knowing the talent of the athlete in his barn and the goal ahead as well as Baffert did, the trainer prescribed sixty days for the colt. He believed the strawberries that were American Pharoah were priceless and he would do everything in his power to prevent them from going bad.

Baffert improvised and adjusted along the way. He kept American Pharoah at his barn in Santa Anita for one, instead of sending him to the more relaxed environment of a rehab farm. He needed to keep the colt light so he would not lose any training time in January. Horses tended to get fat on the satellite farms. At the end of Lookin At Lucky's two-year-old season, the colt suffered a similar setback that put some pressure on his Triple Crown preparation. So Baffert circled the Rebel Stakes at Oaklawn Park in Hot Springs, Arkansas, on his calendar as the targeted return race and went about getting there. He was following that plan now with American Pharoah. After letting the colt down for several weeks, Baffert had American Pharoah's groom, Eduardo Luna, walk him around the shedrow. They began as strolls, a limbering of the legs. They got longer as the days went by and harder when some weights were slung over his back.

Life pretty much went on with American Pharoah mostly under the radar. He returned to the racetrack on the third day of January with his regular exercise rider, Jorge Alvarez, for a short jog. Thirteen days later, he was given the Eclipse Award as the top two-year-old despite missing the Breeders' Cup Juvenile. That race was won by Texas Red, the colt that finished third in the Front-Runner five lengths behind American Pharoah.

It was the first Eclipse for Zayat Stables after being a finalist six previous times. It was some consolation for missing the Breeders' Cup, but with the uncertain future of the star in the barn, what were once potentially life-changing opportunities became less so. Ahmed Zayat never got to go toe-to-toe with the Irish in the way that he had once envisioned. He had no real leverage, because the future of American Pharoah was uncertain. Zayat needed cash and the previous November had sold the colt's mother, Littleprincessemma, who was in foal to Pioneerof the Nile, for $2.1 million at the Fasig Tipton Kentucky Fall season. So, in the middle of January, as American Pharoah's jogs turned to gallops, Zayat sold the colt's stallion rights to Coolmore. It was a fine deal for a two-year-old champion, but not so much for a horse that had the opportunity and potential to win the Kentucky Derby and even the Triple Crown. It was a $10 million deal up front with incentives that bumped that number to $14 million for sweeping the series. There was a possibility of an additional $10 million if American Pharoah captured the Haskell and Travers Stakes as well as the Breeders' Cup Classic and was awarded the Eclipse Award as Horse of the Year, according to two people familiar with the deal.

The Irish were risking a fair amount of money for a horse that may never race again but had gotten in cheap if American Pharoah picked up where he had left off and increased his breeding value by winning the Derby, the Preakness, or the Belmont Stakes. It was a far different horse business than it was fourteen years earlier in 2000 when Coolmore paid $60 million for a colt named Fusaichi Pegasus in the days after he won the Derby. He was beaten, however, in the Preakness and skipped the Belmont altogether. As smart as the Irish were, even they could not predict the outcome of a given horse race or the ability of a stallion to pass on his brilliance. FuPeg, as he was known, has had modest success as a sire and stands for $7,500 a breeding at Coolmore's Ashford Stud.

Zayat was hedging his bet. He had followed the golden rule of horse ownership and had taken the suitcase full of money that was in front of him. Neither he nor Baffert was certain that American Pharoah was going to be fit enough in time to get on the Triple Crown trail, or how he might fare once he got to the prep races. If the colt came back running and became the first Triple Crown champion in thirty-seven years, he was leaving a lot of money on the table.

As January turned to February, all the Zayats could do was wait on word from Baffert on American Pharoah and hope for one of their other three-year-old prospects to stamp himself a classic horse. At Aqueduct, close to their New Jersey home, El Kabeir, a gray son of Scat Daddy, was helping them take their mind off American Pharoah. He was taking the back road to Louisville, having already run seven times and won two graded stakes, from his very wintry home base of New York. He earned a special place in the heart of Justin Zayat, who frequently visited the colt at the barn of trainer John Terranova each weekend because it was an easy trip from New York University as well as an opportunity to continue his education in the horse business.

"We got to see him grow up and develop," Justin Zayat said. "He was a rank, very aggressive, very green two-year-old with a lot of energy. Now he's a totally different horse.

He can relax and he can rate."

He knew he was no real replacement for American Pharoah, but what was a Triple Crown season without hope springing eternal?

"He's really developing at the right time," he said, willing himself to believe it.

Baffert, too, had plenty of things to think about beyond American Pharoah to keep him occupied. That was the luxury of having more than one Ahmed Zayat among your owners. He had made his reputation as a Triple Crown trainer and the men and women who sent him horses did so because they wanted to win the Kentucky Derby and more. The upside was that Baffert was rarely out of bullets as the Triple Crown approached. When one contender fell by the wayside, there usually were two or three to take his place.

On the downside were the volatile personalities Baffert often had to juggle. Each of them could afford to purchase millions of dollars of horseflesh because they were uber-successful in their primary business, which usually meant that they pursued an unshakeable vision, a relentless drive, and were ultra-competitive. Most of them thought if they applied the formula that made them rich to the horse racing business, similar results would follow. That never happened and Baffert has spent countless hours on the phone explaining to the rich what they did not know about horses. In fact, training the owners was far harder than training the horses and sometimes it was easier to fire an owner than waste your time and temper on placating them.

Zayat had fired Baffert first. When Zayat wanted him back into his barn, Baffert thought long and hard about it before saying yes. Zayat had been exhausting the first time around, overly demanding of his time and eager to second-guess Baffert's decisions.

"We agreed that I wouldn't tell him how to build a beer business and he wouldn't tell me how to train horses," Baffert said.

There was another serious horse emerging from the Baffert barn by the name of Dortmund. At seventeen hands, Dortmund was a beast of an animal. He was a bargain, too, costing his owner Kaleem Shah just $140,000 at a Maryland two-year-old-in-training sale. He had the right pedigree as the son of 2008 Derby winner Big Brown, who so far had yet to establish himself as a big-name sire.

Baffert was pleased for Shah as well. He was the son of a prominent horse trainer in southern India who insisted that his son return to the racetrack only after he got an education and only as an owner. Shah came to America in the late 1980s and earned a master of science in computer engineering from Clemson University and an MBA in international finance from George Washington University. He then built an information technology and telecommunications consulting firm called CALNET that morphed into a company with hundreds of millions of dollars of contracts with the United States Defense Department to provide intelligence analysis. He and Baffert were starting to have some success together.

Dortmund was undefeated in five starts, all with Garcia aboard. He had won the Grade 1 Los Alamitos Futurity and the Grade 3 Robert B. Lewis Stakes, and Garcia was riding him tomorrow in the San Felipe Stakes. As good a job as Garcia had done riding Dortmund, his most valuable work had been in the morning over the past month aboard American Pharoah.

It was March 6, 2015, and the Rebel Stakes was eight days away. This would be the sixth workout for American Pharoah in thirty-three days, and Baffert was depending on Garcia to weigh the three-quarter mile that he was about to breeze with the previous five and tell him whether the colt was prepared for the Rebel Stakes. They were already late to the Triple Crown trail and had crammed a lot into a small period of time. There also had been a hiccup after an early workout, and Garcia sensed American Pharoah was uncomfortable on his left front foot rather than the knee. Baffert depended on Garcia to tell him this kind of information.

"That's the way he got the job with me," Baffert said. "Usually, a lot of top jockeys aren't good work riders. He's got a good set of hands, really soft. Horses like him. They run for him. If a horse is a handful, he gets along with them. He's got a lot of horseman in him. He really likes horses. He loves animals. He understands horses."

It turned out that Garcia was right and the colt did have a bruise on his hoof. Baffert was already on a tight schedule and could not afford to miss any more time with American Pharoah. He had a thin aluminum alloy plate cut to fit beneath the horseshoe to protect the triangular frog in his hoof and to act as a shock absorber when American Pharoah's foot hit the ground. So far it did not seem to impact the colt's stride.

Garcia, thirty, was a natural horseman but an accidental jockey. He was born in Veracruz, Mexico, to a teenage father and mother whom he had never met. He was raised by his grandmother and was working in construction at age eleven. In 2003, he came to the United States from Veracruz and ended up as a cook at Chicago's Metropolitan Deli in Pleasanton, California. He spoke no English but understood enough to figure out that the restaurant's owner, Terri Terry, owned some show horses, and he immediately campaigned to get on one.

"I grew up around horses, and I missed them," he said. When Terry relented, she was stunned when Garcia leaped on a horse's back by grabbing a handful of mane and was able to put the jumper through his paces without a saddle or bridle. She knew a former jockey who in turn introduced Garcia to a trainer on California's fair circuit. His education began. He mucked stalls and walked hot horses to cool them down and eventually worked his way up to galloping them in the morning. Within nine months, Garcia was ready to become an apprentice jockey, and on August 17, 2005, he got his first victory in only his third official mount at the Bay Meadows Fair meet. On Mondays and Tuesdays, the racetrack's dark days, he continued to work at the deli where his shrimp salad with jalapeño had quite a following. Within a year, however, Garcia had won the riding title at Golden Gate Fields and was ready to head south to Santa Anita and Hollywood Park to knock heads with California's most accomplished riders.

"He was a real aggressive rider when he showed up here, but he was raw," Baffert said. "He was willing to listen and was a quick study."

The trainer invested hours in Garcia, a powerfully built 5-foot-1, 105-pounder, putting him up on his classiest horses during morning training hours and drilling him on the right and wrong ways to handle them in the afternoon. Baffert sent him to Texas and New Mexico to ride his second-tier stakes horses and he usually came back with the hardware and first-place check. By 2010, he was legging Garcia up on his big horses, winning seven stakes races for Baffert, including the Santa Monica Handicap on Gabby's Golden Gal and the Santa Anita Handicap on Misremembered. Both were rich Grade 1 races, which put him in the top ten in the national jockey earnings standings for the first time with more than $3.3 million in purses won.

Baffert showed his faith in Garcia when he put him on Lookin At Lucky for the Preakness. Until then, Garrett Gomez, who had been the nation's leading jockey in purse money for the previous four years, had the mount. He had won five of six starts to earn Lookin At Lucky honors as the two-year-old champion, but the wheels came off that relationship after Gomez and the colt found trouble in all three of his races as a three-year-old. The colt clipped heels with a rival and nearly fell in the Rebel Stakes; then Gomez tried to bull him through a nonexistent hole up the rail in the Santa Anita Derby. It not only stopped Lookin At Lucky cold but also culminated in a postrace fistfight between Gomez and Victor Espinoza. In the Derby, the duo were the betting favorite but lost all chance when Lookin At Lucky broke awkwardly out of the Number 1 gate and was bounced twice off the rail in the opening eighth of a mile.

So Baffert fired Gomez, put Garcia on Lookin At Lucky, and met him in the winner's circle at Pimlico Race Course to pick up the hardware, the first-place check, and Garcia's first and only victory in a Triple Crown race.

Baffert, however, is a demanding boss and expected Garcia to ride his important horses each morning, which left him little time to cultivate relationships with other trainers to drum up more mounts. In 2012, when Garcia told the trainer that he wanted to ride for other barns, Baffert fired him. Garcia fell out of the top twenty in earnings and later ended his estrangement with Baffert. He had made peace with the fact that he was the test driver to Baffert's crew chief on the barn's most important horses. It meant Garcia returned to near the top of the earnings chart, bringing in more than $10 million in purse earnings even though he had a third fewer mounts than the leaders. It also allowed him to ride extraordinary creatures like American Pharoah.

He and Baffert had been in perfect synch bringing the colt back to the track in February. Early on they were in a holding pattern, letting the colt feel his legs under him and air fill his lungs in a pair of three-eighths-of-a-mile blowouts. As the distances progressed, the wireless communication had become hushed.

"Nice," Baffert said as quietly as if he were in church. "Pick it up a little now."

Garcia, who looks like what little weight he carries is centralized in his cherubic cheeks, would beam a knowing smile when Baffert warned him not to go too fast. American Pharoah was a tough horse to ride in the morning because he was always on go. He galloped kindly for Jorge Alvarez, but once Garcia showed up and he knew that he was going to work, American Pharoah started revving his motor. He wanted to do what he wanted to do.

"Whenever you want to go, however far you want to go, he drags you there," Garcia said.

What amazed Garcia the most was how quickly the colt recovered. Horses that ran as fast as he did were normally blowing and vibrating for at least thirty minutes. American Pharoah needed ten minutes, the time it took to walk back to the barn, and then was in his stall napping twenty minutes after that.

Most of the heavy lifting had been done for American Pharoah's three-year-old debut. Seven days prior, Baffert had put a stout breeze in the colt, stretching to seven-eighths of a mile in 1:23.80. Garcia and American Pharoah were breaking from the gate this morning, and Baffert didn't want to take much out of his colt. The colt popped from the gate and hit every fraction like he was being paced by a metronome before finishing up the three-quarters of a mile in 1:10.40. Baffert was quiet as he waited for Garcia to report in.

"*Patrón,*" said Garcia over the wire. "We were just galloping. He's ready."

It was exactly what Baffert wanted to hear.

Jimmy Barnes had taken American Pharoah to Oaklawn Park in Hot Springs, Arkansas, for the Rebel Stakes, so Baffert watched it from Santa Anita. He was serene and supremely confident. He knew American Pharoah did not need to win the race, but he knew he would. He had watched the colt mature over the winter, getting to see up close his mind at work as he walked around the barn. He was a polite and gentle horse. He seemed to stop for other horses and was curious whenever a new face appeared on the shedrow. He folded himself into his hay to rest with the grace of a ballet dancer. American Pharoah snatched a carrot from the palm of your hand like he was stealing a kiss. Baffert knew this was a special colt and he was more eager than anxious to see his return to the racetrack.

Ahmed Zayat was a wreck. He wanted to believe his trainer that American Pharoah was primed and ready, but he could not beat back his inner handicapper. The colt was coming off an injury, had not run in five months, and was shipping by air for the first time to run outside of California. The weather was miserable to boot. It was cold and rainy and the track was listed as sloppy and looked like the bottom of a bowl of day-old soup. He had called Baffert and asked if they should consider scratching American Pharoah. No way, he was told. There was not any give left in the schedule; it was either run now or miss the Derby.

Baffert told Victor Espinoza to try to go slow early, that there were no world beaters in the field of seven and he did not want American Pharoah to overdo it in his return to racing. The colt was fidgeting when the gates popped and American Pharoah bobbled slightly and tangled his feet. Espinoza kept American Pharoah relaxed and let him find his own stride. He had already splashed to the front when they went under the wire for the first time and American Pharoah was handling the wet going like he had fins on his feet. Espinoza kept the fractions leisurely — :24.41 for a quarter-mile, :49.63 for a half, and 1:15.22 for three-quarters.

In California, Baffert knew that no one was catching him today.

"Once he got to the far turn, he was just in his groove, galloping," said Baffert. "If he's the horse we hope he is, he's in good shape."

He was and Espinoza knew there were no lessons for American Pharoah to learn this afternoon. When he came out of the far turn, Espinoza began massaging the colt's neck and American Pharoah put four more lengths on the field. Espinoza's whip stayed tucked in his fist as he rode American Pharoah home to a six-and-a-quarter-length victory in 1:45.78 for the mile-and-sixteenth distance.

In the clubhouse, Ahmed Zayat hugged his son and anyone else who came within arm's length of his perimeter. His colt had not only successfully returned to the racetrack but he was also clearly better than ever.

"He did it exactly the way you want it; just perfect," Zayat said. "I'm just tickled pink that he's back, he's healthy, and he showed us that he can relax and enjoy very, very hard circumstances."

His mouth was racing along with his thoughts.

"This was not ideal," he said. "The race on paper was his to lose. He hasn't run since last September, but a horse coming off an injury, not running in five months, and shipping in, you're asking a lot of him. We wanted to see how he'd handle it."

When they got American Pharoah to the barn, Barnes discovered that his right front shoe was bent; he had sprung it when he bobbled at the gate. Espinoza looked at the bent shoe and shook his head.

"Most horses when that happens, you can feel something during the race, something not quite right," he said. "With him, I felt nothing different at all, but those kinds of things don't matter to a horse like him. That's why I have so much respect for him."

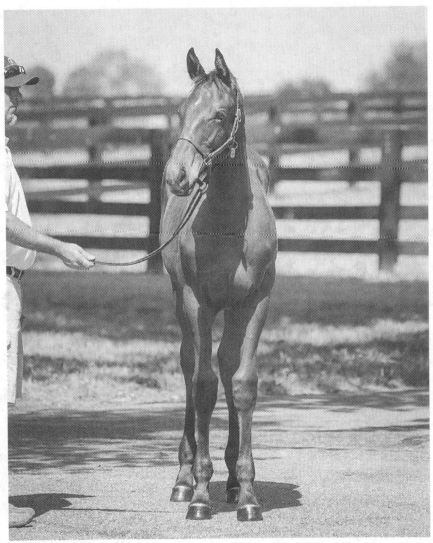

American Pharoah as a weanling in the summer of 2012 at the Vinery, a breeding farm in central Kentucky.

Vinery farm manager Frances Relihan was immediately wowed by American Pharoah's balance, athleticism, and intelligence.

American Pharoah heading to the racetrack and drawing a crowd at Churchill Downs in the week before the 141st running of the Kentucky Derby.

Frances Relihan with her husband, Dr. Joe Schneider, hours before America's greatest race is run.

Victor Espinoza atop American Pharoah moments after winning the Derby. It was Espinoza's third triumph in America's greatest race.

Victor Espinoza gliding American Pharoah around a rain-drenched race-track to victory in the second leg of the Triple Crown.

Ahmed and Justin Zayat take questions as they wait for American Pharoah to arrive from Louisville, Kentucky, to Belmont Park, in New York.

Victor Espinoza acknowledging the thunderous ovation to American Pharoah winning the Belmont Stakes to become only the 12th Triple Crown champion in history.

Ahmed and Joanne Zayat celebrating with their children after American Pharoah crosses the finish line at Belmont Park.

Assistant trainer Jimmy Barnes (left) and groom Eduardo Luna (right) lead American Pharoah to the winner's circle to officially take his place in Thoroughbred history.

Victor Espinoza and Ahmed Zayat hoisting the Belmont Stakes trophy.

The Hall of Fame trainer Bob Baffert leading Triple Crown champion American Pharoah for a walk at Saratoga Race Course in Saratoga Springs, New York.

American Pharoah at his new home at Ashford Stud in Versailles, Kentucky, where he will stand as a stallion for $200,000 per breeding.

CHAPTER ELEVEN:
BARN 33

Kentucky Derby Week, 2015

Once upon a time, barn 33 at Churchill Downs was at the center of the circus that is the Kentucky Derby. It was Baffert's barn and it was easily identified by the three shingles hanging near its entryway in honor of his three Derby winners: Silver Charm, Real Quiet, and War Emblem. From 1996 to 2003, it was the first stop for every celebrity, from New York Yankees manager Joe Torre, to Olympic skier Bode Miller, to the reigning Miss America, as well as Rotary Clubs and Pony Clubs. It was always rimmed with reporters and camera crews waiting for the white-haired trainer to pop out and do a little stand-up. Baffert never disappointed. No matter how much his stomach was turning and whatever ailments, tiny or terrible, in his horses that he and his team were fending off, Baffert always appeared to be relaxed and in command.

Over the next twelve years, though, after bringing twelve middling horses to American horse racing's biggest dance, Baffert's heat had definitely cooled. He never soured and remained a good ambassador, but he was forced to cede the spotlight to new faces like John Servis, who brought Smarty Jones here in 2004, and Michael Matz with Barbaro two years later, and Rick Dutrow with Big Brown in 2008. It hurt. Each of their horses came here undefeated and was the clear favorite to win on the first Saturday in May. Baffert knew better than most that you are only as good as your horses. You're an in-demand genius when they are fast. You are the guy everyone walks past with barely a nod when your horses are slow.

Guess what? The big top was back over the Baffert barn as the 141st running of the Kentucky Derby approached, all because he had brought a couple of big horses here. It was the Wednesday before the race and when American Pharoah and Dortmund left the barn for the racetrack, it was like they were the grand marshals of the Thanksgiving Day parade. Hundreds of people followed en masse with their cell phone cameras aloft. Hundreds more rushed to the rail to secure positions to watch the two gallop. Dortmund, indeed, was a monster. He was tall and broad. Side by side, though, American Pharoah gave nothing away. He stood 16.1 hands, the equivalent of 5 feet, 3 inches at the withers, and weighed 1,170 pounds. He was better put together, more chiseled and majestic. He was Muhammad Ali to Dortmund's George Foreman, LeBron James to Kevin Durant.

Dortmund was unbeaten in six races on the West Coast, where it was widely believed that the best three-year-olds had been competing in the prep races to get here.

On the first Saturday of April, three important prep races were run in a stretch of ninety minutes to determine which horses had a realistic chance to capture the Kentucky Derby in May. When it was over, there was little doubt about the overwhelming favorite at this moment. It was Dortmund, a strapping and fast colt who had just decimated five rivals in the Santa Anita Derby to remain undefeated, which was no small thing for his owner, Kaleem Shah. Before the race, Shah was not only nervous for the first time but was also thinking about history — about two previous Kentucky Derby victors, to be exact: Smarty Jones (2004) and Seattle Slew (1977).

"I was looking to do what Seattle Slew did when he went to the Derby six for six.

Smarty Jones went there six for six," Shah said. "It was critically important that he move forward, not regress."

At Santa Anita, Dortmund certainly looked like he belonged in the same sentence as those two horses. He overcame a stumble out of the gate to lead every step of the way in an emphatic four-and-one-quarter-length victory. He set fast fractions: 46.36 seconds for a half mile, and 1:10.57 for three-quarters of a mile. He finished strong, covering a mile and an eighth in 1:48.73. His rider, Martin Garcia, looked as if he were out for a pleasure ride as Dortmund turned for home. His whip was idle and blowing in the wind like an antenna.

"I didn't do anything," Garcia said. "He just dragged me around there."

How Dortmund won and where he did it mattered greatly. The best three-year-old horses in the nation had resided at Santa Anita Park for the past six months. In Dortmund's case, he shared a barn with a couple of them, American Pharoah and One Lucky Dane. The latter finished second to him and earned a trip to the Kentucky Derby as well. You couldn't forget about Firing Line, either. Twice previously, he had dueled down the stretch with Dortmund, finishing a head behind each time in the Robert B.

Lewis Stakes and the Los Alamitos Futurity. His trainer, Simon Callaghan, knew when enough was enough and sent Firing Line to New Mexico where he crushed the field by more than fourteen lengths in the Sunland Derby.

Still, there were sixteen other horses here in Kentucky lining up against Dortmund and the California contingent, and Baffert had watched on television as they made their case for being considered bona fide contenders. Among them was Frosted, who won the Wood Memorial by going a mile and an eighth in 1:50.31. So far he had shown more potential than results. In his prior race, the Fountain of Youth at Gulfstream Park in Florida, Frosted hit the stretch looking like a winner before pulling himself up and finishing fourth. Afterward, his trainer, Kiaran McLaughlin, had throat surgery performed on the horse, suspecting that Frosted had displaced his soft palate on the floor of the airway near the larynx and partially blocked his airway. If the Wood was any indication, the procedure was a success. McLaughlin's owners, Sheikh Mo's Godolphin Racing, had been trying since 1999 to win the Derby trophy, one of the few premier races on the planet that they had not won.

"We know he has a ton of ability, and the last race really made us scratch our heads, asking why he would go to the lead and throw his head up and stop," McLaughlin said. "We did everything we could to change everything we possibly could."

In the Blue Grass Stakes in Kentucky, Carpe Diem established himself as the class of the East Coast–based horses. He had won four of his five races and impressed his jockey, John Velazquez. He took command at the top of the stretch and rushed on for a three-length victory.

"There wasn't much speed in the race," Velazquez said. "It was a nice slow pace, and I didn't want to fight him very much. Down the lane, I asked him, and he responded right away."

At least a month ago, there was little doubt that Dortmund would be the horse to beat come the first Saturday in May. Horseplayers were always looking for omens and, like his owner Shah, had found it in the fact that Dortmund was undefeated coming to Kentucky, as were his father Big Brown, Seattle Slew, and Smarty Jones. Each of those three found themselves in the winner's circle beneath Churchill's twin spires. Baffert, however, knew not to get ahead of himself. He had lost with seemingly unbeatable horses, including Point Given and Lookin At Lucky.

"Just enjoy the moment because the next race is going to be the one," he kept reminding himself.

Besides, he also knew that the best horse in his barn, in the country, hell, maybe even the world was running the following Saturday in the Arkansas Derby. If you drew a line through the debut race of American Pharoah, the colt was not only a perfect four for four but also had never even been challenged by another horse.

Again, Baffert sent Jimmy Barnes and remained in California. He was taking his new lifestyle seriously and trying to eliminate unnecessary travel. He thought — or at least hoped — that he was in for the full five weeks of the Triple Crown. Baffert knew that sending American Pharoah back to Oaklawn was like sending a bazooka to a knife fight. The colt was full of himself. He told Barnes to pack for a long trip. He and American Pharoah were going straight to Louisville from Hot Springs. He was so sure that the colt was going to win that he called the track announcer at Oaklawn — Frank Mirahmadi, a friend — before the race and told him to get a special call ready.

The colt definitely lived up to Baffert's

expectations. He broke smoothly, but this time Espinoza settled him off the pace set by a horse named Bridget's Big Luvy, who sprinted to a three-length lead in a wicked fast opening quarter of 22.77 seconds.

In the clubhouse, Zayat was confused. In the paddock, neither he nor Barnes had told Espinoza to rate the colt behind other horses. All American Pharoah had ever done was go to the lead. Watching with his wife at home on his couch, Baffert was concerned. The colt was just galloping down the backside.

"Oh, what's happening?" Jill Baffert asked her husband. "What's he doing? He's not running."

"Either he's got him shut down, or he's not going to fire today," Baffert said.

Espinoza had, indeed, shut down American Pharoah. He wanted to teach him how to relax early. It was the only way they were going to win in Kentucky. There was plenty of early speed in this current crop of three-year-olds, and when twenty horses break before more than 150,000 people as they do in the Derby, horses and riders often panic and a game of high-speed bumper cars erupts as the field heads to the first turn. A mile and a quarter is a long way, and Espinoza knew the horse that found its cruising speed quickest and could track panicked front-runners was the one most likely to still be running in the stretch. He wanted American Pharoah to be that horse.

"If I'm going to be in the lead, they're going to go after me," he said.

He had the perfect setup to see if the colt could track other horses. He had to take it. If Baffert got angry, Espinoza would accept the consequences.

American Pharoah understood what he was doing and patiently stalked the front-runner through a still-fast half mile in 45.99 seconds. As they approached the far turn, Espinoza dropped his hands ever so slightly and American Pharoah blew by Bridget's Big Luvy like a rocket. Baffert saw Espinoza pick him up again at the three-eighths pole. He and Jill sank back in their couch. With fifty yards to go, Espinoza eased up on the colt, crossing the wire eight lengths ahead of the field in 1:48.52 for the mile-and-eighth distance.

"He has not been asked the question, but everyone knows the answer!" roared Mirahmadi, making Baffert smile at home.

Afterward, Espinoza phoned Baffert and told him that American Pharoah was the most talented and best-prepared horse he had ever been on heading into a big race.

"The way this horse runs is unbelievable," Espinoza said. "I don't feel like he's running that fast and then I look back and he's so far ahead. He was doing it by himself and doing it easy. We're going to win this thing."

Baffert thought so, too, but he could not say so publicly. Everyone had asked and the trainer did something that did not come naturally: He dodged the question. He had to keep his own counsel. It was wise, of course — Kaleem Shah and Ahmed Zayat, each provided Baffert with an ample number of quality horses. Why alienate one or the other? He had kept the colts apart the past five months to avoid that. So, he kept quiet and enjoyed the comparisons made to the legendary trainer Ben Jones, who brought a couple of iconic colts named Citation and Coaltown here in 1948. Jones was the only trainer to win the Derby six times, including victories with Whirlaway and Citation, who went on to win the Triple Crown in 1941 and 1948, respectively. Baffert was flattered by the comparison to Jones and would be fine with running first and second as Citation and Coaltown had done.

Most everyone roaming the backside of Churchill Downs agreed with Espinoza. It did not happen often that a variety of constituencies rallied around a single horse. This was the Derby, after all, the single greatest betting race on the calendar. It is the only time in American Thoroughbred racing that twenty horses get in the gate. It's the only race on the calendar where the pools are awash with "square," or "dumb," money rather than that of "sharps," or devoted horseplayers. Between the unruly field size that increases the odds for bad luck and the once-a-year players betting on horses' names or the fact that the jockey is a woman, serious money can be made.

In the past twenty-five years, for example, the average payout on a $2 win bet was $28.77; for a $2 exacta ticket, or picking the top two, it was $920.23; for a trifecta, top three, it was $11,131.35; for a super-fecta, top four, it was a whopping $84,860.40. Horseplayers spent the week leading into the Derby looking for "steam," which was any morsel of information ranging from a minor injury to a poor workout to the trainer being distracted by his mistress. Wise-guy picks, or horses talked up because they appear to be overlooked but end up being heavily bet because everyone is talking about them, usually ricochet from the backside to the surrounding bars.

"Who's your Derby horse?" is a question you ask, or are asked, twenty times a day, and usually get twenty different names of horses.

Instead, "American Pharoah" was the answer heard over and over.

It was as if an immortal horse was in our midst. Some of it had to do with the final workout in preparation for the Derby three days earlier on Sunday. With Martin Garcia aboard, the colt went five-eighths of a mile in :58.40, the fastest of thirty-two similar workouts that morning. It was routine for Baffert and Garcia and anyone who had been associated with the colt the past nine months, but it blew the minds of clockers, horsemen, and professional bettors, many of whom were seeing American Pharoah in the flesh for the first time. He ripped through split times: 11.40 for an eighth, :23 for a quarter, :34.60 for three-eighths, and :46.40 for a half, and then galloped out three-fourths of a mile in 1:11 before pounding out seven furlongs in 1:27.

"I have been doing this for thirty-five years," said Gary Young, who clocked horses for betting clients as well as picked out horses for owners. "He might be the best horse I've ever seen. He's simply like Michael Jordan and stays in the air like he did in his rookie year. He stays in the air longer than any horse and you get the feeling that there's not one gear left, but he may have two, three, or four gears."

Mike Welsch has been called the E. F. Hutton of horseflesh. He writes the "Clocker Reports" for the *Daily Racing Form,* long the horseplayer's Bible, and his observations about what goes on in training in the morning have led many a horseplayer to the mutuel windows on Derby afternoon. He looks for a workout from a horse that just screams, "Bet me."

He saw one in American Pharoah's outing. He wasn't just fast, but it looked like the colt did not want to stop: "It's exactly what you want to see: a horse that feels good and you know that is just lengths better than the rest of them."

When he returned to barn 33, Baffert felt a shiver. American Pharoah was not breathing hard. Even a little.

"He's right where we want him to be. He hasn't regressed; he looks great, so it's pretty exciting to come in here," he said. "From here on out, we just keep him happy."

As far as Derby weeks go, Baffert was having a better one than usual. Even though One Lucky Dane was injured in California a couple of weeks earlier and did not make the trip, American Pharoah and Dortmund were holding up well. Most Derby weeks, something pops up — a skin rash, a fever — to unnerve him. The post-position draw was early in the evening and soon Baffert and his rivals would have an idea if their colts had been compromised. So far, all he had to battle was his own neuroses. Baffert was very superstitious, especially about black cats. The morning Real Quiet got beat at the Belmont, a black cat had crossed Baffert's path. The same thing happened with Point Given the week before the Derby.

The other day, driving with Bode, a black cat jumped in front of them. When the trainer slammed on his brakes, Bode asked, "What's wrong, Daddy?"

Baffert hung a U-turn with traffic coming, rattling his son further. He explained his superstition to his son. They went and picked up Jill. Later, while still in the car, he got a call from the barn about Dortmund. He was uncomfortable after his workout. He was getting a little colicky, perhaps from not drinking enough water. After he got off the call, Baffert relayed the situation to his wife.

"That black cat strikes again," Bode Baffert said from the backseat.

Dortmund came out of it and was in Kentucky in fine shape. So was Jill Baffert, keeping her husband calm.

"Every time I start, she just says knock it off," he said. "Come on. Get a hold of yourself. It's nerve wracking. It is a nerve-wracking business we have to go through."

Still, there was an altogether different Derby vibe taking shape, one that had not been hijacked by bombastic owners as when Big Brown arrived to launch his Triple Crown assault. The usually voluble Zayat mostly avoided making any ground pronouncements. He had been smote down by the racing gods thrice before and did not want to think about another heartbreak. He was back, though. In fact, he had three horses here — El Kabeir had earned his way into the field of twenty along with Mr. Z, a colt that had finished third in the Arkansas Derby, a long way behind American Pharoah but good enough to get a shot at the roses.

Every time Zayat got morose or anxious, he tried to think about what Baffert had told him before American Pharoah ever raced.

"I've never seen Bob in the past hype a horse for me," Zayat said, "and day one somehow this horse talked to Bob. He told me, 'Oh my God, this is something. We're going to have a lot of fun with this horse.' He believed dearly in him."

There was no need to manufacture story lines. No, this time the horses were the genuine stars and there was a sense that America's signature race was going to be one for the ages. Much of it had to do with American Pharoah and Dortmund. All week, horsemen had been trekking to Baffert's barn as if it were the Louvre to take a look at what they consider to be the *Mona Lisa* and the *Venus de Milo* of a deep and talented crop of three-year-olds. These were hardboots who knew that even the great horses lose and who declare it often, but they had fallen like schoolboys for American Pharoah.

"He's special," insisted D. Wayne Lukas, who trained Mr. Z for Zayat.

Lukas was as legendary as Ben Jones. Like Baffert, he came from the world of quarter horses and overachieved. Even at seventy-nine years old, Lukas still rocked fringe chaps in the morning and wore a Stetson on horseback, looking as if he'd just galloped out of Monument Valley and a John Ford movie. In the afternoon, the slickest horse trainer of them all pulls a $3,000 suit from his closet, slips on his aviator shades, and turns the racetrack dining room into his office and salon.

Lukas changed the nature of the sport, and his most envied talent was talking rich people out of their money. His passion and charisma had persuaded enough of them to plunk down more than $250 million at horse auctions. He had shed some of the flashier accessories that have been part of his Hall of Fame career. He no longer meets clients in his Rolls-Royce, and his corporate jet has long been replaced by commercial flights. Back in the 1980s, when his stable was 250 strong and he flew his horses all over to win the nation's biggest races, horseplayers used to talk about betting on Lukas's horses when it was a case of "D. Wayne off the plane."

No more. Lukas preferred to ride with his horses in the transport truck when he traveled away from his Louisville base. Two years ago, in 2013, his colt Oxbow won the Preakness, giving Lukas his fourteenth victory in Triple Crown races, making him the most successful trainer in the American classic races. It also ended a thirteen-year Triple Crown drought for Lukas, a string of futility that would have run most out of the game.

"I've been left for dead so many times,"

Lukas said.

As Lukas had grown old, he had also grown up. He was always a proud man who disliked the suggestion that he ever lost his touch. In 1999, in one of those fallow periods, he came to New York with the colt Charismatic and a chance to win the Triple Crown. Instead of enjoying it, however, Lukas drove himself and his help too hard and continued a battle with the news media over whether he was good for the sport after Charismatic finished third and broke his leg in the race.

Lukas knew his horses and was convinced that American Pharoah was the horse to lead the sport out of the Triple Crown wilderness. Mr. Z had finished third, less than a neck behind Dortmund in the Los Alamitos Futurity and eight and three-quarters of a length behind American Pharoah in Arkansas.

"In my opinion, American Pharoah was lengths ahead of Dortmund," Lukas said. "I have not been that impressed with a horse for a long time. We ran at him in Arkansas. We had a perfect trip. We ran right to his neck, and when Victor Espinoza just nudged him, he opened up four or five lengths on us, just wham! Looking at the replay, he lengthened his stride, just cruised. That impressed the hell out of me."

It is the way the colt floated like a cloud around the racetrack that earned Lukas's respect.

"Conformation-wise, just seeing him stand there, he doesn't blow you away," he added. "But when he moves and gets in full flight, he's got an amazing stride. I like the way he's able to go from good speed and then kick it like that. That breaks horses' hearts."

Lukas was not the only seasoned horseman to fall under the colt's spell. Bill Mott, another Hall of Famer, had campaigned the great Cigar to sixteen consecutive victories against top-class competition from 1995 through 1996, the first horse to do so since Citation during a 1948 through 1950 run. When Mott brought Cigar west, Baffert, starting to make some noise with Thoroughbreds, asked Mott, whom he did not know, if he could have a look at his horse. Mott was gracious and let him spend as much time as he wanted with Cigar. Baffert wanted to see him because he had recognized something rarely seen at the racetrack: greatness.

Cigar was considered "America's Horse." He was a ham who posed for the cameras before beating the best of his generation from New York to California, from Massachusetts to Dubai. Cigar's racetrack heroics throughout his streak were many. He was ridden by Jerry Bailey, a Hall of Famer turned broadcast analyst who had been by Baffert's barn often over the spring and shared his favorite stories about the horse. At the Oaklawn Handicap in Arkansas in 1995, Cigar was accidentally hit in the face with a whip by a jockey aboard another horse. Instead of losing momentum, Cigar shook his head, pinned his ears, and spurted away for a sixth consecutive victory. Three months later in the Hollywood Gold Cup, a clod of dirt hit Cigar squarely in the head, making him angry and putting him in a tug-of-war with Bailey. His hands creased by the reins and fingertips numb, Bailey finally surrendered. They won by three and a half lengths anyway, to extend the streak to nine.

Cigar was the inspiration for one of the greatest calls in the history of Thoroughbred racing when he jetted off to win the 1995 Breeders' Cup Classic at Belmont Park to end a perfect ten-for-ten season.

"Cigar! Cigar makes his move, and he sweeps to the lead with a dramatic rush," roared the New York announcer Tom Durkin with a tremor in his baritone as his jockey, Bailey, turned him loose. "Here he is, the incomparable, the invincible, the unbeatable Cigar."

The horse had received a police escort through the streets of Manhattan — accompanied by the Clydesdales and the Knicks' cheerleaders — to Madison Square Garden, where on November 2, 1996, he was thrown a retirement party before the white-gloved set at the National Horse Show. It didn't take long for the great racehorse to demonstrate that he was comfortable among the upper crust. When Bailey lifted in his saddle, Cigar broke into an elegant glide as if he had competed for blue ribbons in a previous life.

Bailey's favorite moment was Cigar's gentlest. After Cigar completed his perfect season in the 1995 Breeders' Cup, Bailey took his son Justin, then three, to check on the horse in Mott's barn. Bailey had the boy in his arms when Cigar suddenly stopped grazing, stepped over, and put his nose to Justin's chest and chin.

"He was just nuzzling on him," Bailey said. "Less than twenty-four hours earlier he was on fire, just a machine, and now he was like a pony in the parking lot of Kmart. He really liked people."

As Baffert listened to Bailey tell his stories, he started to recognize the similarities his horse shared with Cigar. Each seemed to know they possessed star quality. American Pharoah accommodated the photographers who followed him from his barn to the track, stopping purposefully to strike poses, turning his head to insure everyone got a look. He was mellow everywhere but the racetrack, plucking carrots from the opened hands of young children.

Now, on the backside of Churchill Downs, Mott asked Baffert if he could take a look at American Pharoah. Mott, too, recognized the makings of a great horse. He had watched the colt in the mornings and was transfixed by the efficiency of his stride. American Pharoah really didn't hit the ground — he flew over it. Mott told him he had a great horse and to try to enjoy it as he did with Cigar. These were once-in-a-lifetime occurrences.

"I knew what was going on was special and was never going to happen again," Mott said of his run with Cigar. "The really good ones win races when they are not at their best. Whether he was coming off a layup, or had a foot issue, or got caught in a compromising position in a race. Cigar overcame all those."

He told Baffert American Pharoah would, too.

Elliott Walden, a former trainer turned president and chief executive of WinStar Farm, bemoaned his luck for having a highly regarded colt in the same crop as American Pharoah. WinStar was the co-owner of Carpe Diem, who, like American Pharoah, won four of his five starts, earning $1.5 million in purses and decimating the opponents he had faced.

"American Pharoah is a notch above everybody — he glides along so easily, like there isn't any effort," Walden said.

Carla Gaines was saddling a horse named Bolo in her first Derby. She wondered why when she saw American Pharoah one morning at Churchill Downs.

"He breathes different air than other horses," she said. "He's a spectacle to behold on the racetrack. It's like his feet don't touch the ground; he just floats. He kind of sprouts wings. He definitely could be a superhorse."

The closest thing to a flaw to be found in the colt was that part of his name was misspelled: *pharaoh* is correct; *pharoah* is not. How the colt become American Pharoah had become a mystery that was played out in public.

A Missouri woman named Marsha Baumgartner had come up with the name and submitted it in a naming contest on Zayat's Stable's website. She had been a horse racing fan since Secretariat won the Triple Crown in 1973. She settled on American Pharoah for the dark bay colt because his sire is Pioneerof the Nile and his dam's sire was Yankee Gentleman. Even better, Ahmed Zayat is from Egypt. She believed she had submitted the correct spelling.

At first, Ahmed and Justin Zayat said The Jockey Club, which approves all names, had made a mistake. Officials there disputed that and said the name was submitted electronically and it was approved the way it was spelled. One of the more novel theories floated was that the *a* and the *o* were transposed deliberately so the horse would not be mistaken for an idol, especially a Pharaoh, who would not let the Jews go from Egypt.

Even more perplexing was how the strapping and accomplished colt Dortmund had been totally eclipsed by his stablemate. He was one of two undefeated horses in the field, with a victory here the previous November, blitzing eleven rivals by nearly eight lengths. He was the only contender who had been challenged in the stretch when the race was on the line — twice — by a colt here named Firing Line.

252

"We know that Dortmund is probably more battle-tested," Baffert conceded. "He's been in a fight."

Gary Stevens, fifty-two years old and riding with an artificial knee, had the mount on Firing Line. He was the last of the classic American West riders and a keen student of the sport's history. He started his career in his native Idaho and rode in Washington State before establishing himself as a Hall of Famer in California. He had tried to retire three previous times — first to train, then to be a television commentator, and finally to be an actor. He was pretty good at all three and earned rave reviews playing the jockey George Woolf in the movie *Seabiscuit*. The racetrack kept beckoning him back, though. Beyond winning big races, Stevens missed the mornings at Clockers' Corner and the afternoons in the grandstand after he had fulfilled his riding obligations for the day. He enjoyed drinking a beer and smoking a cigarette with the horseplayers who, like him, believed a bad day at the track was better than a good day anywhere else.

Stevens rode his first Derby in 1986 and has won it three times — with Winning Colors in 1988, Thunder Gulch in 1995, and Silver Charm in 1997. He liked Firing

Line's chances. A lot. After the colt had lost those head-to-head duels with Dortmund, they went to New Mexico for the Sunland Derby and blew apart the field. Stevens knew it was going to take a monster effort from Firing Line, American Pharoah, or any other horse to win this Derby.

"This is the best bunch of horses assembled for this race since I've been coming here," he said. "What's even better is most of them haven't seen each other before."

That, too, was adding to the intrigue. There were accomplished horses that could not be ignored and were coming here from all corners of the country. Materiality was the other undefeated horse in the field and had run away with the Florida Derby. In addition to Frosted, Sheikh Mo and Godolphin had sent over Mubtaahij from Dubai. The colt won four of his previous starts on the dirt. His trainer, South African Mike de Kock, was here for the first time. He was not here for the mint juleps, either. He sent only well-meant horses to the world's biggest races and had won many of them.

"I am very impressed by what I see, and I probably picked one of the worst years to try to come to the Derby from another country," he said. "There's some very serious horses. There's not only American Pharoah, there's some proper horses there, so, you know, a healthy respect for them, there's no doubt."

Between the star power of American Pharoah and the depth and talent of his challengers, even the most practical horsemen and cynical horseplayers were finding it hard to shake the feeling that something magical was about to happen along this year's Triple Crown trail.

"Some Derbies, horses that win, no one thought they could," said John Moynihan, the bloodstock agent who picked out Carpe Diem. "That isn't going to happen this year. I don't know if it will be American Pharoah, but a very good horse is going to win. Hopefully, when we get done with the Triple Crown, there's going to be three or four horses that are considered warriors."

There were still seventy-two hours until post time, which was plenty of time for American Pharoah to get cast in his stall, step on stone, tie up his intestines, or any of the dozens of things that can, and do, go wrong for a racehorse as he readies for a big race. Of the most immediate concern for Team Pharoah was the post-position draw that was about to begin. Baffert, Zayat, and Espinoza had all been done in before by a blind draw that matches a horse with a stall in the starting gate. It mattered most here at Churchill Downs, in the Derby's twenty-horse field. Baffert liked to say that the race — and history — was won or lost in the opening quarter-mile run to the first turn. The memory of Lookin At Lucky drawing the Number 1 hole was all too fresh. The colt's chances were compromised as soon as the gate opened, as he was bumped and then pinballed among the cavalry charge before finishing sixth.

Espinoza was especially on edge, which was out of character. Stevens, a friend and a rival, had watched Espinoza grow up in the jockeys' room and had come to admire him as a rider who "just didn't give a shit." He had refused to join the Jockey's Guild, rode how he wanted, and took the sharp words and hirings and firings by trainers with a smile. In fact, Stevens and Espinoza argued about which of them Baffert had fired the most.

Espinoza had managed to stay above the fray in California Chrome's previous year's Triple Crown bid that began in storybook fashion only to unravel messily. One owner, Steve Coburn, was a hard-drinking cowboy who could not keep his mouth shut; the other, Perry Martin, thought his genius as a first-time breeder was responsible for building a better racehorse.

The truth was the two of them got lucky, as in blind dumb luck. Espinoza was more astounded than hurt that Martin never said a word to him throughout their Triple Crown saga, not even offering a simple thank you for his efforts.

It had been a ride of a lifetime that was still paying dividends. The notoriety got him a trip to Royal Ascot, the Queen of England's home track, where he won a stakes race and got a winner's circle audience with Queen Elizabeth II. He was awarded the top jockey award at the previous year's ESPY Award, donning a white dinner jacket for a party where he partied with the likes of the Cleveland Cavaliers' LeBron James and the New England Patriots' Tom Brady. He was put on the ballot for the National Museum of Racing Hall of Fame for the first time, though he did not make the final cut.

"No, I wasn't disappointed," Espinoza said. "It was my first time on the ballot, so that's okay. Maybe voters need me to win another Kentucky Derby or two."

Now he was in the position to join a handful of the sport's giants to win back-to-back Derbies. Only the great Black jockeys Isaac

Murphy (1890–1891) and Jimmy Winkfield (1901–1902); as had Secretariat's rider Ron Turcotte (1972–1973); Eddie Delahoussaye (1982–1983), and Calvin Borel (2009–2010) had done it before. All but Borel are in the Hall of Fame. It was something Eddie Arcaro, Bill Hartack, Laffit Pincay, Angel Cordero, and Bill Shoemaker were unable to do.

He had fallen even harder for American Pharoah than he had for California Chrome and did not want fate and a lousy post to keep the colt out of the winner's circle and derail his Triple Crown bid.

"What are the odds, having a chance to ride the favorite for the Kentucky Derby back-to-back? To come in with more confidence this year than last year is a very good feeling," he said.

Halfway through the draw, however, Espinoza was nauseous, and Baffert was having a flashback to Lookin At Lucky. The Numbers 1, 2, and 3 holes were still empty, and all but two outside posts were spoken for. Baffert's stents were getting a workout. Then they heard American Pharoah's name matched with the Number 18 pole. It was not ideal. Espinoza would have rather had the Number 8 hole that went to Dortmund and Martin Garcia, but Big Brown had won from the 20 hole and I'll Have Another won from 19. Espinoza knew he could control the race from the 18 post. He also knew that two of the most dangerous contenders had lost the race here in a banquet room at Churchill Downs before they ever stepped into the starting gate.

The Blue Grass Stakes champion Carpe Diem and the Florida Derby winner Materiality pulled posts that compromised their chances of finishing the mile-and-a-quarter race ahead of him or anyone else. Mike Battaglia, the Churchill Downs oddsmaker, made Carpe Diem the third morning line betting choice at 8 to 1 despite the fact that he was coming out of the Number 2 hole; Materiality was next door in the Number 3 spot at 12 to 1. The riders of both colts had no choice but to gun their front-running colts early and hope to avoid trouble.

"This doesn't change my confidence in the horses at all," said Todd Pletcher, the trainer of both colts. "You have to work out good trips from any post. It's part of it. We'll be fine."

Baffert had uttered similar comments after Lookin At Lucky's draw. He knew that neither Carpe Diem nor Materiality had a chance. He felt bad for Pletcher. No one was surprised when Battaglia made American Pharoah the 5 to 2 morning line favorite and Dortmund, at 3 to 1, the second choice, least of all Baffert.

"We just have to contain ourselves," Baffert told the assembled media throng. "It's exciting to be here with two good horses, him and Dortmund. In a stampede like the Derby, it's all about the break, so whichever one of them gets out first, I'll focus on. There's more ways to lose this than win it."

It only took about an hour alone for him to churn the possibilities through his head. Yes, he believed in fate. Yes, he had a bad feeling. He believed Pharoah was the one, but he could also make a case for Dortmund. Now he knew how old Ben Jones felt when he was going to walk Citation and Coaltown over there. As his thoughts raced, Baffert barely made sense.

"I believe that something really good is about to happen, or else it's going to be disappointing," he started. "Destiny. Maybe Dortmund is the horse. I don't know how good he is. The farther the better it's going to be for him. He loves this track. He's tough.

"We know Pharoah is brilliant from what he's done. He gallops around there and he really hasn't had to break a sweat. Turning for home, I'd love to see them in first and second. Then see what they're made of.

"Maybe there is another horse. Maybe Carpe Diem is better than them. Or somebody else. That's why we have this race."

Chapter Twelve:
The First Saturday in May

May 2, 2015

It was an hour drive on I-64, and Baffert knew he was going to make it as soon as he learned that Silver Charm was coming home from Japan after a decade to take up residence at Old Friends, a retirement farm for accomplished racehorses in Georgetown, Kentucky. He had two other horses there as well — Danthebluegrassman and Game On Dude. He wanted Jill and Bode to meet him as well. They were not yet a family when Silver Charm gave Baffert his first Kentucky Derby and launched his Hall of Fame career. It was Silver Charm, really, that had given them all they had now.

Baffert teared up as soon as the horse trotted over to the fence, looking every bit as tough as he did two decades ago. Baffert found himself tearing up more often these days. Silver Charm was twenty-one years old and was more white than silver. Like his trainer, he had aged and moved slower than he once did. Jill put her arm around her husband. She understood what this meant.

"He's like your first love," she said.

Baffert believed in fate. He thought back to 1996, his first Derby with Cavonnier and how he bought Silver Charm that week and had him in his barn at Churchill. When Cavonnier hit the stretch with a length lead, Baffert thought that he was going to get one over on the racing gods, bringing home the roses on his very first try. Instead a horse named Grindstone, one of five D. Wayne Lukas trainees in the race, came from the clouds and caught Cavonnier by a nose. Baffert swore right then he was coming back to the Derby. As soon as he did, he worried that he might never have another horse worthy of the race. He needn't have.

Silver Charm was the most competitive horse that had ever come through his barn. Baffert knew that when he led him over to the track, the colt was going to give him everything he had every time.

"He was a fighter, and that was hard on him," Baffert said.

Silver Charm brought him back to the Derby, and in a replay of the previous year before, the colt was in front and looking like a winner when the field hit the stretch.

Gary Stevens and Silver Charm had finally shaken off another gray horse named Free House that had beaten him the previous month in the Santa Anita Derby. Now, however, the Derby favorite, Captain Bodgit, was gearing up and the two were head-to-head.

"I thought, 'Here we go again. I'm going to get beat right on the wire,' " Baffert said.

When he saw Silver Charm digging in, however, he knew that he was wrong to doubt his colt. Silver Charm was not going to let Captain Bodgit by him. They matched strides for seventy-five yards.

"He fought and he just dug in," he said. "He was just a tough, tough horse. He didn't want to win by a lot, but he was a true competitor. It's something you can't measure when you buy them. Like any great athlete, you don't know until they get in that situation."

Two weeks later in Baltimore, Free House, Captain Bodgit, and Silver Charm knocked heads again, thundering down the stretch once more, three wide and inches apart. Free House was inside, Captain Bodgit outside, with Silver Charm between them. When they hit the wire, it took a photo finish to sort out the winner. Silver Charm had gotten the bob.

They were bound for New York and a rare attempt at the Triple Crown, something that Baffert had not really considered a goal. He had not thought much beyond the Derby. He tried to treat it as a free roll, but he felt the weight of not only the sport, but also sports fans who had been waiting nineteen years to witness a transcendent performance that would go in the history books.

In Silver Charm, Baffert knew he had a gutsy colt and a fighting chance. Was it enough? No, it was not. Baffert had the colt ready, and Silver Charm ran his heart out. Both were beaten, however, by the crafty ride of Hall of Fame jockey Chris McCarron on a talented colt named Touch Gold.

They had skipped the Derby and then lost all chance in the Preakness when Touch Gold stumbled out of the gate and went to his knees. He still managed to finish fourth. Everyone thought Touch Gold was a closer, but McCarron had a fresh, tractable horse and believed that the only way he was going to get by Silver Charm was to outfox him. So in the Belmont, he sent Touch Gold to the lead early and then dropped back in the backstretch as if he were spent. He waited and watched as Kent Desormeaux and Free House went throatlatch-to-throatlatch with Silver Charm for the fourth straight race.

Behind them, McCarron swung Touch Gold outside, beyond their vision, and cranked his colt up. Silver Charm didn't see the horse charging on the outside of Free House. By the time Stevens did, with seventy yards to go, it was too late.

"Chris McCarron rode the most brilliant Belmont," Baffert said. "When Free House took off after Silver Charm, he just let them go. Gary thought Touch Gold quit. He decided to take Free House on and once he beat him, here came McCarron. He waited, saved horse, rode a tremendous race."

It was neither of their faults. Eighteen years later, we were all still waiting for a Triple Crown winner. Twice more, Baffert had failed to close the deal. He could have another opportunity this year, but he needed to take the first step on Saturday and win the Derby.

Baffert rubbed the nose of his old friend and thanked him for putting him in this position once again.

Ahmed Zayat kept him and his family busy as they counted down the days and hours until post time. In the mornings, Zayat bounced between the barns where the Derby horses were housed. Mr. Z was with Lukas near the gap to the racetrack. El Kabeir and John Terranova were in borrowed space and grouped with the other out-of-towners. He looked like a man on the verge of a heart attack, but then again he always did. He was either "relaxed, nervous or scared," depending on which media outlet caught him at what part of the day. He was either "confident" like he would grace the winner's circle finally or "afraid" he would forever be a bridesmaid on the first Saturday in May.

Zayat had taken to calling American Pharoah "the Beast" and told anyone within earshot or with a Twitter account that the Beast was "kicking down the barn, jumping out of his skin." He just needed Saturday and the starting gate to get here. The family did make an excursion to WinStar Farm, where Paynter, Bodemeister, and Pioneerof the Nile stood as stallions. When Pioneerof the Nile was brought out of his stall and circled for the group to behold, Zayat went over to him and whispered in his ear, "Your son is going to do it for you."

The reality that no Derby horse (or owner) was assured a place in the Derby until a saddle and rider were on his back in the gate was driven home to Zayat on Friday, the day before the race, when his colt El Kabeir was scratched with swelling in his ankle. Justin had a soft spot for the horse and both he and his father felt bad for John Terranova. He was a young trainer, new to Zayat Stables, and El Kabeir was supposed to be his second ever Kentucky Derby starter. The gray colt was a gritty competitor who had endured one of the worst winters in New York, often training in the snow, to win the Kentucky Jockey Club Stakes here at Churchill as well as the Jerome and Gotham at Aqueduct. Now they were missing the entire Triple Crown.

There was another scratch on the morning of the race when a chip was discovered in the ankle of International Star, the Louisiana Derby winner. The colt's owners, Ken and Sarah Ramsey, were staying at the same hotel as the Zayats, the Hilton near the racetrack. Three Derby dreams were dead. Zayat offered Ken Ramsey a word of comfort in the lobby as they headed for the track.

Frances Relihan looked like one of those women she used to watch as a little girl during the Listowel races. No barn clothes for the Kentucky Derby. She wore a light blue dress beneath a string of pearls and a wide-brimmed hat in a slightly darker shade of blue. She was hewing as close to the color of the Zayat silks as possible. She and her husband, Dr. Joe Schneider, were their guests. Zayat had remembered the young Irish girl who had taken such care of his horses and was the first to tell him that the Littleprincessemma colt was special. The race was still two hours away, but she and Joe had been invited to barn 33 to watch Baffert prepare American Pharoah and Dortmund for the race. The backside had been transformed into picnic grounds as many of the horsemen based at Churchill Downs rolled out barbecue grills and coolers to entertain and watch and bet the races from where they spent the majority of their time: their barns.

There were thousands of people milling around in shorts and flip-flops with beers in their hands, but they were careful to stay clear of where the Kentucky Derby horses were getting ready. Frances watched as American Pharoah gazed above the crowd gathered around him, turning left, then right, and nodding his head slightly. He was something to behold with his rich, velvety bay coat pulled tight over rippling muscles. American Pharoah walked as she remembered him — all precision and purpose without one wasted motion. Dortmund was handsome as well and was tall and long. It was too bad one of them was going to have to lose today and Frances knew which one it was going to be.

"Horsemen, please bring your horses to the paddock for the eleventh race, the Kentucky Derby," came the announcement over a scratchy loudspeaker.

It was delivered in a monotone that failed to capture what those words meant to the dozens of owners and trainers sweating through their suits and beneath their floppy hats. They were about to walk their horses (all of whom they had spent hundreds of thousands, even millions, of dollars on) a quarter mile to the racetrack and perhaps into the record books.

As the Zayats left the barn area, Frances and Joe trailed behind them as they passed through a gauntlet of noisy well-wishers lined up five deep before the gap on the backstretch. They stood in the beds of pickup trucks and cheered them on as they took their first steps onto the racetrack. Frances was honored to be asked to make "the Walk," as it was known, an exhilarating experience for a horseman, second only to winning the Derby itself. It meant you had bred or bought, you had raised or trained, a horse worthy of the sport's grandest stage. It was like being asked to perform at the Grand Ole Opry if you are a country music artist.

270

Her first steps on the track were wobbly because ahead of them was a never ending line of human bodies — more than 170,000 of them — erecting a wall of sound from deep within their lungs. To the right, the infield was packed with more than 50,000 people and was a rowdy city unto itself, kids mostly, more concerned with the mint juleps than fancy hats. The roar began there and rippled through the grandstands and was sustained as one horse and its entourage after another began the promenade clockwise around the track's first turn, to the stretch, and through a tunnel into the paddock. Frances blinked back tears and took in the kaleidoscope of smudged pastels that rendered Churchill Downs and its twin spires something out of a Monet painting.

"This is surreal," she said.

The Zayats flanked American Pharoah. Paul Shanahan and some of the Coolmore lads were in their wake, hoping that the colt was going to win and increase the value of the stallion rights it now owned. Baffert stayed close by his side, a bodyguard daring anyone to get too close. He had traded the cotton balls for the soft, cotton earplugs that show horses often wore. Still American Pharoah was hearing and seeing too much. He was the favorite, the superhorse, and the ovation that he was receiving was deafening. Fans were crushed against the rail with their cell phones, and television camera crews weaved on the racetrack between horses.

American Pharoah fought his groom, Eduardo Luna, for the entire walk, tossing his head, balking, and skittering. He was agitated, working himself into a lather. Baffert did not like what he saw and was getting agitated himself.

He felt like he was walking his horse through Times Square at midnight on New Year's Eve with people yelling and screaming and running next to him.

When they finally arrived in the paddock, American Pharoah was doused with water to soothe and cool him off. Baffert kept him in his stall to unwind. Every other horse was limbering up, circling a postage stamp–sized opening of paddock that was overflowing with people. Baffert backed everyone but Zayat away from the colt. He needed to get him quieted down.

By the time Espinoza showed up in the paddock, the colt was cooling off and Baffert was distracted. The night before, Baffert had given his rider some instructions via text.

"Just send it," he told him. "I don't care.

Just go to the front."

Now in the paddock, Baffert was not so sure.

"Just do whatever you want," he told Espinoza.

In the jockeys' room, Espinoza had planned to do that anyway. He'd put on his silks ninety minutes earlier, set the alarm on his watch, and tried to lie down for a nap like he often did. Stevens, who was sharing a locker with him, smiled, thinking his friend really, really didn't give a shit. Espinoza, however, did not take a nap. He ran the race through his mind. He decided to ride American Pharoah like he was the best horse in the race. In Arkansas, the colt showed that he could wait behind other horses. Espinoza was intent on breaking cleanly. Then he would take whatever the rest of the field gave him. As spectacular a racehorse as American Pharoah had been so far in his career, Espinoza still did not believe that he had seen his true talent.

"I really haven't had a chance to push him, to see what he's really got," he had said before the race. "I know I ride him, but right now, I'm like everybody else. I don't know how good he is."

When Baffert saw Stevens in the paddock, he gave Espinoza a nudge.

"Gary's got his game face on," he said.

Both trainer and jockey knew that Stevens's horse, Firing Line, was a dangerous contender. In fact, he told both Espinoza and Martin Garcia that the colt was sitting on a big race.

"It's going to be you guys and Gary Stevens," he told his riders.

Firing Line had lost by a head twice to Dortmund. In the Robert B. Lewis, Firing Line actually got his head in front of him in the deep stretch before Dortmund rallied to win by a half head. The colt's trip to New Mexico six weeks ago was a confidence booster.

"He's been out of sight, out of mind," Stevens said earlier in the week, "but Baffert knows what I'm sitting on. This horse's strength is his mind. He's a great athlete, but he has the mind to go with it."

Baffert watched first Dortmund and Garcia disappear in the tunnel to the track, and then American Pharoah and Espinoza. He remained behind in the paddock with Jill and Bode and his older boys Taylor, Canyon, and Forest. He would watch the race there with them and a small group of journalists. When the opening chords of the "My Old Kentucky Home" sounded, he knew the horses were on the track and the hard work and triumphs of the past year would come down to this, the greatest two minutes in sports.

"When I hear that song," he said, "I know it's almost over. My job is done."

Baffert had kept American Pharoah and Dortmund apart for five months. He could not do it any longer. In boxes near the finish line were the Zayats and the Shahs. They were about to find out soon enough which of their colts was Citation and which was Coaltown — the two-year-old champion American Pharoah or the undefeated Dortmund. The betting public landed on American Pharoah as the 5-to-2 favorite with Dortmund just behind him at 4 to 1.

As the gate opened and Dortmund, followed by Firing Line, passed the grandstand, the record crowd of 170,513 knew that it would quickly find out which Baffert colt was better on this day. It was the usual Derby mayhem for the inside horses when the gates opened — the undefeated Materiality broke sideways and dropped far off the pace and found walls of horses instead of an open seam whenever he tried to get closer to the front. Espinoza and American Pharoah followed Mr. Z on an angle to the inside, settling into third, just off Firing Line's flank, with Carpe Diem on the inside in fourth. As he angled in, Espinoza heard the riders of the horses that he was cutting off shouting at him. It was always a noisy brawl for position in the opening quarter mile of the Derby.

"I bounced right out of the gate," said Espinoza. "I didn't care."

Behind them horses were getting stopped as Bolo and Danzig Moon were bouncing off each other. As they glided into the first turn, Dortmund was hugging the rail in first place with Firing Line behind and outside of him in his jet stream, and American Pharoah loping effortlessly in their shadow. Baffert was at peace. Garcia was on cruise control. American Pharoah was out of harm's way.

It's our Derby to lose, he thought.

Stevens was having to wrestle a bit with an eager Firing Line and thought about taking over the lead from Dortmund. When he saw that Garcia was strong-arming his colt as well, he decided to wait and try to relax Firing Line.

"I figured if I dropped my horse's head and went on by, Dortmund would start fighting me, and that would set it up for American Pharoah," said Stevens.

Garcia and Dortmund were clipping along at a comfortable pace, hitting quarter poles as if there was a carrot waiting at each of them, a half mile in 47.34 seconds. It was clear halfway down the backstretch that only three horses mattered in this race. Dortmund, Firing Line, and American Pharoah were on a conveyor belt, and the rest of the field was struggling to keep up.

Stevens and Firing Line chased Dortmund into the far turn. Stevens's colt had relaxed down the backstretch and was ready to implement the plan that he had devised to turn the tables on Dortmund and get the jump on American Pharoah. In their previous meeting in the Robert B. Lewis, Firing Line passed Dortmund in the stretch but was quickly reeled in.

"Dortmund is like Silver Charm and likes a fight," Stevens said. "The tighter you get with him, the more he likes it."

In the Lewis, Stevens had moved too early. He was not going to make the same mistake. As they turned for home, Dortmund cut the corner first. Firing Line moved to the middle of the track, and Victor Espinoza, aboard American Pharoah, chose the widest route. For the first time ever in a race, Espinoza felt his colt slowing down and struggling to find his motor.

"So I got into him," he said.

The colt that had rarely seen a whip in his

previous five races was getting well acquainted with one now. Espinoza was paddling him with both hands. Stevens and Firing Line hooked Dortmund first. They matched strides for 10, 20, 30 yards — and then, as if Stevens hit a booster, Firing Line blew by him for good.

"He was on it," Stevens said. "Coming for home, I thought I might get there."

Espinoza moved American Pharoah closer to Firing Line, shaking his reins, making up ground by inches rather than yards. He thought his colt was ready to quit — that he was not fit enough to finish the only race that mattered as he had the previous two.

"That other horse was tough," Espinoza said. "He wasn't going away."

This was the test American Pharoah had yet to take, let alone pass. Espinoza crossed his reins and started fanning his whip. He knew he had to ride him hard. Espinoza whipped him at least thirty-one times. Stevens saw a shadow, then heard Espinoza chirping, and then the Zayat colors went by. He was not surprised. With a sixteenth of a mile to the wire, Firing Line finally buckled. Stevens knew the only flaw in his plan to win his fourth Derby was that American Pharoah may have simply been the better horse.

In his box near the finish line, Ahmed Zayat was swinging his head from his wife, Joanne, who was sobbing, to his horse pounding down the stretch.

"I knew that if he had the lead, nobody would catch him," he said. "He has such brilliant speed. I started getting really, really nervous, and my wife started crying and I understood that they were tears of joy."

Behind him, Frances Relihan recognized in American Pharoah the baby that once took her breath away as he bucked and spun in a field.

"He's got it," she said, digging her nails into Joe's arm.

American Pharoah was the horse that she, Espinoza, and Baffert knew that he was, and the horse that Stevens feared he was. The colt and Espinoza hit the finish line a length ahead of Firing Line, and Dortmund was three lengths behind them in third. Baffert did not match Jones's 1–2 finish with Citation and Coaltown, but he came close. In the paddock walkway, Baffert raised his right fist into the air as his three older boys piled on top of him. Jill Baffert was hugging him, weeping and repeating, "I can't believe it." Bode Baffert was pogoing up and down and screaming at the top of his lungs. The trainer broke away and swept up his youngest son into his arms. In his brief ten years, all Bode had ever witnessed along the Derby Trail was hard work and failure for his father. Three years ago, father and son were so inconsolable when Bodemeister was caught at the wire by I'll Have Another that they fled the paddock in tears.

Now, a few days after meeting his dad's first Derby winner, Silver Charm, he had been with all of Baffert's boys for his fourth Kentucky Derby triumph, one that put him into a tie for second place for the winningest Derby trainer behind Ben Jones and along-side D. Wayne Lukas and Derby Dick Thompson.

Out on the track, NBC's Donna Brothers, the network's sideline reporter, caught up on horseback with an exuberant Espinoza, who was patting American Pharoah on the neck and smiling ear to ear.

"I feel like the luckiest Mexican on earth," he said with a cackle. "American Pharoah, he's special, very special."

With the victory, he now trailed only Bill Hartack, Earle Sande, and Willie Shoemaker for most Derby victories and joined Isaac Murphy, Jimmy Winkfield, Ron Turcotte, Eddie Delahoussaye, and Calvin Borel as back-to-back winners.

In Zayat's box, the family's first victory

after so much disappointment was met with a mosh pit of hugs — and a whole lot more. Joanne Zayat was a puddle. Justin Zayat had gotten sick, throwing up in front of network cameras. Ahmed, meanwhile, asked, "Who finished second? Who finished third?" He was either hoping that Mr. Z had hit the board or that he had hit the exacta or trifecta at the windows.

In the news conference after the race, Baffert acknowledged publicly what he suspected all along: American Pharoah was the bigger of Baffert's two big horses. It was Dortmund's first loss, but he had been dead game.

"He was tough," Baffert said. "I'm proud of him."

American Pharoah was something else altogether, something that may transcend a single race. He was as good as Lukas and Mott had believed. He was a colt worthy of reviving real Triple Crown hopes. Baltimore and the Preakness was two weeks away, but there was a hint of inevitably in the air.

Zayat commandeered the microphone and unleashed a long monologue that said as much about him as his horse. His conviction came through loud and clear. American Pharoah was a gift to him, his family, and the sport at large.

"All this week I was very calm, enjoying it, relaxed," he said. "My wife told me, you are unusually relaxed. I'm kind of a hyper guy. She told me, 'How are you that relaxed?' I said, 'The horse is giving me that confidence, and Bob had that confidence all week.' He trained on this track. He breezed on it. He was doing everything right. Now, comparing him to all the others, I came with good horses, but I felt today I came with a star. I was very cautious of saying that because I wanted the horse to do the talking. It is not about what we feel. It is about the horse."

CHAPTER THIRTEEN:
OLD HILLTOP

May 16, 2015

American Pharoah did what so many had hoped he would in the 141st running of the Kentucky Derby. He did not merely win. He lived up to his promise. The lesson Espinoza taught the colt in the Arkansas Derby had paid off as American Pharoah had stalked Dortmund and Firing Line for a mile before pouncing on them. He had shown fortitude running past them and proved that when challenged he could outwill and outrun tough rivals. Horse racing is a game of opinions, where analysis and hunches and tastes become interchangeable. The doubters saw an American Pharoah that had to run all out to beat Firing Line by a length after getting a perfect trip from Espinoza. The finishing time of 2:03.02 was not very fast. The colt was hard used, as they say, as Espinoza went to his whip incessantly in the stretch, at least 31 times, a fact that was not lost on casual fans and animal lovers who wrote to newspapers and called into radio shows, saying that it had looked an awful lot like abuse. The Kentucky racing stewards at Churchill Downs never questioned Espinoza's ride, determining that he had offered the encouragement in rhythm with American Pharoah's stride, had hit him on his shoulders and hindquarters per regulations, and had ridden well within the rules. The following morning, Baffert led American Pharoah out of his barn and let fans pet him and feed him carrots. The colt was as relaxed and docile as a barn cat and looked none the worse for wear the morning after running a mile and a quarter with a small but powerful man on his back hitting him with a stick.

Now he was in Baltimore for the Preakness Stakes, carrying the heavy weight of Triple Crown hopes in his saddle. Every Derby winner does, but between his performances on the track and the hosannas he was receiving from horsemen and horse lovers alike off of it, the pressure was increased for American Pharoah to make a triumphant stop here en route to his date with history in New York at the Belmont Stakes. Baffert certainly recognized that.

"You know what? I really feel a lot of positive energy because of this horse," he said. "Because I know a lot of people are hoping — they put their hat on something big like this, a horse, like what he's done, there's a certain aura about him. He has caught everybody's attention."

In recent years, the Preakness had been something of a walkover for the Derby winner. While the winner had to come here in pursuit of the Triple Crown, the owners and the trainers of the better horses that failed at the Derby mostly chose to rest their horses five weeks and wait for the Belmont. There they were inevitably joined by late-blooming three-year-olds and the trap was set to spoil yet another horse's bid for immortality. The previous year, one of those, Tonalist, stopped California Chrome's Triple Crown bid, much to the nationally televised chagrin of Steve Coburn, one of Chrome's co-owners and a newcomer to the sport. He melted down before the cameras and called skipping the Derby and Preakness the "coward's way out."

Now the Derby's second- and third-place finishers, Firing Line and Dortmund, were here in Baltimore to try American Pharoah again. The trainer of Firing Line, Simon Callaghan, believed his colt had the edge in freshness. Callaghan, thirty-two, was an

Englishman and up-and-coming trainer who was on the Triple Crown trail for the first time. He was enjoying it. His colt had had six weeks between his three races this year and Callaghan believed he would benefit as well from the Preakness's shorter distance, a sixteenth of a mile shorter than the Derby's mile-and-a-quarter track. His colt had battled deep into the stretch and was only a length behind American Pharoah at the finish.

"I think the spacing that we had in our two prior races is going to help us out," he said. "I think that should enable us to have a slightly fresher horse going forward. He's got a very good cruising speed during his races, and I think that should lend itself to a slight cutback in distance. I think this could be an absolutely perfect distance for him. He earned the right to be here."

More surprising, however, was that Dortmund was here to take on American Pharoah again. Baffert had painstakingly kept the two apart until the Derby, and now they were a couple of stalls apart in Pimlico Race Course's stakes barn and on a collision course once more. The trainer had no reason to discourage Kaleem Shah from entering Dortmund in the Preakness. The colt had run a tremendous race in Louisville in his first career defeat, and his free running style was perfectly suited to a track that rewarded handy horses like Dortmund. When you operated a big barn full of quality stakes horses with owners who wanted to run in the biggest races, inevitably a trainer had to square off with himself. In fact, twenty years ago, D. Wayne Lukas had come here with Thunder Gulch, the Derby winner, and beat him with stablemate Timber Country. He sent them both to New York, where Timber Country spiked a fever the day before the race and Thunder Gulch went on to win it. It meant a training Triple Crown for Lukas but left the owner of Thunder Gulch, Michael Tabor of Coolmore, with two-thirds of the series and wondering perhaps, "What if?"

"It takes a great horse to win the Triple Crown," Baffert said, "and if American Pharoah is great, you can't worry about Dortmund or Firing Line. My job is to get them over here."

As much as Baffert may have wanted, and believed, that the twelfth Triple Crown champion was in his barn, he also understood that horse racing would be just as well served by three competitive races featuring the best horses in training. When Baffert captured his first Derby with Silver Charm, he was part of one of the most thrilling Triple Crown chases ever as Free House and Captain Bodgit challenged the colt in the stretch in the first two legs and Touch Gold finally got by him in the Belmont. Three failed bids had made Baffert a student of the series.

"If you look back at all the Triple Crown runners, they ran a lot," he said. "I think a lot has to do with who you are running against and how tough it is. This was such a tough Derby. This was the toughest Derby I've been in."

In 1978, Affirmed was 12 for 14 coming out of the Derby. American Pharoah had five victories in six starts, which were not exactly golden age numbers but provided a stout foundation when put through the lens of modern times. The paradigm had shifted dramatically over the last fifty years when it came to the durability of a racehorse.

The Hancocks, for example, had been raising racehorses for four generations in the Bluegrass and not too long ago, Arthur III kept to a rule he learned from his father, Bull Hancock Jr.: Never breed to a stallion with fewer than twenty-five career starts. That rule was good enough to produce the Kentucky Derby champions Gato Del Sol in 1982 and Sunday Silence in 1989. Both were strong, sound horses who could run all day. Gato Del Sol turned out to be a bust as a sire, and commercial breeders here ignored Sunday Silence, who had nearly won the Triple Crown but had to go to Japan to become one of the world's leading stallions.

By the time Hancock bred his third Derby winner, Fusaichi Pegasus, in 2000, he had long abandoned the twenty-five-start rule. FuPeg, as the colt was known, was a son of Mr. Prospector, who had raced fourteen times. His mother was Angel Fever, who made it to the track just twice before being hurt and then retired from racing. The match sacrificed heartiness for speed, but that was in demand in auction rings. Hancock sold Fusaichi Pegasus for $4 million as a yearling.

"You got to survive and make money, and you do that by breeding something fashionable that people will buy," said Hancock, who also has sold half siblings of FuPeg for $1 million to $4 million. "I cannot afford to breed the kind of horses that I once did."

So horsemen are getting what they pay for: pedigrees that produce precocious, fast, and fragile runners. American racehorses are less sound than ever. In 1960, for example, the average United States racehorse made 11.3 starts a year; in 2014, the average was 6.2.

When horse racing was a pastime rather than a business, families like the Whitneys and the Vanderbilts and breeding farms like Calumet and the Hancocks' Claiborne made stallions out of the horses that had performed well and over time. It was the era of Iron Horses like the 1941 Triple Crown champion, Whirlaway, who made 60 starts in his career, and the 1946 champion, Assault, who raced as a seven-year-old. In fact, the eleven Triple Crown winners together made 104 starts at age four or older and won 57 of them.

"You used to see a taller Thoroughbred, narrow chested and a bit knock-kneed, who could run forever, but not as fast," said Dr. Larry Bramlage.

Affirmed was perhaps the epitome of this body type. He raced twenty-nine times, won twenty-two, and sired more than eighty stakes winners and nine champions. Over the four decades, the billions spent on horses have put a premium on what Bramlage describes as a "toed-in, wide-chested, lighter-bone horse built for speed."

American Pharoah was not exactly bred any differently than his modern counterparts — yet he was different. Pioneerof the

Nile had made ten career starts, Little-princessemma just two. He was not built like Affirmed, but so far he had demonstrated that he possessed a similar sort of steel. Baffert had quit trying to explain it.

"He was just born with that talent," he said. "He has that long stride. He's quick. He's got a really good mind. He just floats over the ground. He's different, just the way he's made. What we saw in the Derby is that he's not one-dimensional, which is so nice to have."

In other words, the trainer liked the hand that he had been dealt and he was comfortable here in Baltimore. This was Baffert's favorite of the three races, partly because he was coming off the high of the Derby and partly because he always knew he had the best horse. There was no training to do in the two weeks prior to the Preakness; either your horse is in form and fit from the road it had to endure to get here or not. Baffert thought American Pharoah had needed a hard race in the Derby and believed he was now more explosive than ever.

"You have to be in top form to win the Derby, so it's a matter of keeping them galloping and just getting them there," he said. "If your horses are coming off a big effort in the Derby and they've run well, then they're pretty tough to beat."

Six workouts in thirty-three days and two easy races was not the path Baffert normally chose for his contenders. He had no choice, though, after American Pharoah overextended his knee and had to be sidelined. Baffert had watched the replay of the Derby dozens of times and believed the colt was never really in trouble at any part in the race and Espinoza had helped him find another gear that the colt had yet to employ and might need in the future. The Derby was the Derby and the one race Baffert will never tire of winning.

"If you win that race, you can't wait to win it again," Baffert said. "The winner's circle at Churchill Downs must be the most expensive real estate in the world because so much money has been spent trying to get there."

Baffert appreciated the more relaxed atmosphere at Pimlico, a scuffed up old track offering more charm than class or comfort. Lore had it that the name *Pimlico* came from the English settlers who inhabited the 129 acres on which the racetrack was built. They were a nostalgic bunch and yearned for the famous landmark near London that they had left behind: Olde Ben Pimlico's Tavern. Since opening its doors in

1870, the Old Hilltop, as it is called, has been visited by history in odd and significant ways. The United States House of Representatives adjourned on October 24, 1887, so the distinguished gentlemen could watch a horse named Parole beat Ten Broeck and Tom Ochiltree in what has become known as the Great Race. It was here that Seabiscuit defeated War Admiral in a celebrated match race in 1938. Alfred G. Vanderbilt, a former prep school bookie and a sporting scion of one of America's most celebrated families, had orchestrated the race for the track that he owned and a sport he dearly loved.

"Pimlico is more than a dirt track bounded by four streets," he once said. "It is an accepted American institution, devoted to the best interests of a great sport, graced by time, respected for its honorable past."

These days, Baffert considered Pimlico and the Preakness more like going to camp. It was the jeans-and-shirtsleeve stop on the Triple Crown trail, closer to Nogales, Arizona, than New York, New York. The horses all shared the same barn, so Baffert had the opportunity to catch up with fellow trainers like D. Wayne Lukas and mingle with the handful of fans who wandered through each morning. He had chosen stall

30 in the middle of the barn for American Pharoah instead of the spot usually reserved for the Derby winner, stall 40, which was on the corner for all to see. He was taking no chances.

Baffert acted as if he had been turned out to pasture after a hard race himself, speaking to anyone and everyone each morning. He had been asked the same questions a million times by the media but seemed to enjoy reciting the answers all over again, especially when asked by regular fans who had brought their kids to see American Pharoah and play hooky for the day. Who did he like better, American Pharoah or Dortmund?

"They're all like my children," he told a group of them. "They all have their quirks. Dortmund is just a quirky, big, awkward kid. He's also gentle, but he gets a little bit excited and he's quick on his feet, so you want to make sure he doesn't step on your toes."

He also had come up with new material about American Pharoah's sawed-off tail. When he first got the colt, Baffert wanted to correct it with extensions, which are made with real hair. Zayat refused to let him. He liked being able to pick his horse out in the morning and thought the look was distinctive.

"The legend goes that he was running wild in a field, and a mountain lion was chasing him and that's as close as he could get to him," Baffert said, "but nobody really knows."

He also was having fun showing off his favorite horse, Smokey, the buckskin-colored pony he had bought primarily to teach Bode how to ride, but also as a calming companion to the high-strung Thoroughbreds in the barn. Smokey accompanied American Pharoah to the track for his timed workouts and waited there to greet him when training was over and it was time for him to return to the barn. He was also on the track after American Pharoah won the Derby; Baffert had loaned him to NBC's Donna Barton, who does the post-race interview of the winning jockey on horseback. Mostly Baffert himself rode Smokey. It not only relaxed him, but reminded him that he was a former jockey from a border town who owed his life to horses.

Baffert wanted people to know that he was a contented man, one who had tried humility on and found that it fit him. The previous year, Art Sherman had played this role beautifully, primarily because at close to eighty years old, he was comfortable in his own skin, and he knew that another colt like California Chrome coming into his life was highly unlikely. Sherman was not a complicated man and was proud of a life that was longer on memories than it was on bankroll. Sixty years ago, he was a Brooklyn kid in California learning about horses from a crew of cowboys. In 1955, Sherman was a teenage exercise rider who shared a boxcar from California with the colt Swaps for four days on their way to Churchill Downs, where they won the Derby. He survived them and became a jockey, mostly for broke horsemen on both coasts, before finding his true gift on backwater shedrows. Sherman and Baffert knew each other a bit and the Triple Crown newbie asked the veteran Baffert for his advice along the way.

In return, Baffert got to watch how joyously Sherman won his Derby and how gracefully he navigated a journey like no other in their sport. It was another little nudge for Baffert to approach his life and his career differently. He was an old man with a young boy and four older children he wanted to know better. He missed his parents more than he ever thought and wanted his children to feel the same away about him.

"You don't know how much I appreciated

this Derby with my family," he said. "You don't know how grateful I am. The Triple Crown is more for history and the media and New Yorkers. I wanted to win the Kentucky Derby this year. I knew it was mine to lose. I really didn't think I had that many more opportunities left to win another one."

The Zayats were AWOL much of the week leading up to the race. Ahmed was in Egypt for business and then attending a wedding in Israel. The profile of Zayat and his family had risen in the wake of American Pharoah's triumph in Louisville, and one of the most pursued angles in the national and international press was the fact that the family were devout Orthodox Jews. Reports from Cairo to Jerusalem and from news agencies as varied as the Associated Press and the Jewish Standard told of how the Zayats kept kosher and brought in recreational vehicles to racetrack parking lots before Saturday races, as they did here at Pimlico, because they were not permitted motorized travel on the Jewish Sabbath. The RVs often overflowed with friends and family, and the Zayats were clearly having a ball.

However, Ahmed Zayat was uncomfortable being identified publicly as a Jewish Egyptian businessman who had made a fortune selling beer to largely Muslim countries, especially after the Arab spring and the fall of Hosni Mubarak. The government that had helped his family build a fortune was gone. He still had business and family in Eqypt. Zayat tried, and mostly failed, to keep the news coverage mute on that aspect of his life.

Justin was taking his final exams at New York University, where he was graduating in a few weeks with an economics major. His duties as racing manager, however, intruded when D. Wayne Lukas engineered an eleventh-hour purchase of Mr. Z for another of his clients, Calumet Farm. The colt was a well-beaten thirteenth in the Derby and Ahmed and Justin wanted to end his spring season and bring him back in the summer.

Lukas was already in Baltimore with Mr. Z, and he hated missing big races. He knew he didn't have many opportunities left to run in them. Over the past forty years, he had more wealthy owners than any single horse trainer deserves and the latest was Brad Kelley, the billionaire founder of Commonwealth Brands tobacco company and the fourth largest landowner in the United States. Lukas had won this race two years ago for him with Oxbow, and Kelley was willing to take another shot with Mr. Z.

Ahmed's kids had named the colt Mr. Z after their father, but he was not going to let sentiment get in the way of negotiating a deal and putting some money back into Zayat Stables. So on the morning that entries to the Preakness were due, Justin in New York, Ahmed in the Middle East, and Lukas in Baltimore hashed out a deal to sell Mr. Z to Calumet and perhaps deny American Pharoah from winning the Preakness. Business is business.

"Wayne is at the barn at three-thirty and he's eighty years old and who knows how many more Triple Crown races he has left," Zayat said. "If he wins, the first thing I'll do is go over there and give him a big kiss."

So, with Mr. Z switching to the silks of Calumet Farm, a compact field of eight was signed on to contest the 140th running of the Preakness Stakes on Saturday, May 16, 2015, and Vanderbilt's granddaddy of a racetrack was having some problems. It had lost most of its water supply due to a broken water pipe two miles away — not a good thing when you have a record crowd of 131,680 steaming away in thick humidity as rain clouds crowded the sky. On race day, Baffert's backside camp for horse trainers turned into one of the rowdiest and drunkest revelries in all of sports, especially in the infield where rock and hip-hop bands provided welcome distraction from the binge drinking.

Some wacky events have marked the Pimlico's proud heritage as well. On a sweltering day in 1998, a power outage left more than 91,000 people without air-conditioning, working elevators, working escalators, and, worst of all, working betting machines for several hours. The next year, three races before Charismatic secured a Preakness victory for two-thirds of the Triple Crown, a man made his way onto the track from the infield to face down a thundering herd of nine horses in the stretch and take a punch at the 4-to-5 favorite, a horse named Artax.

Horseplayers had been checking the weather radar all afternoon for the storm that was rumbling toward Pimlico. The theory being that a wet track made American Pharoah a lock to win this second leg of the Triple Crown. Baffert wasn't so sure. He knew his colt had sliced his way like a Jet Ski to a six-and-a-quarter-length win two months ago on a sloppy track in Arkansas. Forty-five minutes before the race, the skies were getting scary as Baffert held Bode by the hand and followed American Pharoah from the stakes barn into the indoor paddock area to get his colt saddled. Baffert and his fellow trainers were in a rush, trying to get their horses ready before the coming deluge. They had no control over whether the race would be run before Mother Nature intruded but hurried as if they could beat her.

American Pharoah was acting as if he was a professional racehorse. There were no antics or agitation as there was in Louisville. He turned in circles calmly like a boxer stalking the ring and awaiting the opening bell. Jimmy Barnes and Eduardo Luna led the colt across the racetrack to the turf course with the Bafferts following them. Victor Espinoza sidled up alongside the trainer and told him that he liked what he saw.

"If he fires, you'll win," he said. "If he doesn't, then we just go back and blame it on the rain or whatever."

Espinoza grinned and hopped aboard.

As he and American Pharoah led the post-parade onto the track, a thunder boomer opened up the skies, sending the infield crowd scurrying for cover. Rain was strafing the horses hard enough that Espinoza's light blue and gold silks vanished. So did the pastels of his rivals' silks. Baffert, with Jill and Bode, hustled back to the indoor paddock.

Espinoza, his boots filling up with water, had a moment of clarity. He was drenched and uncomfortable, and as he walked his colt toward the starting gate, he made a decision. He was going to get American Pharoah out of the gate quickly and take this field gate to wire and to victory and to New York and the Belmont Stakes. No mud was going to be kicked in his colt's face. The rain let up a bit as the field approached the starting gate. Espinoza inched American Pharoah into the Number 1 hole and saw before him a rush of water rolling through a ditch that was supposed to be his running path. When NBC showed the river on its telecast, Baffert and his wife winced.

"That's not fair," said Jill Baffert.

When the gates opened, however, the plan that Espinoza had hatched was in trouble. American Pharoah's back end swung out, causing him to leave the gate late. Espinoza crossed his reins, smooched to him, and scrubbed his neck, and suddenly American Pharoah was floating like a swamp buggy atop the water, leaving first Mr. Z and then his stablemate Dortmund in his wake. On the outside, Stevens and Firing Line had fallen out of the starting gate and were staggering five wide. Espinoza knew he didn't have to worry about them. Their race was over.

American Pharoah splashed through the opening quarter mile in :22.90 — too fast but Espinoza had little choice after missing the break. He pulled back on him a touch but still reached the half mile in 46.49 seconds and the three-quarter-mile mark in 1:11.42. It was quick, dangerously quick. Espinoza was in front and beneath him American Pharoah was moving so easily he peeked under his arm to see if any other horse was actually going with him.

Behind him, Corey Nakatani, aboard Mr. Z, believed he had American Pharoah measured. "He was in it," Nakatani thought.

Martin Garcia, atop Dortmund, knew he was in trouble. His colt had never had mud kicked in his face and was ducking his head, trying to avoid it, and was unable to find his best stride.

Espinoza knew the race was over. He dropped his hands and American Pharoah powered off like he was a motorcycle and his pilot had just throttled down. In the paddock, watching the colt gliding down the backside, Baffert was on his toes, feeling a flutter in his heart. He watched American Pharoah's ears go up.

"Oh yeah, oh yeah," he said.

Espinoza was relaxed atop the colt as he leaned toward the rail and braced for the stretch. Baffert's wife, Jill, tugged on her husband's sleeve as a pack of horses seemed to close in on American Pharoah.

"He's waiting, he's waiting, to let him go," Baffert told her.

When Mr. Z got within a half length, Espinoza crossed his reins, gave American Pharoah his head, relaxed, and enjoyed the ride. The rider and his colt hit the stretch four lengths ahead. There was no need for Espinoza to get into American Pharoah here. He waved his whip at the colt one, two, three, four times — not hitting him but like a maestro setting the time for his players. American Pharoah then rolled down the lane with the force of a waterfall. By the time Espinoza crossed the finish line, he and American Pharoah were seven lengths ahead of the long shots Tale of Verve and Divining Rod.

"Great horses do great things," Baffert said, his voice choking. The tears coming again.

In the clubhouse, Lukas was the first to get to Ahmed Zayat. He hugged him and kissed him on the cheek.

Jimmy Barnes found his boss, reached for

his hand, and pulled him close.

"One more time," he told him.

CHAPTER FOURTEEN:
THE SPORT WITHOUT A STAR
IS NOT A SPORT

June 6, 2015

Once more, horse racing aficionados had bounce in their step. For the fourteenth time in the last thirty-six years, a horse was going to pull into Belmont Park with an opportunity to become the twelfth Triple Crown champion and the first since Affirmed in 1978. That phrase had been written countless times, referring to thirteen other horses, including California Chrome the previous year. Three of them were colts trained by Bob Baffert. Now there was a fourth, American Pharoah, the colt that looked like a cigarette boat skimming atop a sloppy track in Baltimore and was coming to New York to try to close the deal on immortality.

Horseplayers are a hardy lot. They have to be, as they have watched a beloved and once royal sport be diminished mainly by its own undoing. In the 1950s, horse racing's shortsighted overlords refused to make races available to television because they were afraid that it would cut into the attendance of the 35,000 to 40,000 people who routinely showed up to the big tracks in New York, California, and Florida. Once the only legal gambling game in town, horse racing lost much of its audience to state lotteries and casinos that popped up in states from coast to coast. There have been, and continue to be, doping scandals. The big money in breeding has turned horses into commodities, which in turn has weakened the breed. With no centralized power or league office, states operate how they want, which meant squeezing the lemon dry by offering year-round races at third-rate tracks with sore horses trained by incompetent and callous horsemen.

For the five weeks of the Triple Crown, though, they get to forget all of that and temporarily become a mainstream sport and hold a place in the national consciousness. There quite simply is nothing better for the sport, or more fun for people who follow it year-round, than a Belmont Stakes with a Triple Crown on the line.

"The sport without a star is not a sport," said Ahmed Zayat.

Within seconds after American Pharoah

had crossed the finish line in Baltimore, the same question was raised by dedicated horseplayers as well as those who had never attended a race in their life: "Is American Pharoah the horse to finally complete one of the most difficult feats in sports?"

The answer? No one had a clue, and the times they thought they did, a horse lost by a bob (Real Quiet in 1998) or was compromised by a questionable ride and got run down in the stretch (Smarty Jones in 2004). Just as most horse owners try to abide by the golden rule of always accepting a better-than-fair price when it's offered for a colt or filly, most horseplayers try, but mostly fail, to honor their own version: that nobody knows nothing.

However, American Pharoah did fit a winning profile. He was the reigning two-year-old champion, as were six of the last seven Triple Crown champs. Like Affirmed, Seattle Slew, Secretariat, Citation, Count Fleet, and Whirlaway, American Pharoah had demonstrated brilliance early in his career, first in the Del Mar Futurity and then in the FrontRunner. He continued to build on that foundation, winning all four of his races as a three-year-old for a record of six victories in seven starts and more than $3.7 million in purses.

American Pharoah had a similar running style to many of the greats before him. In the Derby and Preakness, he showed that he liked to be on or near the front early in the race, possessed a high cruising speed, and had a grittiness that wore down his rivals in the late going. Affirmed, Seattle Slew, and, most memorably, Secretariat took control of the Belmont Stakes from the gate and never gave an inch as each passed the Test of the Champion, as the grueling mile and a half is known. American Pharoah certainly showed that dimension in the Preakness, albeit in the kind of wet conditions at which he had proved adept earlier in Arkansas.

What were his intangibles? He definitely passed the name test; American Pharoah (even misspelled) sounds regal and powerful enough to stand alongside Triple Crown champions like Sir Barton and Gallant Fox, Omaha and War Admiral. You couldn't really say that about Smarty Jones, Big Brown, or I'll Have Another.

American Pharoah also had a distinctive personality and a sharp mind. At least, Baffert believed the colt did.

"The thing is about him, he is the sweetest horse of this caliber that I've ever been around," said Baffert. "I mean, you feed him carrots, and he's like a pet. Usually they're like athletes. They want to get it on. But he's just the sweetest horse. He's spoiled to death."

Affirmed, Seattle Slew, and Secretariat were all based in New York and trained at Belmont Park, so they were familiar with its sandy surface and expansive turns. American Pharoah had been based in California for most of his career, but Baffert always made Churchill Downs his base during the Triple Crown. American Pharoah returned to barn 33 on the Monday following the Preakness and Baffert had decided not to come to New York until the week of the Belmont. He took heat for it, most prominently from Billy Turner, the trainer of Seattle Slew. Why not give American Pharoah some time to get used to Belmont Park, especially when as many as eight rivals awaited him — including the Preakness runner-up, Tale of Verve — along with a very good group of New York horses? Among them was the fourth-place Kentucky Derby finisher, Frosted, and three horses from the powerful Todd Pletcher barn: the Florida Derby champ Materiality, who was sixth in the Derby; the Blue Grass Stakes victor, Carpe Diem, who finished tenth in Kentucky; and Madefromlucky, the winner of the Peter Pan Stakes at Belmont.

Baffert thought about it but stuck to his plan. He knew that a thousand things could happen in the three weeks before the race, most of them bad. He chose to keep the horse at Churchill for his own sanity and that of his team. It was quieter, easier to get around, and far away from the New York media.

"It's going to be tough enough," he said. "I know everybody right now is sharpening their knives, getting ready. I'm staying within my comfort zone."

Jimmy Barnes and his wife, Dana, had been on the road with American Pharoah since March. The couple, along with Eduardo Luna and Jorge Alvarez, knew the colt better than anyone and had tended to his every need. In Louisville, the Barnes family members had everything that they needed: a suite in the Residence Inn near the track, a nearby fluff-and-fold Laundromat, and two rooms with a television in each so Dana did not have to watch Jimmy's endless loop of *American Picker* and *Pawn Stars.*

Jimmy, fifty-five, had been with Baffert since 1999 and Dana, fifty-one, had been exercising horses for him since 1997. He was intense and detail driven when it came to the horses and thought nothing about being with them from 3:30 a.m. until sundown. Baffert called him his drone because he could put his hands on every one of the trainers' high-priced stock and perform any task or procedure associated with training a horse. His colleagues on the West Coast called him "half horse." He was well paid by Baffert to be the backbone of the barn.

Jimmy Barnes had been out on his own and decided that he was not cut out for keeping track of payroll, feed, and tack bills. He was not built, either, for the schmoozing necessary to bring in the top-class Thoroughbreds to his barn.

"I really like to deal with these kinds of horses," he said. "It's less stress."

Dana was far more laid-back but a racetracker nonetheless. They had been married for thirty years and had raised two daughters, despite the fact that the workaholic Jimmy had taken no days off and Dana only one a week. Dana grew up in rural Norco, California, a town where horses were so important that "the McDonald's has a hitching post" and she rode her pony like most kids ride their bikes. Dana had been the main exercise rider on Silver Charm, Real Quiet, and War Emblem. She was Dortmund's exercise rider as well.

Back in January, Jimmy had told Dana

that American Pharoah was going to win the Triple Crown. Now he was calling Baffert in California, telling him the Belmont Stakes was a lock. The Derby had gotten the colt fit, and the Preakness was a maintenance workout. In fact, American Pharoah had gained nine pounds since winning in Baltimore.

"We're all right, man," he kept telling Baffert. "This horse is fresh. The race took nothing out of him."

Alvarez agreed. He once was a jockey in Tijuana but came north and became the top exercise rider for Bobby Frankel, the late Hall of Fame trainer. He had been on American Pharoah's back for the past year for everything from light jogs to strong gallops. Alvarez had been with Baffert seven years and had ridden many of his top horses, including Pioneerof the Nile. American Pharoah had reminded him of his father, except much stronger. When American Pharoah was a two-year-old, Alvarez had to wrestle with him most mornings because he wanted to go too fast. Now he had to pay even closer attention to American Pharoah. He was stronger than ever.

"His long strides cover so much ground and he's always feeling good, so you have to make sure you don't let him go too fast," he said. "When they cover that much ground that easily, you know they're special."

Baffert and Garcia flew into Louisville on May 31, the day before American Pharoah was set for his final breeze before shipping to New York. He usually did not sleep well before the night of an important workout, but with Barnes calling every day, crowing about how well American Pharoah was doing, he was at ease. He decided instead to worry about the Belmont and picked the actual start of the race to obsess over. It was an old habit and familiar enough to Bode Baffert that when the two were talking about how the New York and NBC announcer might call the race, Bode chirped up: "All I know is I hope he says, 'And they're off in the Belmont, and American Pharoah breaks beautifully.' "

Baffert smiled, proud as well as embarrassed.

"That's good," he said. "We want to hear that."

The previous week, Baffert and Garcia had flown in together to test the legs of the colt for the first time after the Preakness. When American Pharoah was finished with his three-quarters-of-a-mile gallop, the trainer's breath was taken away.

"That's beautiful, man," he told Garcia

through the two-way. "Beautiful."

This final workout was designed merely to maintain the colt's fitness, but it was clear as soon as Garcia and American Pharoah broke off from the five-and-a-half-furlong pole that he was in the type of shape that you don't normally see from a horse at this point in the Triple Crown. He went a half mile in 48.60, before Garcia eased up and galloped him out three-quarters in 1:13 and a mile in 1:39.60. This time, it was the jockey's turn to express his admiration.

"*Patrón*, he is ready," said Garcia, breathing harder than American Pharoah. "Man, what a horse."

It was then that Baffert admitted to himself that he really, really wanted American Pharoah to win the Belmont. Fate didn't owe him a Triple Crown as he once thought. It owed this horse.

"Everybody remembers Secretariat, but few remember who trained him," he said. "I couldn't tell you another horse Steve Cauthen rode, but I remember Affirmed. This is all about American Pharoah, not me. I think so highly of him, he's such a good horse, he really deserves it."

Over the course of the spring, Ahmed Zayat had been as gracious an owner of a superhorse as he could be. He and his family had been generous with their time, giving of it equally to small town newspapers and the network morning shows. He had kept his mercurial temper in check and did his best to deflect the attention from him to American Pharoah and his quest to become a Triple Crown champion. It is tough to live in the spotlight for five weeks, and not many owners of Triple Crown contenders have survived unscathed.

The previous year, California Chrome's owners, Perry Martin and Steve Coburn, had a charming tale to tell about the colt they had bred for less than $10,000 and how they named their stable DAP Racing, for *dumbass partners,* and featured a green donkey on their purple racing silks because that is what most thought they were when they projected greatness on the colt. Long before Coburn, a cowboy-hat-wearing machinist, fell apart after the Belmont, the public was starting to sour on the duo, largely because Martin, a brilliant but reclusive engineer and physicist, made his disdain for the media attention known and acted as if he really had employed mind over matter to build a better racehorse rather than gotten extraordinarily lucky as most believed.

In 2012, the colt I'll Have Another

brought his owner, J. Paul Reddam, un-
wanted attention to his mortgage lending
business and loan company, CashCall,
which offered high-risk, high-interest loans
to people who needed cash fast to settle
bills, pay for home repairs, or take a vacation. California governor Jerry Brown had
compared the way Reddam's business operated to loan sharking.

In 2008, Big Brown's majority owner
International Equine Acquisitions Holdings
said it was raising $100 million for a hedge
fund to buy, sell, and breed horses, collecting management and performance fees. Michael Iavarone was the face of the IEAH
stable, and as the Triple Crown chase
progressed, revelations surfaced about how
he had misrepresented himself as a high-
profile Wall Street executive when in fact he
had worked for penny stock firms. He had
also been suspended for Security and Exchange Commission violations. The stable
has been long out of business and in February 2015, James Tagliaferri, an investment
advisor and the money behind IEAH, was
sentenced to six years in prison for defraud-
ing clients out of $120 million by funneling
money to the stable via thinly traded companies in exchange for secret kickbacks.

So in a sport where saints were in short

supply, no one should have been too surprised when Howard Rubinsky resurfaced in Ahmed Zayat's life or at the lawsuit that he filed in a New Jersey federal court alleging Zayat had failed to pay a $2 million debt that he ran up betting via a website in Costa Rica. While American Pharoah had been winning six of his seven races and making his way to New York, Zayat had been contesting a federal lawsuit brought by a felon who had pled guilty in 2008 for his role in an illegal bookmaking operation with Zayat's two former protégés, Michael and Jeffrey Jelinsky.

"Howie," as Rubinsky was known to professional gamblers in Nevada as well as offshore, was working as a shill, or sales associate, for various offshore sportsbooks, bringing bettors to the site in exchange for a commission on their volume of bets and a percentage of their losses. His former protégés and sometime horse advisors, the Jelinsky brothers, had introduced him to Zayat at a breakfast in 2002 at Zayat's home in New Jersey. At first the arrangement worked well — too well, according to Rubinsky. Zayat won so much — $2.8 million — at one website in Costa Rica that the site stopped taking his bets. Then Rubinsky said he had opened a $3 million line of credit for Zayat at Tradewinds Sportsbook. The lawsuit alleged that Zayat, after winning a lot of money, walked away from his debt after an extended cold streak. A year later, in 2004, Zayat went on a payment plan that reduced the debt to $1.7 million, but then he stopped paying altogether, according to papers filed over the last fourteen months.

When Zayat refused to pay, Rubinsky said that his commissions were withheld and that he had personally lost $1.65 million plus interest, according to the documents.

Rubinsky filed the breach-of-contract suit quietly in March 2014 in a District Court in New Jersey, he said, because he only wanted to get paid — not embarrass Zayat. He had been trying to collect the debt for more than a decade — at one point even consulting with a group of Rabbis and suggesting to Zayat they let them arbitrate a settlement.

In a November 19, 2014, deposition, Rubinsky said at one point that Zayat had offered to pay him $1 million if he told the sportsbook that he had died in a car accident. On another occasion, he told Rubinsky that during the investigation of the Jelinsky brothers, a federal agent told him not to repay the debt. Documents showed that agents from the FBI, Homeland Security, and the Nevada Gaming Control Board had visited Zayat's office in New Jersey on May 8, 2008.

Zayat said that he neither placed any bets nor agreed to place bets through Rubinsky. In court papers and testimony, Zayat denied betting with Tradewinds or any other offshore sites and said that his debt did not exist.

"I never asked Rubinsky to put up a line of credit for me anywhere, and I was never aware — and I am still not aware — that he ever did so," Zayat wrote in a March 31, 2015, letter in support of his request for a summary judgment.

Zayat acknowledged betting at times through the brothers and subsequently being "scammed" by them. He said he learned of the deception when the federal agents came to his office and played tapes of wiretaps of the two explaining how they had taken Zayat's money. One brother was telling him to bet on horses that he knew were going to lose, and the other was taking Zayat's bet and holding them himself instead of placing them with a legal Nevada sportsbook.

"So I would lose because they were giving me the wrong horses," he admitted.

In 2008, Rubinsky said he again tried to

collect the money from Zayat. There were transcripts of several text messages between the two men that indicated they had a warm relationship. Rubinsky addressed Zayat as Ephraim, his Jewish name. Zayat called Rubinsky "Howie" and asked that he pray for him. In another, Zayat appears to promise that he will settle the debt and seems to indicate it will come in monthly payments.

In 2007 or early 2008, Rubinsky met with Zayat and said he was sick and had no money and that he had been cheated by the Jelinskys. He said he agreed to give Rubinsky $25,000 and then another $25,000 from the Zayat Foundation made payable to his sister, Donna Rubinsky.

"I do not deny that I gave him that first check — I know that I was willing to help him and I may have given him two checks — but I can say unequivocally that I did not give Rubinsky any money as payment on any debt. I did not, and do not, owe Rubinsky any money. I agreed to give him money because he told me he was ill and broke," Zayat's statement reads.

When Zayat went on the offensive, however, he drew more attention to himself and away from the horse. After suggesting that Rubinsky was trying to shake him down, he said the lawsuit was a fraud.

"It's a scam from A to Z. It's total fiction. It's a total lie," he said.

Within days, Rubinsky's lawyer, Joseph Bainton, filed a $10 million libel suit against Zayat, claiming he had maliciously defamed him when he called the original lawsuit "extortion, a fraud and blackmail." In the complaint, Bainton cited articles in New York's *Daily News,* The Associated Press, and outlets as far away as the *Daily Mail* in London.

"I don't like being called a liar," Bainton said. "I have earned a very good reputation as a lawyer. I don't cotton to being called a criminal. I think it's finally time for Zayat to be held in account for his conduct."

Zayat had plenty of defenders. Mary Ellen Modico was among his most fervent supporters, having seen a side of him that was not captured in court filings. She had never met him and had spoken to him only a couple of times, but she was going to be in the grandstand at Belmont Park with her husband, Kenneth, and was certain American Pharoah was going to make history. Her son Nick had been the captain of the 2008 state champion baseball team at John F. Kennedy Catholic High School in Somers, New York, a member of the National Honor Society, and a horseplayer like his parents.

"He learned percentages and odds as a young boy at Yonkers," Modico said.

In 2012, while he was a student at Boston College, Nick learned he had Ewing's sarcoma, a rare bone and soft tissue cancer found in teenagers and young adults. It was not Nick's nature to brood or rue circumstances. Instead, he wrote uplifting blog posts, finished his degree in finance and marketing, and continued to pursue his passion for horse racing.

Between bouts of crippling radiation and chemotherapy, Nick managed a trip to Keeneland, the stately racetrack in Lexington, Kentucky, where he picked a long-shot winner on TVG, a horse racing network, and struck up a friendship with Zayat. They talked horses by text and on the phone. Mr. Zayat even offered to fly him to California for the Breeders' Cup world championships at Santa Anita Park. At the time, Nick was too ravaged by his treatments, so Mr. Zayat asked him to name a colt of his, a son of Giant's Causeway. Nick's baseball jersey at Kennedy was 37.

"He took it seriously and came up with Thirtysevenliveson," Modico said. "It was one of the highlights of his life."

Nick did not live to see the horse run — he died in March 2014. Modico was missing American Pharoah's try for the Triple Crown.

"Ahmed Zayat helped our son out in our darkest hour," she said. "It meant so much to Nick and our family. It actually gave him something to live for — people deserve to know the kind of guy Ahmed is."

CHAPTER FIFTEEN:
TEST OF A CHAMPION

June 6, 2015

Victor Espinoza knew that it was an odd stop on his itinerary, this visit to the grave site in Queens of Rabbi Menachem Mendel Schneerson, the rebbe of the Lubavitcher group of Hasidic Jews. Since Schneerson died in 1994, Jews from all over the world have made a pilgrimage to Montefiore Cemetery to pay homage to the charismatic rebbe, considered one of the most influential Jewish leaders of the twentieth century. Espinoza, of course, was not Jewish but considered himself spiritual. He prayed several times a day as well as meditated. Espinoza had scheduled the stop after receiving a blessing from a rabbi before the Preakness.

It was Thursday, the Belmont was two days away, and Espinoza was feeding off the energy of the grave site as people from all over the world, many of them clad all in black in the attire of the sect, wrote notes on small pieces of paper and tossed them onto the rebbe's grave, asking him to deliver the messages to God.

"I was just curious," he said. "To me, life is all about learning."

The *New York Post* had already welcomed Espinoza to town in distinctive tabloid fashion, attempting to stir up some controversy with photos of the five-foot-two-inch jockey alongside "good-luck charm, leggy nineteen-year-old equestrian beauty Kelly Kovalchick," a five-foot-seven blonde he had allegedly been seeing since the previous year, unbeknownst to his longtime girlfriend and now fiancée Stephanie Kunkel. He took the gossip good-naturedly, laughing it off as the tabloid having some fun.

Espinoza wrote a prayer in Spanish and lit a candle before ripping the paper into pieces and tossing it on the grave site. He read King David's Book of Psalms. He walked backward out of respect when he left the grave site. He even bought the book *Rebbe: The Life and Teachings of Menachem M. Schneerson, the Most Influential Rabbi in Modern History* at the visitors' center. He swore that he was not a superstitious guy.

"So whatever happens, if it's meant to be, it's meant to be," he said. "If not, then I move on like last year. We have a value system in our life, and that is a priority in our family: God comes first, family, country, and all the others — all the others, you can put horse racing in them."

Lessons and understanding that divine intervention is a hope, not a horse had come naturally to Espinoza. In two days, he would become the first jockey in history to have three chances at winning the Triple Crown. He was devastated after War Emblem but accepting that he was on a tired California Chrome the previous year, and now he was eager and happy to have another opportunity. The ripped up prayer that he left for the rebbe was not to win the Belmont aboard American Pharoah.

"I prayed for health and safety for all of us," he said, another smile creasing his face. "It's more important than a horse race."

Espinoza had one more stop before he returned to his hotel. He wanted to see Anna's House, the day-care center for the children of backstretch workers at Belmont Park. Ahmed Zayat had just donated $100,000 to the facility, which was the only one of its kind on an American racetrack. Many of the fifty-plus children being cared for were from Mexico and had parents who, like him, had come to America for the promise of a better life. They had nothing else — no friends or family or the ability to speak the language of what would become their new country. When Espinoza first arrived in America as a teenager, he had lived in a tack room and shared a communal bathroom at Bay Meadows and Golden Gate Park in Northern California.

His post-Preakness comment about being the "luckiest Mexican on earth" was not meant to be flippant. He had once been like the children at Anna House, happily at play, unaware how hard their parents worked to make a meager living. Espinoza knew they would probably have to grow up too fast like he did and find work to help their families. He knew that he was fortunate to find the path that led to a job he had learned to love and was well compensated for and that gave him the fortitude to overcome his circumstances, his limitations, and his fears.

As Espinoza painted and colored with the children, exchanging bursts of Spanish that often ended in laughter, he wanted to believe — he had to — that some would find their own path to a happy, successful life in whatever they chose. Either way, Espinoza was having a good day. The kids were fun. They were interesting. They said what they felt.

Conspiracy theorists, soothsayers, and experts of all stripes feel truly at home in few places. The racetrack is one of these premier locales. The times when this assemblage of dreamers balances anxiety and gloom, hope and despair with the fervor of true believers are rarer still. The eve of a Triple Crown bid is such a time.

It was a wonderful day at the racetrack on the eve of the Belmont Stakes, as theories and opinions about the prospect of American Pharoah's winning the 147th running of the Belmont Stakes and sweeping Thoroughbred racing's Holy Grail were lobbed and volleyed with enthusiasm. They started in the morning on the backside, drifted onto the rail by early afternoon, and worked their way up to the third-floor clubhouse bar and finally to the press box.

People agreed on only two things: One, it had been far too long to have not minted another Triple Crown champion, and two, some of the arguments would be validated by 7:00 p.m. or so on Saturday after American Pharoah ran the Belmont's mile-and-a-half route and either passed or failed the Test of the Champion.

Those who believed American Pharoah would succeed leaned on the fact that he was the two-year-old champion last year, meaning he was stamped as the best of his generation. They also were buoyed that Baffert had been in this situation on three previous occasions, and Espinoza had twice before — just last year. The feeling was that they had learned a great deal from those experiences, from the best way to condition a horse for the grueling three-race, five-week schedule to when exactly in the race to move him on this distinct mile-and-a-half oval with its sweeping turns and sandy surface.

No one argued how great American Pharoah looked since arriving here on Tuesday. He was a ripped and muscled bay cannonball that looked at home on Big Sandy, as the Belmont surface is known, as soon as he stepped on it. All the heavy lifting was done, but when Jorge Alvarez galloped him on Thursday morning, American Pharoah floated around the racetrack like an old soul. He was even better on Friday morning. The *Daily Racing Form*'s Mike Welsch perhaps summed up the case for American Pharoah strongly and succinctly in his final Clockers' Report on the Belmont field.

"The most talented horse in the field also is training the best coming into the race," he wrote. "There are not enough superlatives to describe his awesome work at Churchill Downs on Monday, when he cruised an absolutely effortless five furlongs in 1:00.08 before galloping out like a monster, six furlongs in 1:12.82, seven-eighths in 1:25.94, and a mile in 1:39.59. He was just as sharp and eager to train during his first two training sessions at Belmont and seemed to have adapted well to his surroundings. Considering the way he's thrived since the Preakness, if there's ever going to be a Triple Crown winner in our lifetime, he sure seems like the one."

The doubters of American Pharoah — and there were plenty — argued that in a deep crop of promising three-year-olds, it was too early to proclaim him the best. He was all-out to win the Derby by a length; he benefited from a sudden drenching of Pimlico, which gave him his preferred running surface in the Preakness; and he lacked the pedigree to go this long distance. They conceded that Baffert and Espinoza are seasoned but wonder how much either had learned. For the fourth time, Baffert trained his Triple Crown contender at Churchill Downs in Kentucky rather than getting him acclimated here. Why wouldn't Espinoza come here a couple of weeks early to pick up some mounts and increase his knowledge of the local track?

Andrew Beyer, the longtime horse racing columnist for the *Washington Post* and the creator of the Beyer Speed Figures, was perhaps the most forceful detractor. He noted that the average price of the Belmont winner since 2000 was 17-to-1 and that the pedigree of American Pharoah suggested that the colt would be staggering down the stretch. No American horses were bred to run a demanding mile and a half on the dirt, and with a female bloodline dominated by sprinters with minimal stamina, American Pharoah was less so. Beyer argued that the colt's Derby and Preakness looked better visually than it did on the stopwatch and his figures.

"It may have appeared that he was finishing strongly in these two victories, but he wasn't," he wrote. "He ran the final quarter-mile of the Derby in a slow 26.57 seconds, and the final fraction of the muddy Preakness in the equivalent of 27.62 for a quarter-mile — hardly an indication that he wants to go a longer distance."

Finally, there were a couple of other fresh and accomplished horses among the seven Belmont challengers, namely the Florida Derby winner Materiality and the Wood Memorial champion Frosted. Both overcame terrible trips to finish strong in Kentucky — Materiality sixth, Frosted fourth. Both were based here and were impressive-looking specimens. Both have classic distance pedigrees that scream they will still be running that last quarter of a mile.

So, who was going to win? The three hardest things to predict the outcome of are a ballgame, a love affair, and a horse race. Some horse and rider were going to get lucky; another couple were going to taste misfortune. Someone would be right; most would be wrong.

Either way, this was an exciting weekend to be at Belmont Park. There was no way Frances Relihan was going to miss seeing American Pharoah achieve what she had long ago predicted for him. The morning following the Derby, she told her husband, Joe, that she was buying their Belmont tickets that morning and would book flights as well. Relihan was that certain American Pharoah was going to win the Preakness easily and bring her to New York for a date with destiny.

She had watched the second leg of the Triple Crown in the Bluegrass at a party at Chanteclair Farm alongside her childhood friend Pat Hayes. They had grown up riding ponies together in Listowel, and Hayes now managed Chanteclair, one of its owners being John Moores, the former owner of the San Diego Padres baseball team. She was on her toes clapping at the television as American Pharoah rolled to victory on the sloppy track, validating her confidence in the colt. As Relihan boarded the train to Belmont at Penn Station Saturday morning, she grabbed her husband's hand and assured him that this was going to be a day to remember.

On the backside of Belmont Park, Ahmed Zayat and his family and friends had circled their wagons — or at least four RVs — behind barn 8. About 10:00 a.m., Zayat led his family in the Sabbath Prayer and reminded them that they had much to be grateful for. In the previous forty-eight hours, a federal judge in New Jersey ruled that the statute of limitations had run out on Howard Rubinsky's breach of contract lawsuit and dismissed it. Zayat had been comforted when the daughter of Affirmed's owner, Louis Wolfson, had reached out to Joanne Zayat and told her to ignore the unfavorable stories that had been written about her husband. Her father had served nine months in federal prison for conspiracy and illegal stock sales, an episode revisited often through Affirmed's Triple Crown. It had been upsetting, but she told Joanne Zayat not to let the attention ruin the experience. They needed to enjoy the moment.

It had rained in the early morning hours at Belmont Park, and now the track was drying out, which could mean trouble if it became deep out and tiring as the day went on. It was something else to worry about beyond Zayat's control, so he banished it from his thoughts. He watched as his family and friends dove into the whitefish and bagels and lox and spoke enthusiastically about a day that could very well be one to remember. Zayat was proud of himself. He had been in the horse business only since 2006, and here he was on the precipice of a Triple Crown. He had lost a fortune in the game and was in the process of trying to make some of it back. He had been tortured by close finishes in the Derby, but here he had a colt that he had born and bred — "Zayat blood from A to Z" — trying to do something special. Mostly, Zayat understood that he had been blessed with American Pharoah. There were so many things that had gone right. The injury to the suspensory tendon could have been career-ending. The bruise to the foot in February could have been worse and meant missed training.

Instead, American Pharoah was getting stronger, faster, and smarter here in New York while the thirteen horses that had tried and failed to win the Triple Crown prior to his colt arrived here tired, beat up, and ultimately defeated by what it took to get here.

Across the parking lot, inside that grand old racetrack on Long Island, the anticipation of something perhaps extraordinary occurring built throughout the day. The New York Racing Association, which operated Belmont, had capped attendance at 90,000 in the hopes of avoiding the overcrowding that had marred the previous year's race. A crowd of 102,199 came to see California Chrome's attempt and by the time the race went off at 6:51 p.m., concession stands were out of water, beer, hot dogs, and everything else, and people were hot and cranky from an afternoon spent pushing through crowds. It got worse when thousands of people had problems leaving Belmont Park by the Long Island Railroad and were stranded there for hours.

The cap had been effective at thinning out the crowd, and sunny skies and breezy 76-degree weather had lulled Belmont Park into its usual big day rhythm. It was a day for pastel sports coats and form-fitting dresses and porkpie hats along with wide-brimmed ones made from lace. Mostly it was an afternoon dedicated to the finest racing in America as seven stakes races, five of them Grade 1s, worth a combined $5.9 million, led into the $1.5 million 147th running of the Belmont Stakes. Every twenty-eight minutes, what already was a steady roar became a crescendo of hopes and passion as the horses pounded down the stretch toward the wire with track announcer Larry Collmus laying down the narration as bettors sang their own choruses in seeming harmony.

"Get there wire!"

"Come on 7!"

"Hold on, Javier!"

"Yes, yes, yyyyyyes!"

Then, suddenly, the racetrack apron emptied as winners skipped to the windows to collect and losers headed back to seats and Daily Racing Forms to get it all back in the next race.

In the press box — where many of the same cast of characters had gathered on previous June Saturdays like this one, only to be disappointed again — a search was on that spoke volumes about the expectations set for American Pharoah. Tim Layden of

Sports Illustrated asked if there was a journalist in attendance and was working when Affirmed won horse racing's last Triple Crown thirty-seven years ago. Layden had been covering the horses, among other things, for three decades and worked off a list of contemporaries. It took longer than expected before he came across Jerry Izenberg, eighty-four years old, who still wrote columns on occasion for Newark's *Star-Ledger.*

"I was here for Affirmed," Izenberg said. "Secretariat and Seattle Slew, too."

Down the hall in a glass-enclosed booth, Larry Collmus was preparing for what might become a historic race call. This was his fifth year calling all three legs of the Triple Crown for NBC, but his first as the track announcer for New York Racing. He replaced Tom Durkin, who had retired after twenty-five years of being the signature voice of horse racing. His baritone was mellifluous and his word pictures were often poetry. Durkin, however, was 0 for 7 when it came to Triple Crown bids — and 0 for 8 if I'll Have Another's scratch is counted. He was in this crow's nest for all three of Baffert's failed attempts. The defeat that stung Durkin the most came in 2004 when Smarty Jones was caught at the wire by Birdstone.

The colt had pulled into New York undefeated, and Durkin wanted to be prepared for a transcendent performance. So he took a surveyor's tape out to the track and measured 31 lengths — Secretariat's record-setting margin of victory in 1973 — and made a mark on the rail so that if Smarty Jones turned in a record-setting performance, he could say so. New York Racing officials subsequently put a pole at that location to honor Big Red. It was Durkin's call, however, that lives as a memorial to the heartbreak of near greatness.

"And Smarty Jones enters the stretch to the roar of a hundred and twenty thousand!" he intoned. "But Birdstone is going to make him earn it today! The whip is out on Smarty Jones! It's been twenty-six years — it's just one furlong away!" Then, a second later: "They're coming down to the finish! Can Smarty Jones hold on? Here comes Birdstone!"

When Birdstone passed Smarty Jones in the last 70 yards, Durkin, along with most everyone else at Belmont, was crushed. When California Chrome came up short the previous year, a frustrated Durkin tossed his headset in the booth. It was a hole in a Hall of Fame resume that would never be filled.

Now here Collmus, forty-eight and having honed his craft over thirty years at racetracks from Alabama to Massachusetts and Florida to California, had an opportunity to crown a champion less than six months into his new job. He had a couple of possible phrases ready if the feat occurred, but he did not want to be overly scripted. Collmus spent much of the day praying for clouds to roll in, because as dusk settles on sunny days at Belmont Park, the horses are completely backlit as they turn for home. On sunny days, the silks, which Collmus relied on to identify the horses, turn black, shadows set in, and he cannot see for certain who's who until mid-stretch.

With ninety minutes before post time, there was not a cloud in the sky.

In the Baffert barn, things were getting busy as well as strange. In the week before the race, the Zayats, Baffert, and Espinoza all entertained deal offers from sponsors eager to have their products linked with what was hopefully the twelfth Triple Crown Champion. The winners were Monster Energy drink; Wheels Up, a luxury jet share company; and Burger King. Wearing a logoed ball cap, as Zayat and Espinoza did for Wheels Up, was one thing, but letting the fetching Monster Girls lead American

Pharoah into the saddling paddock was quite another. The Monster people had hoped to put its logo on American Pharoah's bridle, reins, or shadow roll. That was a non-starter as Baffert, ever superstitious, worried the slightest alteration to the colt's routine would change his luck. With sponsors, media members, and fans milling around, Baffert rubbed Smokey's head for luck as he did before all big races and headed to the racetrack.

In the jockeys' room, Espinoza was running on the treadmill. He had gone to bed early the night before and slept in until 10:30 a.m. He was also relaxed enough to catch a mid-afternoon nap. Espinoza had had two mounts earlier in the card, including a third-place finish aboard Sky Kingdom in the Brooklyn Handicap; that was an important race because it was the exact mile-and-a-half distance of the Belmont. This was the only mile-and-a-half oval in America and was a tough track to navigate for visiting jockeys. The turns were long — 1,000 yards versus Churchill's 770 yards. They were so sweeping that Espinoza often felt that he was not on a turn at all. Belmont Park rewarded the patient and precise rider who could fight the impulse to hurtle his horse into the turn or even turn him loose on the top of it. Instead, more often than not, a winning ride was launched coming out of the turn and into its never-ending stretch. Much had been made of Espinoza's poor record here. He had won only four races in seventy-nine mounts, and the rides he was most remembered for here were War Emblem and California Chrome's failed bids. However, Espinoza knew that he had never been here with a horse like American Pharoah and was confident he was about to make a lasting memory.

Jimmy Barnes led American Pharoah into the paddock at Belmont Park while thousands of people lined up ten deep to get a look at the colt. The Monster Girls, indeed, were in tow and dressed almost demurely in black. Baffert made the walk from his barn to the paddock with his family. He had Bode by the hand, and Taylor, Canyon, Forest, and his daughter Savannah trailed behind them. In 1998, he had held four-year-old Savannah in his arms as they watched Real Quiet stagger down the stretch to get caught by a nostril by Victory Gallop. This was the first time ever that Baffert had all of his children at a Triple Crown race, which meant more to him now than whatever happened. Everything felt just right. Baffert knew he was having a good day when he passed a group of Jamaican horse-players he recognized from his three previous bids. Instead of heckling Baffert as they had in the past, telling him that they were going to bet against his horse, they offered encouragement: "It's your day, mon."

Earlier in the day, he had spoken with Penny Chenery, who bred and owned Secretariat. It was her horse that set the modern standard for greatness in a racehorse on June 9, 1973, when he won the Belmont by thirty-one lengths, breaking the margin-of-victory record set by Triple Crown winner Count Fleet in 1943. He also ran the fastest mile and a half on dirt in history, at 2:24. Secretariat broke the stakes record by more than 2 seconds, and his time works out to a speed of 37.5 mph for his entire performance.

"Secretariat is widening now! He is moving like a tremendous machine!" is how CBS television announcer Chic Anderson described the colt's stretch run.

Now ninety-three, Chenery had been coming to this race for thirty-seven years, waiting for one more horse and its owner to join this small and select fraternity. None had done so.

Zayat, surrounded by his family and friends, stood near the statue of Secretariat in the center of the paddock, trying to contain himself. He could not. His colt was the 3-to-5 favorite to win the race on the tote board and was 1-to-9 in his, and most people's, hearts. He turned to Joanne.

"Are you ready to become the owner of the twelfth Triple Crown champion?" he asked her.

Espinoza emerged from the jockeys' room with his six rivals and friends — all wearing polished boots, white pants, and Day-Glo silks and caps. Gary Stevens, Kent Desormeaux, and Mike Smith were colleagues from California and each was in the Hall of Fame. John Velazquez was as well but was based in New York, as were Irad Ortiz, Joel Rosario, and Javier Castellano. They stopped beneath a tree and arranged themselves around some wrought-iron chairs for the traditional photo portrait of the Belmont jockeys. When they were finished, Espinoza accepted the murmurs of "good luck" from them with a nod and went to find Baffert.

Espinoza thought the trainer was calmer than he had been in Louisville and Maryland. He was confident, too.

"Dude, he is ready. Go ahead and ride him with confidence," Baffert told Espinoza. "That's the only way, ride him with extreme confidence, put him on the lead. Go for it. If he doesn't make it, don't worry about it; we tried."

Barnes grabbed Espinoza's leg and vaulted him atop American Pharoah and off they went to the racetrack, escorted by a convoy of television cameras and still photographers. Espinoza heard the song "New York, New York" and the voices of 90,000 people singing along with Frank Sinatra before they made it to the breezeway.

And find I'm A number one . . .
Top of the list . . .
King of the hill . . .
A number one!

Espinoza allowed it to wash over him as he paraded American Pharoah past the grandstand. It was electric. He gave his colt a nudge and American Pharoah bowed his neck, pricked his ears, and galloped into the backstretch.

In a box on the second-floor clubhouse, the Bafferts took their seats with Jill and Bode flanking Bob, and Forest, Canyon, and Savannah a row behind them. They were joined by the costumed, plastic-headed "Burger King." The fast-food company had paid Baffert $200,000 for their character to stay close enough to be in camera shots — money the trainer had pledged to four horse

345

charities, including Old Friends and the Permanently Disabled Jockeys Fund.

Nearby, the Zayats were on their feet in a knot, with Justin behind with both hands on his father's shoulders.

As Espinoza and American Pharoah shuffled into the Number 5 post, Collmus asked the question that everyone was awaiting the answer to.

"Is today the day? Is he the one?"

They would have the answer in less than two and a half minutes.

Suddenly, the bell rang and the gates swung open, but it startled American Pharoah and he snapped back on his heels. Just as quickly, Espinoza felt the colt uncoil and spring forward and within two jumps, they had catapulted ahead of his seven rivals and glided into the first turn like a marble circling a roulette wheel. Espinoza knew the race was over then. Beneath him was a horse that he barely recognized, one with a new depth of power. American Pharoah was hitting the ground as if he were walking on clouds. He was stretching as supplely as a yogi.

Behind him, Velazquez on Materiality sensed Espinoza was sitting on a ton of horse. He was just cruising along, running unhurried quarter miles at 24-second clips.

He was on a fresh horse; now he needed to find out how fast Materiality was. He asked his colt to start chasing American Pharoah down the backstretch. Espinoza let Materiality get within a head but smooched in his colt's ear and shook him off at the mile mark.

"Steady, steady," he whispered to American Pharoah.

Mubtaahij, from Dubai, took a run at him on the far turn but got within only three lengths before peeling back. Revving up outside him, however, was the late-running Frosted. American Pharoah was pulling on him, wanting to go. Espinoza gave him a little rein but slowly reeled him back in. He didn't want to choke him down. Frosted's jockey, Joel Rosario, scrubbed the gray colt's neck and got within four, three, and two and a half lengths.

As American Pharoah came out of the far turn and squared his shoulders, Espinoza stared down the long withering stretch of Belmont Park as a sense of inevitability surged through its mammoth old grandstand. It was go time, and the crowd strained on the tips of their toes and let out a roar from deep in their souls. It was going to end, finally, please — this thirty-seven-year search for a great racehorse. This battered old sport needed another immortal Thoroughbred, one worthy to stand alongside Sir Barton and Gallant Fox, Omaha and War Admiral, Whirlaway and Count Fleet, Assault and Citation, Secretariat, Seattle Slew, and Affirmed. In the time it took to find a twelfth Triple Crown champion, America had elected five presidents, fought three wars, and lived through at least three economic downturns.

As American Pharoah bounded into the stretch amid a deafening roar, the memories of the gritty Affirmed, the speedy Seattle Slew, and that tremendous machine Secretariat were summoned from backside to grandstand, and rightfully so. No one doubted that American Pharoah was about to enter the history books. He was bouncing down the lane as if jumping from one trampoline to another, and no one was going to catch him.

Baffert was transported. He had come here before, certain that he had a horse that belonged among the giants of racing, only to feel his heart ascend to his throat. That was not going to happen here today, though. He had watched Secretariat win the Belmont with his father on a little television set with rabbit ears in a VFW lodge in Arizona. God, he wished the Chief and his mom, Ellie, were here to see this. The crowd was thundering and Baffert was a fan again, not a Hall of Fame trainer.

In the saddle, Espinoza felt a rush that had twice eluded him. He dropped the reins on his colt and let the muscled bay take him home. When he was a boy in his native Mexico, Espinoza had been afraid of horses, but now more than ever he felt the gift they had given him. Beneath him, American Pharoah's strides were getting longer and longer, but Espinoza felt as if he were riding the colt in slow motion.

Far behind him, Stevens, Velazquez, Ortiz — every rider except Rosario aboard Frosted — had their heads tilted to the infield, watching the stretch run on the giant screen there. Stevens felt the tears stinging his eyes as they gathered in his goggles. Espinoza hit American Pharoah with his right hand once, twice — more like taps than thumps — three, four, and five and snapped off to a four-length lead. At the sixteenth pole, Collmus had seen enough and let loose the phrase that had been tumbling in his mind for days: "The thirty-seven-year wait is over. American Pharoah is finally the one."

When Espinoza crossed the finish line five and a half lengths ahead, he finally allowed a smile to curl at the corner of his mouth and the raucous celebration to reverberate deep in his bones. Flowers cascaded down from the upper tiers of the clubhouse and tears spilled along with beers as strangers fell into each other's arms, ecstatic.

"Holy shit!" Espinoza said after powering the colt down on the first turn and being gathered up by an outrider. "Wow. Wow. He's just an amazing horse."

He turned and galloped American Pharoah the length of the grandstand and let a thunderstruck crowd cheer the sublime performance of a once-in-a-lifetime athlete. Espinoza could barely catch his breath.

In the clubhouse, Jill Baffert swung her arms around her husband and buried her wet cheeks into Bob's chest. He could not talk as other trainers pushed through the crowd to congratulate him.

"That horse is too good," said Todd Pletcher, the trainer of Materiality.

Kiaran McLaughlin, the trainer of Frosted, shook his hand.

Ahmed Zayat was a puddle by the time he got his trainer in a bear hug.

In the breezeway near the winner's circle, Frances Relihan had goose bumps listening to the thunderous ovation the colt was getting, a colt she knew as a weanling in the quiet of the Bluegrass. Jimmy Barnes was stoic, holding a tearful Dana, until he saw Espinoza returning American Pharoah from his victory lap. He ran onto the track, grabbed hold of the colt, and burst into tears.

"We all wanted it," Zayat said when they finally converged in the winner's circle. "We wanted it for the sport."

CHAPTER SIXTEEN: THE VICTORY LAP

August 2, 2015

Everyone knows there is no cheering in the press box, and crying is frowned upon as well. Both rules were violated as American Pharoah thundered down the stretch and into the record books. It was a perfect moment that the sport had been longing for, and it was clear that Ahmed Zayat, Bob Baffert, and Victor Espinoza understood that.

"He's the one that won — it wasn't me," Baffert said, still fighting back tears. "It was the horse. We were passengers."

The following morning, Baffert and Espinoza were on NBC's *Weekend Today* with American Pharoah standing behind them eating carrots from the trainer's hand. The colt looked in better shape than his human connections. Espinoza had been out all night and had not slept a wink. He had a first pitch to throw out at the New York Yankees game and an appearance on *The Tonight*

Show Starring Jimmy Fallon still ahead of him.

Baffert was hoarse and ready to catch a flight back to California in the afternoon. Jimmy and Dana Barnes were taking American Pharoah back to Louisville for a well-earned vacation at Churchill Downs.

So now what? Coolmore had purchased the stallion rights for American Pharoah to stand at Ashford Stud, but Zayat had retained the right to race him through the rest of the year. He insisted that he was going to do so.

"I take this very responsibly. I think it's a huge, huge honor and privilege, and we owe it to the sport to do the right thing," he said.

By winning the Triple Crown, American Pharoah had just given horse racing a badly needed shot in the arm. More than 18.6 million people watched the race on television, the third highest rated Belmont Stakes in history. The colt was home page news globally on websites and in newspapers, celebrated on sports channels, and on network television, and his performance was dissected and relived on radio talk shows. It was not solely that a Triple Crown sweep had been a long time coming that attracted the attention of casual sports fans. It was how American Pharoah had done it:

with grit in the Derby, brilliance in the Preakness, and dominance in the Belmont.

American Pharoah's final time of 2:26.65 was the sixth fastest Belmont of all time, but Penny Chenery, ever protective of the legacy of Secretariat, characterized it as "not fast enough."

Neither Secretariat nor the four others horses that ran faster in the Belmont — Gallant Man (1957), Risen Star (1988), Easy Goer (1989), or A.P. Indy (1992) — had run the final quarter mile faster than the :24.32 American Pharoah did after leading every step of the way. In fact, none of them had run the final two quarters as fast as he had.

"Every time he runs, he shows me something we've never seen," Baffert said.

Even the most casual sports fan recognized and was moved by sublime athletic achievement, and over the previous five weeks, American Pharoah had reminded them what an ethereal creature a Thoroughbred was and how beautiful it was in full flight. The colt had graced the cover of *Sports Illustrated* and had crashed the NBA finals of a sort. After game three of the series, Steve Kerr, the Golden State Warriors coach, was asked if there was a better athlete than LeBron James. "Maybe American Pharoah," he said.

The colt had extinguished the talk of changing the distances or giving horses more time to rest between the three races. Even Baffert had started thinking that it never was going to be achieved again under the current system, that the breed had become too weak. Now he knew the sport had to wait on superior horses, and American Pharoah had proven that they don't come around that often.

Baffert, too, felt beholden to show off his Triple Crown champion. He also understood that the health and the reputation of American Pharoah were his first responsibility.

He and the Chief had been heartbroken when a horse named Onion defeated Secretariat in the Whitney Handicap the August following Big Red's Triple Crown sweep. He had seen Affirmed and Seattle Slew get beat as well after winning the Triple Crown. In fact, the three most recent Triple Crown champions won only five of their combined eleven races as three-year-olds.

"I don't want to see that," he said. "I want to make sure that when you see him out there, you can feel good about it."

Zayat, on the other hand, had something to sell as well as share with the sporting world: the Big Horse. So far, American Pharoah had won seven of eight races for more than $4.5 million purses. It was no secret Coolmore wanted the colt retired immediately to Ashford Stud rather than risking injury or perhaps even diminishing his value with a poor performance or two. With the bonuses for winning the three legs of the Triple Crown, Coolmore had $14 million invested in the colt. No stud fee had been set for American Pharoah, but it was projected to be at least $150,000 a breeding. Do the math — if American Pharoah was booked to 150 mares, which was likely, Coolmore was due to collect $22.5 million, or $8.5 million in profit the first year alone.

Keeping American Pharoah on the racetrack, however, allowed Zayat to cash more win checks and collect more appearance fees to offset the fact that he left money on the table by selling the stallion rights so early. He had plenty of suitors in racetrack executives who were swooning at the mere thought of the colt circling their oval before a full house. The belief was that American Pharoah would increase attendance, lift the amount wagered on the track's races, and provide untold publicity.

Seven days after American Pharoah won the Belmont, for example, more than 30,000 showed up at Churchill Downs just to watch the colt be paraded between races. They oohed and aahed and snapped photos.

"Oh my God!" one woman yelled from the crowd. "It's gorgeous."

The following morning, Cecil Seaman visited American Pharoah outside Barn 33 at Churchill Downs. He took his tape measure out and began stretching and wrapping around various parts of the colt's body — fifteen specific measurements in all — as he has done for more than 108,000 Thoroughbreds, including the previous four Triple Crown champions, over forty-five years. It had already been established that American Pharoah's stride reached 26 feet and he could cover approximately 55 feet per second. Seaman, a bloodstock consultant, had developed a system to evaluate the biomechanics of Thoroughbreds. Among his comprehensive database were the measurements of 850 champions, 2,000 G1 winners, 750 earners of at least $1 million, 50 Kentucky Derby victors, and more than 25 winners each of the Epsom Derby and Prix de l'Arc de Triomphe.

Seaman was hardly surprised that American Pharoah graded out A+ in his system alongside 447 other horses — or less than half of one percent of all he has measured.

He was taller and had a longer body than Affirmed, Seattle Slew, and Secretariat. Seaman found him more aerodynamic than three previous Triple Crown champions as well as most of the other horses in his top tier. American Pharoah's biomechanics were optimally suited for distances from one mile to a mile and three-quarters. He had already proved that he could run on dirt, but Seaman thought he could also be successful racing on turf.

What did surprise Seaman, however, was American Pharoah's bright mind and serene nature. As he wrapped his tape around his girth, the colt turned and looked curiously at what Seaman was doing. He then swung his head to Dr. William McGee, at ninety-eight the oldest living equine veterinarian, who was in a wheelchair in front of him feeding him carrots.

"Here's this champion and he acts like the kindest old riding horse," Seaman said.

American Pharoah proved it when Seattle Slew's jockey, Jean Cruguet, got on his back. He was there, too. Cruguet swung his seventy-six-year-old frame onto the colt's back and simply marveled: Slew was high-strung and would have never allowed a stranger on his back.

Zayat had picked the William Hill Haskell

Invitational at Monmouth Park on August 2 for the return of American Pharoah. It was a Grade 1 race, and the track was on the Jersey Shore in his home state. Zayat had negotiated a $2 million bonus from Coolmore if American Pharoah won there, another $2 million for winning the Grade 1 Travers Stakes in Saratoga, and $4 million for the Breeders' Cup Classic.

Besides offering a $1 million purse, Monmouth gave $25,000 to the owner and the trainer of the winner of each Triple Crown race. That meant Zayat and Baffert were each guaranteed $75,000. There was also very little risk that American Pharoah would lose. The Haskell should be renamed the Bob Baffert Invitational because his horses had appeared in it eleven times, won seven, finished second three times, and third once. It was an easy spot because the trainers of the better East Coast three-year-olds were aiming to capture the Travers and preferred to prep their horses in the Jim Dandy Stakes in Saratoga, which ran the day before the Haskell.

Monmouth was not alone in looking to attract racing's biggest star, whose presence would increase attendance and help lift the amount wagered on the track's races, and put them on the map as a destination for horse people. Canterbury Park offered to move its Mystic Lake Derby from the turf to the dirt, where American Pharoah is more comfortable, and provide a $2 million purse if Pharoah would go to Shakopee, Minnesota. Executives at Parx Racing near Philadelphia had a more lucrative bonus structure in place than Monmouth: $50,000 each for the winning owner and trainer of a Triple Crown race, guaranteeing Zayat and Baffert $150,000 each to show up for the Pennsylvania Derby. Plus, it was willing to raise its $1 million purse. New York, too, was trying to come up with extra purse money for the $1 million Travers to attract American Pharoah.

While Zayat sifted through racetrack deals, Baffert tried to restore some order to his barn and American Pharoah's routine. The colt had returned to California in the middle of June, transforming barn 5 into the center ring of what was becoming a circus. Friends, fans, and strangers stopped by at all hours to get a look at the Triple Crown champ. Baffert and his staff were accommodating, at first perhaps too accommodating, but now the trainer was eager to shut down the "petting zoo" and get American Pharoah back to work. The colt was losing weight and was acting more anxious.

Baffert agreed to parade him at Santa Anita on Saturday, June 27, but afterward the colt was put on lockdown.

So two days after more than 21,000 people showed up to show their appreciation for American Pharoah, the colt returned to the racetrack with Martin Garcia aboard after a brief twenty-three-day vacation. As soon as Baffert saw American Pharoah get into stride for a three-eighths-of-a-mile breeze, he knew he had done right by his horse, something that he was having a hard time articulating to people who asked him, "Hasn't the colt done enough?" In a testament to how popular American Pharoah had become, Baffert found himself answering that question a lot, most recently on a flight and from Cheech Marin and Tommy Chong, the comedy duo that pioneered and built an audience out of marijuana-based humor. They had watched the race, fallen for the horse, and asked why not quit while he's ahead.

"He's happiest when he is on the racetrack," Baffert explained. "He loves to run. He loves to train. There's no guarantee where he's going to run next because he has to tell me, 'Hey, I'm ready; I'm sitting on gold.' As long as he's sitting on gold, he'll run.

"If I see something in the morning — he doesn't want to train — then you won't see him in the races. As long as he's doing well, you're going to see Pharoah."

One month later, after his sixth workout in the past thirty days, Baffert declared American Pharoah fit and ready for the forty-eighth running of the William Hill Haskell Invitational.

"I think he's getting faster," Baffert said. "He gives me goose bumps."

The day before American Pharoah was scheduled to leave Del Mar, a group of parents with their kids showed up at the barn asking if they could get a look at the colt. Jimmy Barnes told them no; he was getting good at playing the bad cop. Somehow, however, they persuaded Baffert to bring him out for a photo. Barnes waited for them to leave before scolding Baffert.

"Ridiculous," said Jimmy.

"No, it's a good omen," replied Baffert. "One of them was named Haskell."

Shortly after Air Horse One, as the 727 American Pharoah shared with other horses is known, touched down at the Atlantic City Airport, Monmouth officials announced that they were increasing the purse for their marquee race to $1.75 million. They denied it was a quid pro quo but acknowledged that

Zayat and Baffert were aware that the pot would be sweetened for them if they, indeed, brought American Pharoah east from California. They were not finished, either. The racetrack promised to create a $1 million race for American Pharoah in September on the date and at the distance Baffert specified.

Even though second place was now worth $330,000 and third $150,000, only six horses signed on to face American Pharoah. None of them were in the colt's league, but that is not why a record crowd of 60,983 showed up to revel in the sunshine and sea air. American Pharoah was becoming a full-blown phenomenon. When he stepped onto the track to the full-throated strains of the Haskell anthem, Bruce Springsteen's "Born to Run," there was a roar that rivaled the one that he received winning the Belmont.

It scared Baffert. He started his day the same way he had on his eleven previous trips here for the Haskell — by having lunch at Max's Famous Hot Dogs in nearby West Long Branch, a ninety-nine-year-old landmark whose walls had signed photos from Frankie Valli and Joe Pesci and the Boss. He wolfed down a classic Max's with mustard, ketchup, and relish. He didn't anticipate being this anxious, but Baffert took his role as the protector of American Pharoah's legacy seriously. He did not want to get his horse beat, especially not here by far lesser horses. It had been fifty-seven days since the Belmont, and Baffert had given the colt seven stout timed workouts since his Belmont victory, each more breathtaking than the last. However, Secretariat, Seattle Slew, and Affirmed had all managed to get beat.

"Every time we run him and work him, he keeps showing he's getting faster and stronger," Baffert said, reassuring himself.

Still, Baffert's stomach churned throughout a long day spent mostly extricating himself from one mob of well-wishers to the next. He has long been one of the most recognizable figures in horse racing, but now he was a Triple Crown–winning trainer. While the Zayats entertained more than one hundred friends and neighbors in a banquet room high above the track, Baffert signed autographs and posed for pictures. In the paddock, Victor Espinoza could tell the trainer was on edge.

"Don't worry," he said. "Looks like you got him even bigger and stronger."

After saddling American Pharoah, Baffert barely made it back to his seat in time to see the start of the race. As soon as American Pharoah broke from the gate, however,

Baffert's anxiety gave way to awe. Mike Smith aboard Competitive Edge had gotten the jump on American Pharoah and shot out to the lead. Smith's colt had won the Grade 1 Hopeful Stakes at two and the Grade 3 Pat Day Mile earlier in the year, but Espinoza knew the horse had never been more than a mile and was far more comfortable sprinting at shorter distances.

So he sat on American Pharoah as relaxed as if he were on a Sunday trail ride as they tracked one length behind Competitive Edge around the first turn and into the second. When Smith looked over and saw Espinoza still on his flank after going three-quarters of a mile in a rapid 1:09.60 seconds, he knew he was running for second-place money. American Pharoah was running like the 1-to-5 favorite and Triple Crown champion that he was.

"He was on me, and he was on me, loaded," Smith said. "I was in a full drive and he was galloping, man."

American Pharoah blew by without Espinoza even asking him. He let the colt slingshot around the far turn and then Espinoza peeked beneath one shoulder, glanced over the other, then narrowed his eyes between his colt's ears and stared down the stretch. The colt's ears were wiggling.

They hit the stretch with a five-length lead, and Espinoza powered American Pharoah down to preserve his brilliance for another day. As they loped home, behind them a horse named Keen Ice was running full throttle but barely making up ground.

"No one can keep up with a horse this fast," Espinoza said.

The two-and-a-quarter-length victory brought a triumphant end to a lucrative day for Zayat Stables. It earned them a $1.05 million first-place check, lifting American Pharoah's career earnings to more than $5.5 million as well as a $2 million kicker from Coolmore. Plus, the $75,000 Monmouth paid Zayat and Baffert for making the trip.

Afterward, all anyone wanted to know was where American Pharoah was going to run next. Justin and Ahmed Zayat were pushing for the Travers Stakes in twenty-seven days. The New York Racing Association announced that it would raise the purse to $1.6 million if American Pharoah ran in the Midsummer Derby. Baffert, however, insisted he was taking American Pharoah's schedule one race at a time. He was taking the colt back to California, where he would assess his fitness and attitude before deciding where he went next.

"He was on my schedule for the Triple

Crown, but now I'm on his," he said. "The last thing we want to do is embarrass the horse."

CHAPTER SEVENTEEN: THE GRAVEYARD OF CHAMPIONS

August 29, 2015

They take their Midsummer Derby seriously here in Saratoga Springs, New York. So shortly after noon on Sunday, August 23, 2015, when Larry Collmus excitedly announced to racegoers at the nation's oldest racetrack, "Yes, he's coming — he'll be here at the Spa," they knew exactly what he was talking about: American Pharoah would be here the following Saturday for the 146th running of the Travers Stakes. The news was met with sustained applause and high fives being exchanged along the apron of the racetrack and throughout its bucolic backyard. It ended a rumor-filled week of expectation, in which supposed sure signs that Pharoah's owner, Ahmed Zayat, intended to run him here (he booked a block of hotel rooms) and that Baffert had finally agreed (he had a seat on a private jet) did battle with the natural pessimism of horseplayers.

Why would Baffert take his prized colt to a racetrack that he has shown little fondness for, a track that has earned the nickname of the Graveyard of Champions over its storied 150-plus years? It was here, after all, that the Triple Crown winner Gallant Fox was beaten by 100-to-1 Jim Dandy in the 1930 Travers and another Triple Crown champion, Secretariat, was defeated in the 1973 Whitney by a horse named Onion. Don't forget Affirmed, either. He came here for the Travers and beat his fierce rival Alydar at the wire but was disqualified for interference on the grandstand turn. It was a hollow victory for the connections of Alydar, who finished second to Affirmed in all three Triple Crown races, but it only enhanced the unforgiving reputation of this racetrack.

Besides, Baffert had made no secret that he found the track surface here deep and demanding. He had started five horses in the Travers, winning only once, with Point Given in 2001. A month earlier that same year, Baffert and Gary Stevens had brought a colt named Congaree here as the heavy favorite for the Jim Dandy Stakes. Congaree had finished third in the Kentucky Derby and Preakness and had won the Grade 1 Swap Stakes in California the previous month. Baffert was shocked when the colt stopped running in the stretch and was passed by a 12-to-1 long shot named Scorpion. On their flight the following day to New Jersey, where Point Given was running in the Haskell, Baffert swore to Stevens that he would never bring a horse to Saratoga unless he was certain it was ten lengths better than the rest of the field.

Whether or not American Pharoah was ten lengths better than his rivals would be determined within a week. Ahmed and Justin Zayat had been vocal all summer about wanting to race the Triple Crown champ here at the nation's premier meet. The $850,000 first-place check and the $2 million kicker from Coolmore were powerful motivators as well. Baffert was feeling the pressure. He had preferred a more prudent route to the Breeders' Cup Classic, one that took them to the outskirts of Philadelphia in mid-September to compete in the Pennsylvania Derby. The spacing was better for training American Pharoah — seven weeks after the Haskell and six weeks leading into the Classic. Parx, the track, was connected to a casino and Zayat and Baffert had been assured that the $1 million purse would be raised in addition to the $150,000 each was promised for showing up. He was looking for a reason to scuttle the trip to New York.

Instead, earlier that morning at his summer home in Del Mar, California, American Pharoah threw down another sizzling workout that the trainer could not ignore. The colt rolled through seven-eighths of a mile in 1:23.20 and punctuated the drill by blowing past another trainer's horses, which had started their workouts well ahead of American Pharoah. It was enough to convince Baffert.

"If you have a seat at Saratoga, I wouldn't sell it," he said.

No one did. New York Racing officials once more capped the crowd, this time at 50,000 people due to Saratoga's smaller grounds. As a consolation, however, Zayat and Baffert allowed them to advertise a public gallop on the day before the race. At Monmouth, more than 5,000 had come. Baffert knew there would be a lot more than that in New York.

"I feel like I'm bringing The Beatles to town," Baffert said.

He was and it was apparent as soon as American Pharoah stepped feistily off the airplane in nearby Albany, New York, on the Wednesday before the race. The colt stopped on the Jetway, as if it were a model's runway, so the gaggle of photographers could get their shots. In winning eight straight races over the previous year, American Pharoah had been a road warrior. He had traveled 18,750 miles to run on seven different racetracks, and this was his second coast-to-coast trip in twenty-four days. Horses were not supposed to be able to log miles like that without wearing down, and despite his outward confidence, Baffert worried that they had shipped American Pharoah too far and too much.

Saratoga was just damn glad he was here. The colt had been the talk of the taverns that surround Saratoga Race Course as well as the tonier restaurants off Broadway, its main drag. That American Pharoah was here for the 146th running of the Travers Stakes was almost too good to be true.

"We have never seen a horse like this" is how the discussions usually began, to the soundtrack of ice tinkling the sides of tumblers and the clink of wineglasses.

This was the Vatican of horse racing, after all, and American Pharoah was being treated like the pope by horse lovers and like the heavyweight champion of the world by horseplayers. These two worlds coexist in a sport that can be both beautiful and brutal. The colt was already the 1-to-5 morning-line favorite for the Midsummer Derby on Saturday. The horse lovers were pulling for another exquisite performance from the colt. The gamblers? They were going to bet on Texas Red, the Breeders' Cup Juvenile winner, or Frosted, the Belmont runner-up, in pursuit of a financial score.

On Friday morning, the two factions sat side by side — more than 15,000 strong — to watch American Pharoah circle the racetrack. They came from Boston and Los Angeles, Atlanta and Cincinnati, and places in between, all to see the Big Horse, a title long thrown around lightly but now deservedly worn by American Pharoah.

No horseman likes to concede that they are running for second-place money, but the trainer of Texas Red, Keith Desormeaux, declared that American Pharoah was from "another planet." Keith Mason, one of the owners of Keen Ice, was simply grateful to have a horse in a race with the Triple Crown champion. His colt finished third to American Pharoah in the Belmont and second in the Haskell Stakes earlier this month.

"I feel fortunate to be at a place like Saratoga to run against a horse like American Pharoah," said Mason, an Atlanta lawyer. "The sport deserves something like this."

When the gates opened at 7:00 a.m., there

was a stampede to the clubhouse to secure box seats. Ten minutes later, those boxes were filled. By 8:00 a.m., so were the seats along the stretch. When American Pharoah took to the track at 8:45 a.m., people were standing six deep along the rail.

As the chiseled bay colt galloped, a hush descended on the racetrack. Binoculars were trained on American Pharoah. Cell phone cameras were held aloft to capture the moment. On the rail in the winner's circle, Bob Baffert leaned sideways so he could watch his colt as well as the crowd behind him. He confessed that this was the greatest moment in his career as a horse trainer to see how a knowledgeable crowd had appreciated the work of art before them.

The reverence and awe shown American Pharoah washed over him. He thought about Seabiscuit and Secretariat and more recently the great race mare Zenyatta, who drew big crowds to racetracks while running her record to 19-to-0 from 2007 to 2010.

"People want their kids to see this horse," he said. "It means a lot to them."

Then the trainer got quiet. He saw something in American Pharoah that concerned him. This was supposed to be an easy gallop, but Jorge Alvarez was wrestling a bit with American Pharoah. The colt was on edge. In his barn after the gallop, Baffert paraded American Pharoah in a courtyard, to the delight of fellow horsemen and news media members. When it was time for American Pharoah to return to his stall, the colt — clearly enjoying the attention — put up a fight. He stamped his feet like a child before being gently nudged. As magical as racehorses are in motion, Baffert had felt most privileged to experience American Pharoah at rest for the past year.

"I think I know how it feels to be a Secret Service agent," he said, "and to have to protect a precious package."

Even though both were fully aware of this historic racetrack's reputation for felling iconic horses, the next day Baffert met Victor Espinoza beneath an oak tree in the paddock and told him if ever a horse existed that could dance atop the Graveyard of Champions, he was about to get on him and join Whirlaway (1941) as the only other Triple Crown Champion to win the Travers. He had spoken with Alvarez after the previous morning's workout and the exercise rider conceded that American Pharoah had been keyed up and had galloped far more aggressively than he should have. Baffert blamed himself. He had sent American

Pharoah to the track with Smokey, which gave the colt mixed signals. American Pharoah thought he was going to the track for a timed workout. He then was frustrated at being made to only gallop.

American Pharoah looked even fitter than he did on the first Saturday in May at Churchill Downs. He was maturing. Baffert noticed that he was growing longer and his neck, shoulder, and hip were marbled with muscle. He was the picture of a perfect racehorse. So when the gates opened to the roar of more than 50,000 people and Espinoza throttled American Pharoah past the old wooden clubhouse a comfortable length ahead of the field, Baffert had no reason to suspect that the Spa was going to add another monumental heartbreak to its résumé.

Espinoza, however, was already concerned. The colt had warmed up poorly and began to sweat as the pair made their way to the starting gate. His mane was so drenched that Espinoza had to use his whip as a squeegee to get him dry. His colt was agitated, spent, and not ready to run. American Pharoah had never been like this before. He glided him into the clubhouse turn and hoped to settle into an unhurried run down the backstretch in the hope of getting the colt to relax. Instead, he felt Jose Lezcano, the rider of Frosted, beside him, determined to make American Pharoah run hard every step of the way. He put his gray colt right on Espinoza and stayed on Pharoah's flank like a nightclub bouncer hustling an unruly patron out the door. Not only was this a change of tactics from Frosted, who had heretofore mounted late runs to finish fourth to American Pharoah in the Derby and second in the Belmont, but also Lezcano had never been on the colt before. He had inherited the mount on Frosted a little more than an hour before the race, and only because the colt's regular rider, Joel Rosario, fell off a horse earlier in the card and was taken to Albany Medical Center with lower back pain.

Lezcano was forcing the tempo of the race, making American Pharoah go 23.18 in the race's third quarter mile and 23.60 in the fourth. Behind them, Javier Castellano was riding Keen Ice, another late runner, for the first time. Dale Romans, the colt's trainer, had instructed him to change tactics as well.

"Let's put him in the race," Romans told Castellano before giving him a leg up.

At the half-mile pole, Espinoza knew he was in trouble. He asked American Pharoah for some oomph, but horse and rider could not separate from Frosted. The colt's energy was not the same; he was running on fumes. Worse, Lezcano and Frosted banged into American Pharoah with enough force to knock him off stride, then continued to bounce the Triple Crown champion as if they were riding bumper cars as they dueled into the far turn. He was trying to rattle Espinoza as well as American Pharoah. He was trying to intimidate them and force them into making a mistake. It was perfectly legal and often employed in big races.

In the clubhouse, Baffert saw Espinoza struggling and American Pharoah sputtering and got worried. This was not his colt's A game on display. "He didn't have the power he usually has," Baffert said. "His tank wasn't as full as we'd hoped."

As they turned for home, Lezcano lifted Frosted past American Pharoah, and horse and rider looked intent on turning the tables on their nemesis. American Pharoah refused to lose — he vaulted a half-length ahead as they neared the eighth pole to the full-throated roar of a crowd that sensed an upset had been thwarted.

Baffert understood American Pharoah had repelled the challenge on pure guts but doubted he could withstand another one.

Closing fast were Castellano and Keen Ice. Castellano knew Frosted had softened American Pharoah up . . . but how much?

"When I got closer to him, and I didn't see him take off, I knew I had a chance," Castellano said. Keen Ice kept coming. He put a nose, a neck, and finally three-quarters of his body ahead of American Pharoah at the wire.

The final chart shows that Keen Ice covered the mile-and-a-quarter route in 2:1.57, or fast enough to earn his owners, Donegal Racing, an $850,000 first-place check. His backers scored, too, getting back $34 for a $2 bet. The history books, however, were going to tell an altogether different but epic tale about how a hallowed racetrack saw a brave performance from another Triple Crown horse but rewarded a winning one, Keen Ice.

Everyone in American Pharoah's camp was stunned. Baffert staggered down to the track to check on his colt and talk to Espinoza.

"I'm not used to being in this position with him," Baffert said. "It's hard to digest right now."

Zayat looked shell-shocked, and his family in mourning, as they made their way through the crowd to the postrace news conference. He didn't wait for a question.

"You have to ask yourself is the show over?" he said. "Is it the time? My gut feeling, time to go out on a high note. My gut feeling right now, without being outspoken, is to retire him."

Neither American Pharoah nor Baffert looked worn out or deflated the next morning. Outside his barn, the trainer smiled as he led his big bay colt, stopping to let a little girl feed him carrots. American Pharoah's defeat did not stop people from wanting to catch one more glimpse of him. The colt stomped his foot once and then twice in appreciation. He was a happy horse. Baffert was disappointed but satisfied with his colt's gritty performance. He also made it clear that he didn't want American Pharoah retired.

"He was valiant in defeat," he said. "If he would have stopped running and finished fifth or sixth, you would have scraped me off the track. I would have been so mad at myself. You begin to feel like they're invincible, and you forget they all get beat."

They all do get beat at horse racing's highest levels. Zenyatta suffered her only loss in her final start, at the 2010 Breeders' Cup Classic. Only Personal Ensign, another great mare, managed to retire with a perfect 13-

for-13 record at the sport's elite level; she punctuated a spectacular career by capturing the Breeders' Cup Distaff in her final start, in 1988. That is where Baffert wanted American Pharoah to say farewell — Lexington, Kentucky, on Halloween in the Breeders' Cup Classic. He believed that the colt earned one more race to take on the best older horses in the world and to prove he was a horse for the ages.

"No regrets," Baffert said. "I'm glad we brought him."

He refused to blame Lezcano's tactics for the ride.

"I found the ride a little bit odd, and it probably did both of them in, but that's horse racing," Baffert said. "If you can't beat him one way, try another. We almost did it."

American Pharoah was beaten, but he hardly embarrassed himself, and the applause that greeted him as he was led off the racetrack Saturday evening was a testament to the awe and the respect he has stirred in horse lovers. Later Saturday night, Bob and Jill Baffert were greeted with a standing ovation when they were seated for dinner at the Wishing Well, a local institution.

In fact, after sleeping on it, Baffert called

it the most "positive loss" of his career. He had a plan: get the colt home to California for a couple of weeks of rest and then train him up for the Breeders' Cup Classic for a final and potentially history-making race.

"I can do it," Baffert said.

CHAPTER EIGHTEEN:
CALIFORNIA DREAMING

October 31, 2015

When he returned to California, Bob Baffert knew he had to give American Pharoah a break from training. He had done this long enough to know that you learn more about your horse when you lose. In American Pharoah's debut, Baffert discovered his colt was anxious when bombarded by sounds. He needed earplugs. In Saratoga, Baffert learned that American Pharoah needed his routine. Sending Smokey, the pony, to the racetrack with him for the public gallop was not the only mistake he had made. Baffert was mad at himself for putting American Pharoah on a flight to Saratoga that was stopped in Kentucky to pick up other horses. It was too much commotion for the colt. It was too much time in the air. He had upset American Pharoah's rhythm and had paid for it.

Now he needed to shut him down. Baffert

needed to completely reboot him. He began by allowing American Pharoah only light jogs, short and easy spins on the racetrack. Then, he eased the colt in with some controlled gallops. Mostly, Baffert fed him. American Pharoah needed to have his nerves calmed and some weight put back on his frame.

The goal was the Breeders' Cup Classic on Halloween eight weeks from now. At $5 million, it was the richest race in North America and the one that annually attracted the best horses in training from around the world. It would be the first time that American Pharoah took on older horses, which was a significant step up for any three-year-old. The colt's elders were physically more developed, mentally more experienced and battle tested. In the previous thirty Classics, three-year-olds had won it just ten times. The Breeders' Cup was founded in 1984 with races in many divisions as a sort of series of championships to determine who was the best sprinter or turf horse, the most accomplished two-year-old, the champion filly and mare. The Breeders' Cup had not penetrated the consciousness of casual fans as deeply as the Triple Crown races, but it offered two afternoons of the finest racing in the world that were eagerly devoured by horse aficionados around the world. Of the thirteen races, the Classic, at a mile and a quarter, was the Breeders' Cup's marquee race and had been previously won by a who's who of great horses — Sunday Silence, A.P. Indy, Cigar, and Zenyatta.

For the first time ever, the Breeders' Cup was being held at Keeneland Racecourse, 147 acres of bluegrass and limestone in the heart of America's Thoroughbred breeding industry and the home of one of the world's most prestigious auction houses. This was the home track of the sport's blue blood breeders and owners. It held a race meet for three weeks each October and three weeks each April, and it was the place to be for everybody who was anybody in the Thoroughbred horse business. The irony of a former quarter horse trainer from Nogales, Arizona, bringing a Throughbred owned by an Egyptian American owner — a relative newcomer — to plunder one of the sport's most revered cathedrals was not lost on Baffert. He knew that many of the same people for whom he had bought millions of dollars of horses on behalf of his clients might be rooting against him.

Zayat had rethought his post-Travers sentiment and decided not to retire American Pharoah as Baffert knew he would. The trainer had known the owner too long and had watched him speak before he thought things through. Zayat cried. He screamed. He lived life's drama to its fullest. Baffert also knew that Zayat had fallen hard for his horse for reasons other than the money and the fame. One afternoon earlier in the summer, Baffert watched Zayat lie down in the stall with American Pharoah, who nuzzled and licked him. It was captured by Justin in a photograph that went viral on Twitter.

"An incredible moment," Zayat said. "It was just total love, total passion."

Baffert had fallen hard for the horse, too. He had been around some of the best racehorses there were and had never had one like this. American Pharoah had a security camera in his stall and sometimes, when he was away from the barn, Baffert dialed the livestream up on his phone to watch the colt and wonder what he did to deserve him. "He ships, he flies," he said. "There's no excuse. He just goes. He shows up. I've had horses that were maybe, on a given day, they were as fast as him, but they had a small window. His window has been wide open the whole time."

Silver Charm, Real Quiet, War Emblem, and Point Given — Baffert believed he had something to do with their success. He had brought them along, figured them out, and put them in a position to succeed. He thought Bode could have trained American Pharoah. He meant it when he said it. The colt had different mechanics, was so efficient with his stride, and so determined in competition. American Pharoah was a gift from the heavens and Baffert wanted to share him. He wanted to send him out as a horse for the ages.

Zayat wanted Baffert to consider a prep race at Churchill Downs, the D. Wayne Lukas Classic on September 26. It was a mile-and-an-eighth race, and the racetrack had agreed to offer a $1 million purse if American Pharoah showed up. Baffert instead persuaded him to allow him to let American Pharoah down for a month and then train him up to the Classic. It was a similar schedule he had employed to get the colt ready for the Rebel Stakes and his Triple Crown campaign. Baffert did agree to send the colt to Churchill Downs in October to complete his final training.

One of the positive outcomes of American Pharoah losing in the Travers was that the traffic through Baffert's barn virtually disappeared. No more lurkers trying to catch a glimpse of the Triple Crown champ. The Baffert barn had the horse back to themselves, even though they knew their days with the colt were numbered. American Pharoah's stall was near Jimmy Barnes's office, and he was the first horse Barnes checked in on each morning and the last he said good-bye to. He could not imagine the day the colt would be gone for good, or who might inherit his stall. Barnes knew it had to be a good one but that he would never find a better one.

Martin Garcia resumed his duties on the back of American Pharoah and at the other end of Baffert's radio. Over fourteen months, Garcia had ridden the colt nearly thirty miles in workouts and knew better than even Victor Espinoza what he was capable of. Zayat and Baffert had thanked him publicly after each race and he had been compensated, along with all of American Pharoah's team, with a percentage of the colt's purse winnings. Did he ever stay up at night and wonder why it was not him who was aboard the horse for his historic Triple Crown campaign? He had and had come to terms with the role he had played.

"It is what it is," he said. "Maybe with me on him, none of this would have happened."

The month-long vacation Baffert had planned for American Pharoah was cut short by a week. He had become aggressive in the morning and clearly wanted to return to work. Baffert brought him back on September 21, and again six days later — two easy breezes to clear his lungs out. Garcia was aboard him on the morning of October 3, 2015, when Baffert got the first signal that his plan to burnish the legacy of American Pharoah was on track. It was just after 6:30 a.m. and the sun was colliding with the San Gabriel Mountains, bathing Santa Anita in the sepia tones from another era. It was the third time Garcia had been on the colt since the Travers but the first time that he felt like the American Pharoah of the spring. His bay coat shimmered and was soft to the touch and the colt felt serene and strong beneath him. Garcia and American Pharoah clicked off a swift five-eighths of a mile in :59.80, but it was the gallop out that was more telling. For the first time in months, the colt was relaxed and reaching out with his stride, asking to do more. They galloped out three-quarters of a mile in 1:12.40 and seven-eighths in 1:25.80.

The real American Pharoah was back. Baffert had booked him on a flight to Louisville in two days, but he changed his plans. He had the colt the way he wanted him. He did not need to get on another airplane yet. The weather in California was beautiful, and

Kentucky was getting cold and wet. Routine. American Pharoah had one here.

"I got to trust my gut," Baffert said.

Besides, Baffert wanted to keep him close for a few more weeks. He knew once American Pharoah went to Kentucky, he was never coming back.

"I got to trust my gut," Baffert said.

CHAPTER NINETEEN: THE LAST WALTZ

October 31, 2015

In the pages of the *Daily Racing Form,* the past performances of his rivals showed that American Pharoah had his work cut out for him to win the Classic. Tonalist had won the previous year's Belmont Stakes and the Grade 1 Jockey Club Gold Cup four weeks ago in New York. Honor Code, also New York based, already had won the Grade 1 Metropolitan and Whitney handicaps. Gleneagles was here from Europe, where he had won the English and Irish 2,000 Guineas and the St. James's Palace Stakes. Beholder was the two-time American champion filly, and was a perfect five-for-five for the year. She had beaten the West Coast's best older male horses by more than eight lengths in the Pacific Classic at Del Mar. Keen Ice, the only horse to vanquish American Pharoah this year, was here, too.

As accomplished as those horses were,

however, they were no more than bit players in the drama that most wanted to see: the Coronation of American Pharoah. Baffert was certain the colt's last waltz was going to be a memorable one. The Travers loss had drained him of any fear. American Pharoah had not been at his best but had run gamely and barely got beat. Baffert survived, as did Espinoza and Zayat. The colt was fit and ready. In fact, after arriving here on the Tuesday before the race, Baffert acted not only like he was on a farewell tour but also as if he was here to play an exhibition game. He was proud of American Pharoah and wanted his contemporaries to know that he was a great horse.

"I just wanted to share him with my friends in the sport," he said.

He had been after Gary Stevens all summer to come by and get on American Pharoah, only because he knew how much his friend would appreciate the colt's effortless stride. Stevens did not think it was appropriate and refused the offer. One morning, he urged the trainer Todd Pletcher to grab a hold of American Pharoah's shank and walk with him.

"Even the way he walks, it's incredible mechanics," Baffert told him.

Either out of respect for Baffert or fearing

that something would go wrong, Pletcher declined to take the shank but agreed to walk alongside Baffert and the colt.

By Thursday, the chances of American Pharoah running away with the Classic increased, on paper at least, when Beholder had to be scratched from the race. She had shipped to Kentucky two weeks ago in preparation but spiked a fever as soon as she stepped off the plane. Her trainer, Richard Mandella, thought he had it under control but a scope of her lungs found blood, indicating that she had an infection. He did not want to put Beholder under the pressure of a race. Like American Pharoah, the mare had a high cruising speed and was expected to make him run early, as Frosted did in the Travers.

With her out of the race, that task fell to Smooth Roller, a late-developing four-year-old horse that had run away with the Grade 1 Awesome Again Stakes at Santa Anita Park. The morning of the race, however, Smooth Roller was scratched from the race by state veterinarians who had detected tendon problems in his left foreleg.

When Espinoza was told the horse had been scratched, he was matter-of-fact.

"Really?" he asked. "Oh, then, we are home free."

The Classic, with its field of eight, was its smallest since 1989 when Sunday Silence turned back rival Easy Goer for the third time. Really, there was only one horse that mattered in this edition of the Classic, and as Barnes led him into the paddock, the backyard of this usually stately racetrack erupted as if the Kentucky Wildcats had scored a touchdown nearby at Commonwealth Stadium.

American Pharoah circled the crush of people inside the paddock like an old pro. Zayat was looking at him admiringly as he passed and received either a message or omen from the colt.

"He literally stopped and looked at me and my family," he said. "Like I'm ready. I'm going to get it done. It's just . . . it was an incredible thrill."

When Espinoza arrived, he exchanged a glance with Baffert.

"He's sharp," is all the trainer had to say.

It had been a damp and overcast day, and it began to mist as the horses headed to the racetrack. The backyard and paddock drained like a bathtub as people went inside to make their bets and to return to their seats to see, they hoped, something extraordinary. Baffert was misting up as well.

"I've never been so damn emotional about

running a horse," he said.

"Stop crying," Jill Baffert told him.

They remained in the paddock, as did the Zayats and scores of other people — some they knew, most they didn't — who all wanted to be close if American Pharoah triumphed as they hoped. As American Pharoah and his seven rivals edged into the starting gate, Baffert and everyone else in this historic racetrack in the heart of the Bluegrass State became deafeningly quiet. You could hear deep breaths. Nothing much was at stake — except the legacy of a horse and the definition of greatness.

When the gates opened for a final time, Espinoza bounced American Pharoah out of the Number 4 hole and to the rail like they had been pulled by a magnet.

"Let him run, Victor!" Baffert said as he watched the big screen.

That is exactly what Espinoza had vowed to do. In each of his previous nine trips aboard American Pharoah, he had been careful to leave something in his tank, save a little something for the next race or the one after that. Even in Saratoga losing the Travers, Espinoza was careful not to push his colt for nothing. He knew American Pharoah was tired and vulnerable and rode him that way. Espinoza was on a two-prong mission — to keep American Pharoah safe and to let the colt go all out in his final spin around a racetrack.

He did not have to worry about fulfilling either one. He and American Pharoah were ahead by one length at the half-mile mark, three lengths at the three-quarter-mile mark, and five lengths when they hit the stretch. No other horse had gotten near him. It was the most boring and beautiful race that the 50,155 people on their feet and roaring had ever seen.

"I am gone," Espinoza told himself.

In the paddock, Zayat closed his eyes and refused to watch the final eighth of a mile. He knew this race, this run, was over and he was relieved, ecstatic, and sad all at once.

Zayat was hardly alone. In the past year, American Pharoah had made people remember that horse racing is America's oldest sport and that rare was the man, woman, or child who did not become short of breath when watching a racehorse running a hole in the wind. In a world filled with smartphones, brain-rattling NFL hits, and presidential debates as spectator sport, there is something soothing and old world about watching a horse rocket around an oval ahead of others just because he can. He reminded them that horse racing is an easy game to love and too often a hard one to like. Horses are beautiful animals. The humans around them mostly are, but in Thoroughbred racing particularly, the miscreants who drugged them, mistreated them, and traded them like commodities degrade the sport and create distrust.

American Pharoah made most people forget about the cheaters and the hard hearts. He restored the magic to horse racing. It was how he did it that was so mind blowing: bounding out of the gate, begging the other horses to chase him, hitting the ground with elegance and efficiency. When American Pharoah crossed the finish line six and a half lengths ahead of a 33-to-1 long shot named Effinex, he had nothing left to prove. He was triumphant and adored.

The colt had earned the sustained ovation that he received as Espinoza brought him back to the grandstand. He deserved the tears people spilled for him in the grandstand and the clubhouse here as well as in the living rooms around the nation.

When Espinoza finally got American Pharoah to the winner's circle, Baffert reached to offer his rider a handshake.

"We'll never have another son of a bitch

like this," he said.

No, they would not.

EPILOGUE

January 18, 2016

Two days after ending his racing career triumphantly in the Breeders' Cup Classic, American Pharoah was given a police escort to Ashford Stud to begin his career as a stallion. The Bafferts — Bob, Jill, and Bode — Jimmy Barnes, George Alvarez, and Eduardo Luna went with him to say their good-byes. He walked off the van and into his retirement shortly after 8:30 a.m. with a media throng looking on for one final time. Baffert kept a bag of baby carrots close and lovingly doled them out to the Triple Crown champ. He could not help feeling like a father dropping his child off at camp. He knew he was leaving American Pharoah in good hands and in a nice place, but it did not make the farewell any easier. When it was time to catch a plane home to California, Baffert leaned into American Pharoah for a final hug before the colt was led back to his barn to adjust to a quieter life.

He spent his initial weeks alongside Thunder Gulch, the 1995 Kentucky Derby and Belmont winner, now twenty-four years old. The old-timer's assignment was to teach American Pharoah about life not on the run. New stallions want to play and sprint a lot. If they have company, it only encourages them to do so. Not Thunder Gulch. He was there to teach American Pharoah the finer things in stallion life such as eating grass, whiling away an afternoon on the farm, and saving energy for the mares. Each day the colt was turned out into the fields at daylight, then brought in before lunch and groomed. When the breeding season begins each February, American Pharoah will perform his duties three times daily: at 7:30 in the morning, 1:30 in the afternoon, and 6:00 p.m. in the evening.

Initially, those will be lucrative assignations. Not long after arriving at Ashford, Coolmore set a stud fee of $200,000 for the first Triple Crown champion available to breeders since Seattle Slew died in 2002. There was no guarantee that American Pharoah would be able to pass on the same genetics that made him a horse for the ages, but the steep price hardly scared anyone away. Ashford had more than 200 applications for the 150 bookings it was allowing for American Pharoah's first season, which was more than enough to recoup its investment in the horse and make a handsome profit. Among them were some of the most accomplished mares in the sport, such as Take Charge Lady, the dam of 2013 champion three-year-old Will Take Charge and a War Front weanling filly who sold for a record $3.2 million at the Keeneland November sale; Charming, the dam of Take Charge Brandi, the champion two-year-old filly of 2014 who was sold for $6 million at the Keeneland at the same sale; and Rags to Riches, who in 2007 became the first filly since 1905 to win the Belmont Stakes.

On Saturday, December 19, Frances Relihan had a long-awaited reunion with American Pharoah at Ashford Stud. She had recently resigned as farm manager at Haras Don Alberto and was heading home to Ireland for the holidays to regroup before deciding on what was next for her in the horse business. It was a crisp, sunny morning, and American Pharoah looked magnificent and appeared to be settling nicely into farm life. It was the first one-on-one time she had with him in nearly two years and she thought he remained "full of class."

"I'd like to think he remembered me," she

said. "But it is enough to have had the opportunity as a farm manager to have watched him develop and mature as a young horse, before exceeding all imaginable expectations to become one of racing's all-time greats. To have this personal connection with him is of course very special. But I find myself equally humbled in his presence and in awe of him now as a lifetime racing fan."

American Pharoah also made an impact beyond the Thoroughbred industry. He was the overwhelming choice of sports fans to be named *Sports Illustrated*'s Sportsman of the Year, getting 47 percent of the vote — a total of 278,824 — and outpolling the World Series champion Kansas City Royals nearly 2 to 1. When the magazine editors instead named Serena Williams as its honoree, it touched off a noisy brouhaha that kept the debate alive for several days.

"Total BS," Justin Zayat tweeted. "Why have a poll if you totally ignore it? Serena FAILED at winning the Grand Slam. AP once-in-a-lifetime horse."

The Associated Press righted that wrong somewhat when its voters selected American Pharoah's Triple Crown sweep the sports story of the year. It was a clear winner over the "Deflategate" scandal that ensnared

Super Bowl–winning quarterback Tom Brady of the New England Patriots in allegations that he had directed the doctoring of his footballs.

Ahmed Zayat had not only campaigned a great horse, but also stabilized the finances of his business. He retained some shares in American Pharoah and was further rewarded when the stud fees of Pioneerof the Nile were more than doubled to $125,000 for 2016.

Baffert and Espinoza were on an extended victory lap through much of 2015, each picking up a variety of honors and enjoying the perks of fame. Baffert was the celebrity college football picker on ESPN's *College GameDay,* and Espinoza appeared on *Dancing with the Stars,* though it was evident whatever rhythm he had in the saddle didn't transfer to the ballroom. He was the second contestant voted off the show.

Both men had experienced a lifetime of memories over the previous year and were coming to terms with their roles in what American Pharoah accomplished.

For Baffert, it was simply getting the right horse at the right time. He had learned from mistakes on his three failed Triple Crown bids and had benefited from decades of training high-quality horses. When he was growing up, Baffert and his father, The Chief, were in agreement that Secretariat was the greatest horse they had ever seen. He would let other people decide where American Pharoah fit among the immortals, but Baffert was proud that his colt now belonged in the same sentence as Big Red.

"I never felt like I got to the bottom of Pharoah in a work or race," Baffert said. "He did everything effortlessly. It's the damnedest thing I have ever seen."

On January, 16, 2016, at Gulfstream Park in Hallandale, Florida, the Thoroughbred industry gathered for the forty-fifth annual Eclipse Awards and to celebrate one of the greatest years in the history of American horse racing. American Pharoah was the unanimous winner of Horse of the Year.

Baffert took honors for champion trainer and Zayat for owner and breeder. Espinoza inexplicably finished second in voting for champion jockey, but shrugged off the slight.

Espinoza did not need it. He pointed to his ride on the colt in the Kentucky Derby as the finest moment of his career. He thought they were going to lose and he was forced to push American Pharoah to give all he had.

"It was the hardest I ever rode in my

career," he said. "I earned the Triple Crown in that race. In my opinion, if anyone else had ridden American Pharoah, he would not have won the race and there would not be a Triple Crown."

ACKNOWLEDGMENTS

Only the incredibly fortunate get paid to hang out at a racetrack, and I have been among them for nearly two decades. I have made more friends than enemies there (though some will dispute that) and I am grateful to them all for being sources, educators, friends, drinking buddies, and fellow railbirds. There are far too many of you to namecheck, but from Saratoga to California, New York to Kentucky, and every other place where Thoroughbreds are revered, you know who you are. I thank you for making my life (if not exactly my bank account) richer.

I could not have spent as much time at the track, made as many friends, or learned as much about our nation's oldest sport without the indulgence and support of a succession of sports editors at the *New York Times,* Jason Stallman being the latest. Jason et al. have encouraged me to pursue many lines of reporting that have enriched my personal experiences and, I hope in some cases at least, our readers. I am proud to work alongside a talented bunch of editors and reporters in the Sports department. I'm gratified that many of them also are true friends. I need to offer a special shout-out to a couple of them. Melissa Hoppert joins me on the Triple Crown trail each year and appreciates the athletes and people as much as I do. Bob Goetz is equally adept at talking trainer trends and good stories. Fern Turkowitz, I miss you. Carl Nelson, the Big Fella, thank you and ——— ! You are an American Original.

My editor at Hachette Books, Mauro DiPreta, made this book better with his keen insights and deft editing touch. Thank you, Mauro — now we may move from horses and the racetrack to saints and the Vatican. Ashley Yancey at Hachette kept me on track and scolded me gently when I fell off it. I am lifted by the energy and enthusiasm that Betsy Hulsebosch, Hachette's director of marketing, had for this book. I appreciate the hard work she and the whole marketing and sales team continue to give it.

Hank Forcier is my friend, my lawyer, and one of the few people I have known personally who has hit trifectas at Rockingham Park as well as Churchill Downs. Besides making school drop-offs and Dads' Night Out far more fun and interesting, Hank helped me when I needed it most and put this deal together. Bob Curran has newspapers in his pedigree and horses in his blood. He kindly and bravely read the initial drafts of the book to make sure I was factually correct and stylistically defensible.

I am blessed to have good friends here in New York as well as Kansas City and Texas and other random places. You offer wise and not-so-wise advice, but mostly you make me think, laugh, and feel. Thank you.

I am bountifully blessed by a large, often unruly family of Drapes and Kennedys, which includes in-laws and out-laws, and nieces and nephews. You are not only big fun, but you have shown Jack Drape what the warm embrace of family means.

I love you all.

Mary Kennedy, I owe you everything. Jack, you got the best mom ever and, because of you both, I am the luckiest man in the world.

GLOSSARY OF
HORSE RACING TERMS

apprentice Rider who has not ridden a certain number of winners within a specified period of time. Also known as a "bug," from the asterisk used to denote the weight allowance such riders receive.

apprentice allowance Weight concession given to an apprentice rider: usually ten pounds until the fifth winner, seven pounds until the thirty-fifth winner and five pounds for one calendar year from the thirty-fifth winner. More rarely, a three-pound allowance is allowed to a rider under contract to a specific stable/owner for two years from his/her first win. This rule varies from state to state. Apprentices do not receive an allowance when riding in a stakes race. All jockeys going from track to track must have a receipt from the clerk of scales from their track verifying the jockeys' most recent total number of wins. Also known as a "bug," from the asterisk used to denote the weight allowance.

apron The (usually) paved area between the grandstand and the racing surface.

bay A horse color that varies from a yellow-tan to a bright auburn. The mane, tail, and lower portion of the legs are always black, except where white markings are present.

bit A stainless steel, rubber, or aluminum bar, attached to the bridle, which fits in the horse's mouth and is one of the means by which a jockey exerts guidance and control. The most common racing bit is the D-bit, named because the rings extending from the bar are shaped like the letter D. Most racing bits are "snaffled (snaffle bit)," which means the metal bar is made up of two pieces, connected in the middle, which leaves it free to swivel. Other bits may be used to correct specific problems, such as bearing in or out.

blaze A generic term describing a large, white vertical marking on a horse's face. The Jockey Club doesn't use blaze, preferring more descriptive words. Also known as snip; star; strip.

blinkers A cup-shaped device to limit a horse's vision to prevent him from swerving from objects or other horses on either side of it. Blinker cups come in a variety of sizes and shapes to allow as little or as much vision as the trainer feels is necessary.

breeze (breezing) Working a horse at a moderate speed.

claiming race A race in which each horse entered is eligible to be purchased at a set price. Claims must be made before the race and only by licensed owners or their agents who have a horse registered to race at that meeting or who have received a claim certificate from the stewards.

classic (1) A race of traditional importance. (2) Used to describe a distance. A race at the American classic distance, which is currently one and a quarter miles. The European classic distance is one and a half miles.

conformation The physical makeup of and bodily proportions of a horse; how it is put together.

cover A single breeding of a stallion to a mare. For example, "He covered seventy mares."

dam The female parent of a foal.

dam's sire (broodmare sire) The sire of a broodmare. Used in reference to the maternal grandsire of a foal.

dorsal displacement of the soft palate A

condition in which the soft palate, located on the floor of the airway near the larynx, moves up into the airway. A minor displacement causes a gurgling sound during exercise, while in more serious cases the palate can block the airway. This is sometimes known as "choking down," but the tongue does not actually block the airway. The base of the tongue is connected to the larynx, of which the epiglottis is a part. When the epiglottis is retracted, the soft palate can move up into the airway (dorsal displacement). This condition can sometimes be managed with equipment such as a figure-eight noseband or a tongue tie. In more extreme cases, surgery might be required, most commonly a "myectomy."

Eclipse Award Thoroughbred racing's year-end awards, honoring the top horses in eleven separate categories; the leading owner, trainer, jockey, apprentice jockey, and breeder, as well as members of the media who have demonstrated excellence in their coverage of the sport. Their namesake is Eclipse, the great eighteenth-century racehorse and sire who was undefeated in eighteen career starts and sired the winners of 344 races. Any Eclipse Award winner is referred to as a "champion."

fetlock (joint) Joint located between the cannon bone and the long pastern bone, also referred to as the "ankle."

graded race Established in 1973 to classify select stakes races in North America, at the request of European racing authorities, who had set up group races two years earlier. Always denoted with Roman numerals I, II, or III. Capitalized when used in race title (the Grade I Kentucky Derby). See *group race.*

group race Established in 1971 by racing organizations in Britain, France, Germany, and Italy to classify select stakes races outside North America. Collectively called "pattern races." Equivalent to North American graded races. Always denoted with Arabic numerals 1, 2, or 3. Capitalized when used in race title (the Group 1 Epsom Derby). See *graded race.*

handily (1) Working in the morning with maximum effort. (2) A horse racing well within itself, with little exertion from the jockey.

homebred A horse bred by its owner.

maiden race A race for horses that have not won a race.

quarter horse The American Quarter Horse is an American breed of horse that excels at sprinting short distances. Its name came from its ability to outdistance other horse breeds in races of a quarter mile or less.

shadow roll A (usually sheepskin) roll that is secured over the bridge of a horse's nose to keep it from seeing shadows on the track and shying away from or jumping them.

sire (1) The male parent. (2) To beget foals.

socks Solid white markings extending from the top of the hoofs to the ankles.

stakes A race for which the owner usually must pay a fee to run a horse. The fees can be for nominating, maintaining eligibility, entering, and starting, to which the track adds more money to make up the total purse. Some stakes races are by invitation and require no payment or fee.

stallion A male horse used for breeding.

stallion season The right to breed one mare to a particular stallion during one breeding season.

stallion share A lifetime breeding right to a stallion; one mare per season per share.

stick A jockey's whip.

stockings Solid white markings extending from the tops of the hoofs to the knees or hocks.

teaser A male horse used at breeding farms to determine whether a mare is ready to receive a stallion.

416

toe-in A conformation flaw in which the front of the foot faces in and looks pigeon-toed, often causing the leg to swing outward during locomotion ("paddling").

toe-out A conformation flaw in which the front of the foot faces out, often causing the leg to swing inward during locomotion ("winging").

Source: Equibase Company

■ ■ ■ ■

APPENDICES

■ ■ ■ ■

APPENDIX A:
THE PEDIGREE OF AMERICAN PHAROAH

AMERICAN PHAROAH
Bay Colt; foaled 2012

			Unbridled
		Empire Maker	Toussaud
	Pioneerof the Nile		Lord At War (ARG)
		Star of Goshen	Castle Eight
AMERICAN PHAROAH			Storm Cat
		Yankee Gentleman	Key Phrase
	Littleprincessemma (2006)		Ecliptical
		Exclusive Rosette	Zetta Jet

By PIONEEROF THE NILE (2006). Black-type winner of $1,634,200, CashCall
Futurity **[G1]** (HOL, $400,000), etc. Sire of 3 crops of racing age, 223 foals,
138 starters, 9 black-type winners, 85 winners of 172 races, earning
$16,195,735, including champion American Pharoah (Triple Crown,
$8,650,300, Breeders' Cup Classic **[G1]** (KEE, $2,750,000)-ntr, etc.),
Midnight Storm ($562,110, Del Mar Derby **[G2]** (DMR, $180,000), etc.),
Cairo Prince ($562,000, Holy Bull S. **[G2]** (GP, $240,000), etc.),
Jojo Warrior **[G2]** ($396,231).

1st dam
LITTLEPRINCESSEMMA, by Yankee Gentleman. Unplaced in 2 starts. Dam
of 3 registered foals, 2 of racing age, 2 to race, 2 winners--
   AMERICAN PHAROAH (c. by Pioneerof the Nile). Champion, see record.
   Xixixi (r. by Maimonides), 2 wins at 3, placed at 4, 2015, $83,299.

EXCLUSIVE ROSETTE, by Ecliptical. 3 wins at 2 and 3, $27,281, Florida Thoroughbred Charities S.-R (OTC, $15,000). Set ncr at Atlantic City, about 5 fur. in :57 1/5. Dam of 10 other foals, 9 to race, 8 winners, including—

STORM WOLF (c. by Stormin Fever). 3 wins in 5 starts at 3, $147,840, Lazaro Barrera Memorial S. **[G2]** (HOL, $90,000). Sire.

MISTY ROSETTE (f. by Stormin Fever). 4 wins in 8 starts at 2 and 3, $184,021, Old Hat S. **[G3]** (GP, $60,000), Crank It Up S. (MTH, $33,000), Sandpiper S. (TAM, $27,000), 3rd Darley Test S. **[G1]** (SAR, $25,000), Forward Gal S. **[G2]** (GP, $16,500). Producer.

Vintage Red. 2 wins at 3, $73,584. Dam of 5 winners, including—

Red Raffles (g. by Bold n' Flashy). 5 wins, 3 to 5, $309,125, in Canada, 2nd Vice Regent S.-R (WO, $25,000), etc. (Total: $290,530).

3rd dam

ZETTA JET, by Tri Jet. Dam of 10 foals, 8 to race, all winners, including—

EXCLUSIVE ROSETTE. Black-type winner, above.

4th dam

QUEEN ZETTA, by Crozier. Sister to **MIAMI SUN** ($277,365, sire), **MIA MOOD** ($74,815), **Miami Game**. Dam of 2 other foals to race, including— Plantation Queen. Winner at 2, $11,162. Producer.

RACE RECORD: At 2, champion 2-year-old colt, 2 wins (Del Mar Futurity **[G1]** (DMR, $180,000), FrontRunner S. **[G1]** (SA, $180,000)) in 3 starts: at 3, 2015, Triple Crown, 7 wins (Breeders' Cup Classic **[G1]** (KEE, $2,750,000)-ntr, 1 1/4 mi. in 2:00, Kentucky Derby **[G1]** (CD, $1,418,800), William Hill Haskell Invitational S. **[G1]** (MTH, $1,100,000), Xpressbet.com Preakness S. **[G1]** (PIM, $900,000), Belmont S. **[G1]** (BEL, $800,000), Arkansas Derby **[G1]** (OP, $600,000), Rebel S. **[G2]** (OP, $450,000)), once 2nd (Travers S. **[G1]** (SAR, $270,000)) in 8 starts. Totals: 9 wins, once 2nd in 11 starts. Earned $8,650,300.

Foaled in Kentucky.

APPENDIX B:
THE OFFICIAL CHART FOR
THE 2015 KENTUCKY DERBY

Kentucky Derby Presented by Yum! Brands (Grade I)

Purse: $2,000,000 Guaranteed

11th Race CHURCHILL DOWNS - Saturday, May 02, 2015

Stakes Track Condition: Fast

FOR THREE YEAR OLDS. With an entry fee of $25,000 each and a starting fee of $25,000 each. A minimum $500 jockey mount fee will apply to starters that finish beyond third place. Supplemental nominations may be made upon payment of $200,000 and in accordance with the rules set forth herein. All fees, including supplemental nominations, in excess of $900,000 in the aggregate shall be paid to the winner. Churchill Downs Racetrack (CDRT) shall guarantee a minimum gross purse of $2,000,000 (the "Guaranteed Purse"). The winner shall receive $1,240,000, second place shall receive $400,000, third place shall receive $200,000, fourth place shall receive $100,000 and fifth place shall receive $60,000 from the Guaranteed Purse (the Guaranteed Purse to each place to be divided equally in the event of a dead heat). Starters shall be named through the entry box on Wednesday, April 29, 2015, at 10:00 am Eastern Daylight Time (the "Closing"). CDRT, in its sole and absolute discretion, may set the number of starters up to a maximum of twenty (20) and the number of horses that are also-eligible to start up to a maximum of four (4). Colts and Geldings shall each carry a weight of one hundred twenty six (126) pounds; Fillies shall each carry one hundred twenty one (121) pounds. Supplemental Nominees may enter and will be treated equal to any Original Nominee without preference of one over the other. If the number of nominees exceeds the number of available starting positions and also-eligible positions set by CDRT (the "Number of Starting and AE Positions") at the Closing, these conditions shall be applied to determine which nominees will be allowed to start and which nominees shall be designated as also-eligible to start. In the event that more than the Number of Starting and AE Positions pass through the entry box at the Closing, the starters and also-eligible horses shall be determined at the Closing from Original Nominees and Supplemental Nominees if starting and/or also-eligible positions are still available, with preference given to those horses that have accumulated the most points pursuant to the Road to the Kentucky Derby Point System. For purposes of this preference, the Road to the Kentucky Derby Point System shall mean the point values assigned to the first four finishing positions in each race comprising the Road to the Kentucky Derby as published by Churchill Downs Racetrack.

Notwithstanding the foregoing, CDRT may, at its sole discretion, allocate one or more starting and/or also-eligible positions or otherwise give preference to winners of a designated race or races provided, however, that any such designated race or races may not include restrictive provisions relative to which a horse may enter such race or races, other than by sex or age. In the event of any ties resulting from the Road to the Kentucky Derby Point System or should additional horses be needed to bring the field to the Number of Starting and AE Positions, the remaining starters and also-eligible horses shall be determined at the Closing with preference given to those horses that have accumulated the highest earnings in non-restricted sweepstakes. For purposes of this preference, a "non-restricted sweepstakes" shall mean those sweepstakes whose conditions contain no restrictions other than that of age or sex. In the case of remaining ties resulting from preferences or otherwise, the additional starter(s) and/or also-eligible horses shall be determined by lot. Any horse excluded from running because of the aforementioned preference(s) shall be refunded the $25,000 entry fee and the $200,000 supplemental fee, if applicable. After the Closing, CDRT shall designate in order of preference the nominees that are also-eligible to start in accordance with these conditions ("Also Eligible Horses"). If a starter is scratched from the Kentucky Derby before 9:00 a.m (Eastern Standard Time or EST) on Friday, May 1, 2015 ("Scratch Deadline"), then the Also Eligible Horse with the highest preference (if any) as determined by these conditions shall become a starter. All starters and Also Eligible Horses must be stabled at Churchill Downs by 8:00 a.m. on Wednesday, April 29, 2015 Post positions shall be determined by a nontransferable lot number being drawn for each horse named as a starter at the Closing. The lot number drawn for each starter shall determine the post position of such starter. Horses having common ties through ownership or training shall each be treated separately for purposes of determining post position. In the event of one or more scratches after the determination of post positions and prior to the Scratch Deadline, then (i) starters with post positions higher than the post position of the scratched starter will be moved to the next lowest empty post position (i.e. toward the inside rail of the

Available Money: $2,178,800

Value of Race: $2,178,800 1st $1,418,800, 2nd $400,000, 3rd $200,000, 4th $100,000, 5th $60,000

Pgm	Horse Name (Earned)	Last Race	S/A	Wgt	Med	Eqp	Odds	PP	1/4	1/2	3/4	1m	Str	Fin	Jockey
18	American Pharoah ($1,418,800)	11Apr15 OP 11	c 3	126	L		*2.90	15	$3\frac{1}{2}$	3hd	$3\frac{1}{2}$	3^3	1hd	1^1	Victor Espinoza
10	Firing Line ($400,000)	22Mar15 Sun 11	c 3	126	L		9.50	9	2^1	2^1	2^1	2hd	$2\frac{1}{2}$	2^2	Gary Stevens
8	Dortmund ($200,000)	04Apr15 SA 8	c 3	126	L		4.30	7	1hd	1^1	$1\frac{1}{2}$	1hd	3^4	3nk	Martin Garcia
15	Frosted ($100,000)	04Apr15 Aqu 10	c 3	126	L	b	10.30	12	14^2	$14\frac{1}{2}$	15^1	$7\frac{1}{2}$	$4\frac{1}{2}$	$4^3\frac{1}{2}$	Joel Rosario
5	Danzig Moon ($60,000)	04Apr15 Kee 10	c 3	126	L	b	22.60	5	6hd	$6\frac{1}{2}$	5^1	4^2	5^3	$5^1\frac{1}{4}$	Julien Leparoux
3	Materiality	28Mar15 GP 14	c 3	126	L		11.50	3	13^1	$13\frac{1}{2}$	14^1	17hd	13hd	6^1	Javier Castellano
14	Keen Ice	28Mar15 FG 11	c 3	126	L		45.80	11	17^2	17^2	16^1	$12\frac{1}{2}$	14^1	$7\frac{3}{4}$	Kent Desormeaux
6	Mubtaahij (IRE)	28Mar15 Mey	c 3	126			14.40	6	12^2	10^1	$9\frac{1}{2}$	9^2	$6^2\frac{1}{2}$	$8\frac{3}{4}$	Christophe Soumillon
13	Itsaknockout	28Mar15 GP 14	c 3	126	L		30.60	10	$11\frac{1}{2}$	12^2	$13\frac{1}{2}$	11hd	10^2	$9\frac{3}{4}$	Luis Saez
2	Carpe Diem	04Apr15 Kee 10	c 3	126	L		7.70	2	$5\frac{1}{2}$	$4\frac{1}{2}$	4^2	$6\frac{1}{2}$	$8\frac{1}{2}$	10^1	John Velazquez
21	Frammento	04Apr15 Kee 10	c 3	126	L	b	69.50	18	16hd	$16\frac{1}{2}$	$17^1\frac{1}{2}$	$13\frac{1}{2}$	11hd	$11\frac{1}{2}$	Corey Nakatani
9	Bolo	04Apr15 SA 8	c 3	126	L		31.90	8	4hd	5hd	$6\frac{1}{2}$	$8\frac{1}{2}$	9^1	$12^2\frac{1}{2}$	Rafael Bejarano
17	Mr. Z	11Apr15 OP 11	c 3	126	L		36.60	14	$7\frac{1}{2}$	$7\frac{1}{2}$	8hd	10^1	12hd	13hd	Ramon Vazquez
1	Ocho Ocho Ocho	04Apr15 Kee 10	c 3	126	L		26.10	1	$8\frac{1}{2}$	8^1	7^2	5^1	$7\frac{1}{2}$	14hd	Elvis Trujillo
20	Far Right	11Apr15 OP 11	r 3	126	L		39.20	17	18	18	18	16hd	16^4	$15^3\frac{1}{2}$	Mike Smith
16	War Story	28Mar15 FG 11	g 3	126	L		45.30	13	$15^2\frac{1}{2}$	$15^2\frac{1}{2}$	$12\frac{1}{2}$	$15\frac{1}{2}$	15^2	$16^{15}\frac{1}{2}$	Joseph Talamo
4	Tencendur	04Apr15 Aqu 10	c 3	126	L	b	52.30	4	$10\frac{1}{2}$	$9\frac{1}{2}$	10hd	18	18	$17^{25}\frac{1}{2}$	Manuel Franco
19	Upstart	28Mar15 GP 14	r 3	126	L		15.70	16	9hd	$11\frac{1}{2}$	$11^1\frac{1}{2}$	14^1	17^1	18	Jose Ortiz

Off Time: 6:43

Fractional Times: :23.24 :47.34 1:11.29 1:36.45 2:03.02

Start: 3,15   Track: Fast   Weather: Clear

Mutuel Payoffs

18	American Pharoah	7.80	5.80	4.20			
10	Firing Line		8.40	5.40			
8	Dortmund			4.20			

Total WPS Pool: $56,536,752

$1 Pick 3 (4-5-18)	$105.60	Total Pool:	$1,241,298
50 Cent Pick 3	$84.80	Total Pool:	$830,113
(OAKS/WDFRD/DERBY 7-5-18)			
$1 Pick 4 (3-4-4/5/6/8-18)	$1,054.90	Total Pool:	$2,827,330
50 Cent Pick 5 (3-3-4-4/5/6/8-18)	$2,452.90	Total Pool:	$1,532,280
$2 Pick 6 (11-3-3-4-4/5/6/8-18)	$64,925.60	Total Pool:	$1,089,971
$2 Pick 6 (11-3-3-4-4/5/6/8-18)	$561.20	Total Pool:	
10 Cent Pick 7 Jackpot	$27,767.83	Total Pool:	$140,006
(6-11-3-3-4-4/5/6/8-18)			
$1 Daily Double (5-18)	$21.20	Total Pool:	$1,025,842
$1 Daily Double (OAKS/DERBY 7-18)	$27.30	Total Pool:	$2,562,510
$2 Exacta (18-10)	$72.60	Total Pool:	$24,287,575
50 Cent Consolation Pick 3	$25.20	Total Pool:	
(OAKS/WDFRD/DERBY 7-5-12)			
50 Cent Consolation Pick 3	$3.20	Total Pool:	
(OAKS/WDFRD/DERBY 7-8-12)			
50 Cent Consolation Pick 3	$9.60	Total Pool:	
(OAKS/WDFRD/DERBY 7-8-18)			
$2 Future Wager (EXACTA POOL 1 - 1-24)	$58.00	Total Pool:	$8,093
$2 Future Wager (EXACTA POOL 2 - 1-24)	$96.80	Total Pool:	$108,472
$2 Future Wager (EXACTA POOL 3 - 1-24)	$123.80	Total Pool:	$121,927
$2 Future Wager (EXACTA POOL 4 - 1-24)	$109.80	Total Pool:	$144,456

$2 Future Wager (POOL 1 - 1)	$27.00	Total Pool:	$163,492
$2 Future Wager (POOL 2 - 1)	$23.00	Total Pool:	$340,126
$2 Future Wager (POOL 3 - 1)	$18.20	Total Pool:	$300,403
$2 Future Wager (POOL 4 - 1)	$13.00	Total Pool:	$273,016
10 Cent Superfecta (18-10-3-15)	$63.41	Total Pool:	$13,250,865
$1 Super High Five (18-10-3-15-5)	$6,658.30	Total Pool:	$583,474
$2 Trifecta (18-10-8)	$202.00	Total Pool:	$30,749,967
$1 Consolation Double (OAKS/DERBY 7-12)	$7.20	Total Pool:	

Winner: American Pharoah, Bay Colt by Pioneerof the Nile - Littleprincessemma Bred in Kentucky

AMERICAN PHAROAH in range 5w,edge up 5/8,5w bid 5/16,duel,led 1/8,brush,driving FIRING LINE prompted 3wd,bid between,led past 5/16,duel,drifted late,brushed DORTMUND quickly to front,towards inside,joined 3/8,battled to 1/8,willing FROSTED rank,rate back start,angled 3/4,sweeping 5wd move,churned on late DANZIG MOON exchanged bumps,in tight 1m out,chase,3w move 5/16,bid,flattened MATERIALITY hesitated start,off pace 4wd,shifted in with run 3/16,recovered KEEN ICE dove to rail,settled,advance 5/16,wait 5wd upper,altered,bump,bid MUBTAAHIJ (IRE) rate back between,angled in,hard ride chasing 5/16, toiled on ITSAKNOCKOUT steadied 1m,angled 3/4,3wd between 1/2,5-6wd upper,no rally CARPE DIEM firm hold saving ground,moved 2wd,chased,mild move 1/2,flattened FRAMMENTO lagged back,7wd upper stretch,bumped late stretch,no factor BOLO exchanged bumps,in tight early,chase 3wd,faded,steady late MR. Z checked repeatedly off heels 1m,chased 4-5wd,gave way 5/16 OCHO OCHO OCHO hard hold along rail early,asked 1/2,slight move 3/8,angle,weaken FAR RIGHT unhurried off rail, very wider upper stretch, no headway WAR STORY steadied, in close between early, angled to rail, no impact TENCENDUR saved ground chasing pace, dropped back 2nd turn UPSTART 4 wide 1st turn, stopped after mile, eased, walked off

Owners: (18) Zayat Stables, LLC; (10) Arnold Zetcher LLC; (8) Kaleem Shah, Inc.; (15) Godolphin Racing LLC; (5) John C. Oxley; (3) Alto Racing, LLC; (14) Donegal Racing; (6) Essafinaat Limited; (13) Starlight Racing; (2) WinStar Farm LLC and Stonestreet Stables LLC; (21) Mossarosa; (9) Golden Pegasus Racing, Inc. and Mack, Earle I.; (17) Zayat Stables, LLC; (1) DP Racing, LLC; (20) LaPenta, Robert V. and Rosenblum, Harry T.; (16) Loooch Racing Stables, Inc., Ellis, Glenn K. and Dunn, Christopher T.; (4) Philip S. Birsh; (19) Evans, Ralph M. and WinStar Farm LLC, Lessee

Trainers: (18) Bob Baffert; (10) Simon Callaghan; (8) Bob Baffert; (15) Kiaran McLaughlin; (5) Mark Casse; (3) Todd Pletcher; (14) Dale Romans; (6) Michael de Kock; (13) Todd Pletcher; (2) Todd Pletcher; (21) Nicholas Zito; (9) Carla Gaines; (17) D. Lukas; (1) James Cassidy; (20) Ron Moquett; (16) Thomas Amoss; (4) George Weaver; (19) Richard Violette, Jr.

Late Scratches: Tale of Verve; El Kabeir; International Star; Stanford

APPENDIX C:
THE OFFICIAL CHART FOR
THE 2015 PREAKNESS STAKES

Xpressbet.com Preakness S. (Grade I)
Purse: $1,500,000 Guaranteed

13th Race PIMLICO - Saturday, May 16, 2015

Stakes   Track Condition: Sloppy

For three-year-olds. $15,000 to pass the entry box, starters to pay $15,000 additional. 60% of the purse to the winner, 20% to second, 11% to third, 6% to fourth and 3% to fifth. Weight 126 pounds for Colts and Geldings, 121 pounds for Fillies. A replica of the Woodlawn Vase will be presented to the winning owner to remain his or her personal property. 1 3/16 Miles (Run Up 50 Feet)

Available Money: $1,500,000

Value of Race: $1,500,000 1st $900,000, 2nd $300,000, 3rd $165,000, 4th $90,000, 5th $45,000

Pgm	Horse Name (Earned)	Last Race	S/A	Wgt	Med	Eqp	Odds	PP	ST	1/4	1/2	3/4	Str	Fin	Jockey
1	American Pharoah ($900,000)	02May15 CD 11	c3	126	L		*0.90	1	5	1^1	$1^{2\frac{1}{2}}$	$1^{1\frac{1}{2}}$	1^4	1^7	Victor Espinoza
5	Tale of Verve ($300,000)	23Apr15 Kee 3	c3	126	L		28.50	5	6	8	8	5^2	$4^{\frac{1}{2}}$	2^1	Joel Rosario
7	Divining Rod ($165,000)	11Apr15 Kee 10	c3	126	L		12.60	7	7	4^1	$4^{3\frac{1}{2}}$	4^8	2^3	$3^{7\frac{1}{2}}$	Javier Castellano
2	Dortmund ($90,000)	02May15 CD 11	c3	126	L		4.50	2	4	$3^{1\frac{1}{2}}$	3^2	$3^{3\frac{1}{2}}$	3^1	$4^{1\frac{1}{2}}$	Martin Garcia
3	Mr. Z ($45,000)	02May15 CD 11	c3	126		b	16.40	3	2	2^4	2^3	$2^{2\frac{1}{2}}$	5^6	5^1	Corey Nakatani
4	Danzig Moon	02May15 CD 11	c3	126		b	13.40	4	3	$7^{5\frac{1}{2}}$	7^4	7^2	6^8	$6^{26\frac{3}{4}}$	Julien Leparoux
8	Firing Line	02May15 CD 11	c3	126	L		3.00	8	8	6^1	$5^{2\frac{1}{2}}$	6^1	7^7	$7^{3\frac{3}{4}}$	Gary Stevens
6	Bodhisattva	18Apr15 Pim 9	c3	126	L	bf	29.90	6	1	$5^{2\frac{1}{2}}$	6^2	8	8	8	Trevor McCarthy

Off Time: 6:21

Start: 8

Fractional Times: :22.90   :46.49   1:11.42   1:37.74   1:58.46

Weather: Rainy   **Track:** Sloppy

Mutuel Payoffs

1	American Pharoah	3.80	3.40	2.80
5	Tale of Verve		19.00	8.80
7	Divining Rod			5.20

50 Cent Pick 3 (2-2-1) $35.10   Total Pool: $656,312
50 Cent Pick 4 (9-2-2-1) $269.35   Total Pool: $2,433,241
50 Cent Pick 5 (5/7/8-9-2-2-1) $1,144.85   Total Pool: $1,423,287
10 Cent Pick 6 Jackpot

Total WPS Pool: $10,502,706

(13-5/7/8-9-2-2-1)

$2 Daily Double (2-1)		Total Pool:	$557,000
$2 Daily Double (BLK EYED SUSAN/PREAKNESS 9-1)		Total Pool:	$672,521
$2 Exacta (1-5)		Total Pool:	$124.40 ... $9,013,256
$1 Superfecta (1-5-7-2)		Total Pool:	$1,906.90 ... $6,485,174
$2 Trifecta (1-5-7)		Total Pool:	$985.00 ... $11,682,912

Winner: American Pharoah, Bay Colt by Pioneerof the Nile - Littleprincessemma Bred in Kentucky

AMERICAN PHAROAH clear into first turn, pace 2 wide 1/4, asked 3/16, ridden out TALE OF VERVE no speed, 2 wide 1/4, 4 wide 3/16, altered in 1/16, rallied DIVINING ROD rail move far turn, 3 wide 1/4, drifted out 1/16, weakened DORTMUND rated back,rail first turn, angled 3/4, 4 wide move 3/8, faltered MR. Z outside winner early, rebid 3 wide 3-1/2, angled in 1/4, tired DANZIG MOON rail, steadied 7-1/2, well back, 3 wide 1/4, no factor FIRING LINE stumbled start, 4 wide first turn, no factor, eased stretch BODHISATTVA some early speed, 2 wide first turn, done 1/2, eased

Owners: (1) Zayat Stables, LLC; (5) Charles E. Fipke; (7) Lael Stables; (2) Kaleem Shah, Inc.; (3) Calumet Farm; (4) John C. Oxley; (8) Arnold Zetcher LLC; (6) Jose Corrales

Trainers: (1) Bob Baffert; (5) Dallas Stewart; (7) Arnaud Delacour; (2) Bob Baffert; (3) D. Lukas; (4) Mark Casse; (8) Simon Callaghan; (6) Jose Corrales

APPENDIX D:
THE OFFICIAL CHART FOR
THE 2015 BELMONT STAKES

Belmont S. presented by DraftKings (Grade I)

Purse: $1,500,000 Guaranteed

11th Race BELMONT PARK - Saturday, June 06, 2015

Stakes Track Condition: Fast

FOR THREE YEAR OLDS. By subscription of $600 each, to accompany the nomination, if made on or before January 17, 2015, or $6,000, if made on or before March 23, 2015. At any time prior to the closing time of entries, horses may be nominated to The Belmont Stakes upon payment of a supplementary fee of $75,000 to the New York Racing Association, Inc. $15,000 to pass the entry box and $15,000 additional to start. All entrants will be required to pay entry and starting fees; but no fees, supplemental or otherwise shall be added to the purse. The purse to be divided $800,000 to the winner, $280,000 to second, $150,000 to third, $100,000 to fourth, $60,000 to fifth, $45,000 to sixth, $35,000 to seventh and $30,000 to eighth. Colts and Geldings, 126 lbs.; Fillies, 121 lbs. The winning owner will be presented with the August Belmont Memorial Cup to be retained for one year as well as a trophy for permanent possession and trophies to the winning trainer and jockey. 1 1/2 Miles (Run Up 68 Feet)

Available Money: $1,500,000

Value of Race: $1,500,000 1st $800,000, 2nd $280,000, 3rd $150,000, 4th $100,000, 5th $60,000, 6th $45,000, 7th $35,000, 8th $30,000

Pgm	Horse Name (Earned)	Last Race	S/A	Wgt	Med	Eqp	Odds	PP	1/4	1/2	1m	1 1/4	Str	Fin	Jockey
5	American Pharoah ($800,000)	16May15 Pim 13	c3	126	L	a	*0.75	5	1¹	1½	1½	1²	1²½	15½	Victor Espinoza
6	Frosted ($280,000)	02May15 CD 11	c3	126	L		4.10	6	3hd	5hd	5¹	2⁴	2⁴	2²	Joel Rosario
7	Keen Ice ($150,000)	02May15 CD 11	c3	126	L		17.20	7	5½	4½	4hd	5¹	4²	3nk	Kent Desormeaux
1	Mubtaahij (IRE) ($100,000)	02May15 CD 11	c3	126			14.10	1	4½	3hd	3¹	3³	3¹½	4⁷½	Irad Ortiz, Jr.
4	Frammento ($60,000)	02May15 CD 11	c3	126	L		21.70	4	8	8	7hd	4½	5⁴	5²½	Mike Smith
3	Madefromlucky ($45,000)	09May15 Bel 3	c3	126	L		14.60	3	6⁴	6³½	6²	6¹	6¹½	6²½	Javier Castellano
2	Tale of Verve ($35,000)	16May15 Pim 13	c3	126	L		19.90	2	7²	7½	8	8	7¹½	7¹½	Gary Stevens
8	Materiality ($30,000)	02May15 CD 11	c3	126	L		5.40	8	2½	2¹	2nd	7hd	8	8	John Velazquez

Fractional Times: .24.06 .48.83 1:13.41 1:37.99 2:26.65

Weather: Clear

Off Time: 6:52

Start: Good for all   Track: Fast

Mutuel Payoffs

5	American Pharoah	3.50	2.80	2.50
6	Frosted		3.50	2.90

$2 Pick 3 (9-7-5)	$503.00	Total Pool: $1,085,893
$2 Pick 4 (9-9-7-5)	$4,595.00	Total Pool: $4,060,635

Total WPS Pool: $29,139,175

$2 Pick 6 (1/2/11-6-9-9-7-5)	$908.00	Total Pool: $756,482
$2 Daily Double ((BEL GOLD CUP-BELMONT STAKES))	$15.00	Total Pool:
$2 Daily Double (7-5)	$71.50	Total Pool: $879,266
$2 Exacta (5-6)	$13.60	Total Pool: $14,720,160
$2 Superfecta (5-6-7-1)	$570.00	Total Pool: $10,353,238
$2 Trifecta (5-6-7)	$109.50	Total Pool: $19,593,860

Winner: American Pharoah, Bay Colt by Pioneerof the Nile - Littleprincessemma Bred in Kentucky

AMERICAN PHAROAH quick control,rate kind ins,let out,drew clr FROSTED well reserve 2p to 1/4,rail on 2nd,angle out upper,no match KEEN ICE 3-4w to 1/4,swung 5w into lane, rallied to get up for show MUBTAAHIJ (IRE) track ins,light hand urge,tip 2p 1/2,had no rally FRAMMENTO quick tuck rail,rail run 2nd,urged 4w into lane, no headway MADEFROMLUCKY 3w 1st, hung out 4w & asked 2nd turn, tired TALE OF VERVE off inside,asked 2nd,cut corner into lane, empty MATERIALITY 3w turns, attended 2p, gave way

Owners: (5) Zayat Stables, LLC; (6) Godolphin Racing LLC; (7) Donegal Racing; (1) Essafinaat; (4) Mossarosa; (3) Cheyenne Stables LLC and Nichol, Mac; (2) Charles E. Fipke; (8) Alto Racing, LLC

Trainers: (5) Bob Baffert; (6) Kiaran McLaughlin; (7) Dale Romans; (1) Michael de Kock; (4) Nicholas Zito; (3) Todd Pletcher; (2) Dallas Stewart; (8) Todd Pletcher

APPENDIX E:
THE OFFICIAL CHART FOR
THE 2015 BREEDERS' CUP
CLASSIC

Breeders' Cup Classic (Grade I)
Purse: $5,000,000 Guaranteed

11th Race KEENELAND - Saturday, October 31, 2015

Stakes Track Condition: Fast

FOR THREE-YEAR-OLDS AND UPWARD. Northern Hemisphere Three-Year-Olds, 122 lbs.; Older, 126 lbs.; Southern Hemisphere Three-Year-Olds, 117 lbs.; Older, 126 lbs. All Fillies and Mares allowed 3 lbs. $50,000 to pre-enter, $50,000 to enter, with guaranteed $5 million purse including travel awards of which 55% to the owner of the winner, 18% to second, 10% to third, 6% to fourth and 3% to fifth; plus travel awards to starters not based in Kentucky. 1 1/4 Miles (Run Up 34 Feet)

Available Money: $5,000,000

Value of Race: $4,550,000 1st $2,750,000, 2nd $900,000, 3rd $500,000, 4th $300,000, 5th $100,000

Pgm	Horse Name (Earned)	Last Race	S/A	Wgt	Med	Eqp	Odds	PP	1/4	1/2	3/4	1m	Str	Fin	Jockey
4	American Pharoah ($2,750,000)	29Aug15 Sar 11	c 3	122	L		*0.70	4	1 1	1 1	1 2	1 3½	1 5	1 6½	Victor Espinoza
6	Effinex ($900,000)	03Oct15 Bel 10	c 4	126	L	b	33.00	6	2 2½	2 3	2 1	2 2	2 3½	2 4¼	Mike Smith
9	Honor Code ($500,000)	03Oct15 Bel 5	r 4	126	L		4.70	8	8	8	8	5½	5 1½	3 1½	Javier Castellano
2	Keen Ice ($300,000)	29Aug15 Sar 11	c 3	122	L		9.70	2	5 1½	5 1½	5½	7 2	6 hd	4 ns	Irad Ortiz, Jr.
1	Tonalist ($100,000)	03Oct15 Bel 10	c 4	126	L	f	6.00	1	3 1½	3 hd	4 6½	4 4	4 2	5 ns	John Velazquez
8	Hard Aces	26Sep15 SA 10	h 5	126	L	b	72.80	7	7 3	7 5	6½	6 1	7 4	6 hd	Joseph Talamo
3	Frosted	19Sep15 Prx 10	c 3	122	L	b	11.30	3	4 1½	4 4½	3 hd	3 1	3 3½	7 12½	Joel Rosario
5	Gleneagles (IRE)	17Oct15 Asc	c 3	122	L		11.10	5	6 hd	6½	7 2½	8	8	8	Ryan Moore

Off Time: 5:52

Start: 5   **Track: Fast**

Fractional Times: :23.99   :47.50   1:11.21   1:35.47   2:00.07

Weather: Cloudy

Mutuel Payoffs

Pgm	Horse			
4	American Pharoah	3.40	3.00	2.40
6	Effinex		14.20	6.60
9	Honor Code			3.40

$2 Pick 3 (13-9-4)		$453.00	Total Pool: $846,773
50 Cent Pick 4 (7-13-9-4/7/10)		$765.00	Total Pool: $3,802,438

Total WPS Pool: $6,269,156

$2 Pick 6 (11-5/13-7-13-9-4/7/10)	$674.40	Total Pool:	
$2 Daily Double (9-4)	$45.60	Total Pool:	$832,209
$2 Daily Double (DISTAFF/CLASSIC 4-4)	$14.00	Total Pool:	$705,623
$2 Exacta (4-6)	$76.40	Total Pool:	$4,553,714
$2 Superfecta (4-6-9-2)	$1,224.00	Total Pool:	$2,411,198
$1 Super High Five (4-6-9-2-1)	$1,715.10	Total Pool:	$290,125
$2 Trifecta (4-6-9)	$322.60	Total Pool:	$4,070,105
$2 Consolation Double (DISTAFF/CLASSIC 4-7)	$6.40	Total Pool:	

Winner: American Pharoah, Bay Colt by Pioneerof the Nile - Littleprincessemma Bred in Kentucky

AMERICAN PHAROAH opened clear, tucked in, responded gallantly, widened EFFINEX shadowed leader 3w, moved in kind, unable to make headway HONOR CODE settled, tail of field, roused 7/16, sweeping move 5w, willingly KEEN ICE rated back, shifted out, under pressure, angled in, belatedly TONALIST rank to place inside, bumped, hit rail, flattened HARD ACES allowed to settle, 4w, came under a ride, lacked a response FROSTED settled in hand, bid between horses, bumped 5/16, faltered GLENEAGLES (IRE) off slow, angled in, saved ground, no factor

Owners: (4) Zayat Stables, LLC; (6) Tri-Bone Stables; (9) Lane's End Racing, Dell Ridge Farm LLC and Teresa Viola Racing; (2) Donegal Racing; (1) Robert S. Evans; (8) Hronis Racing LLC; (3) Godolphin Racing LLC; (5) Tabor, Michael B., Magnier, Mrs. John, and Smith, Derrick

Trainers: (4) Bob Baffert; (6) James Jerkens; (9) Claude McGaughey III; (2) Dale Romans; (1) Christophe Clement; (8) John Sadler; (3) Kiaran McLaughlin; (5) Aidan O'Brien

Late Scratches: Beholder; Smooth Roller

APPENDIX F:
AMERICAN PHAROAH'S
LIFETIME PAST
PERFORMANCES

Lifetime Past Performance for American Pharoah

Powered By EQUIBASE COMPANY

In United States

Year	Age	Starts	1st	2nd	3rd	Earnings (USA$)
2014	2	3	2(2)	0	0	$361,500
2015	3	8	7(7)	1	0	$8,288,800
Totals		11	9(9)	1	0	$8,650,300
			(BlkType)			

Owner: Zayat Stables, LLC
Trainer: Bob Baffert
Owner & trainer as of 10/31/15

American Pharoah

Bay Colt by Pioneerof the Nile (06) -- Littleprincessemma (06) by Yankee Gentleman (99) -- Bred in KY by Zayat Stables (Feb 02, 2012)
(SPR=99; CPI=172.5)

Date	#Track	Dist	Run Up	Temp Rail	Splits	Type/Value/Clm		Points of Call	Jockey	W	First Three Finishers	Comments	Earned (USA$)
103115	11KEE	ft 1¼m	34		47^{50} $1{:}35^{47}$ $2{:}00^{07}$	BCClasicG1	118	4 1^{1} $1^{3\frac{1}{2}}$ 1^{5} $1^{6\frac{1}{2}}$	EspinozaV	122 L *0.70	American Pharoah$^{6\frac{1}{2}}$,Effinex$^{4\frac{1}{2}}$,Honor Code$^{1\frac{1}{2}}$	gallantly, widened	$2,750,000
082915	11SAR	ft 1¼m	48		48^{30} $1{:}35^{08}$ $2{:}01^{57}$	TraversG1	110	2 $1^{\frac{1}{2}}$ 2^{hd} $1^{\frac{1}{2}}$ $2^{\frac{3}{4}}$	EspinozaV	126 L *0.35	Keen Ice$^{\frac{3}{4}}$,American Pharoah$^{2\frac{1}{4}}$,Frosted$^{2\frac{1}{2}}$	repelld foe1/8,caught	$270,000
080215	12MTH	ft 1⅛m	56		46^{14} $1{:}09^{60}$ $1{:}47^{95}$	HskllnvG1	112	3 1 2^{1} 2^{1} 1^{5} $1^{2\frac{1}{4}}$	EspinozaV	122 L *0.10	American Pharoah$^{2\frac{1}{4}}$,Keen Ice^{3},Upstart$^{3\frac{1}{2}}$	took charge, easily	$1,100,000
060615	11BEL	ft 1½m	80		48^{83} $1{:}37^{99}$ $2{:}26^{65}$	BelmontG1	112	5 1^{1} 1^{2} 1^{3} $1^{5\frac{1}{2}}$	EspinozaV	126 L *0.75	American Pharoah$^{5\frac{1}{2}}$,Frosted^{2},Keen Ice^{nk}	ins,ask upr,drew clr	$800,000
051615	13PIM	sy 1$\frac{3}{16}$m	50		46^{49} $1{:}11^{42}$ $1{:}58^{46}$	PrknssG1	111	1 5 $1^{2\frac{1}{2}}$ $1^{1\frac{1}{2}}$ 1^{4} 1^{7}	EspinozaV	126 L *0.90	American Pharoah^{7},Tale of Verve^{1},Divining Rod$^{7\frac{1}{2}}$	ridden out	$900,000
050215	11CD	ft 1¼m	34		47^{34} $1{:}36^{45}$ $2{:}03^{02}$	KyDbyG1	111	15 3^{2} 3^{hd} 1^{hd} 1^{1}	EspinozaV	126 L *2.90	American Pharoah^{1},Firing Line^{2},Dortmund^{nk}	5wd turns,brushed late	$1,418,800
041115	11OP	ft 1⅛m	70		45^{99} $1{:}10^{54}$ $1{:}48^{52}$	ArkDbyG1	107	6 2 2^{3} 2^{1} $1^{5\frac{1}{2}}$ 1^{8}	EspinozaV	122 L *0.10	American Pharoah^{8},Far Right$^{\frac{3}{4}}$,Mr. Z^{nk}	moved at will,handily	$600,000
031415	10OP	sy 1$\frac{1}{16}$m	50		49^{63} $1{:}15^{22}$ $1{:}45^{78}$	RebelG2	108	4 1 1^{1} 1^{1} 1^{4} $1^{6\frac{1}{4}}$	EspinozaV	119 L *0.40	American Pharoah$^{6\frac{1}{4}}$,Madefromlucky$^{2\frac{1}{2}}$,Bold Conquest$^{1\frac{1}{4}}$	bobble strt,kicked clr	$450,000
092714	6SA	ft 1$\frac{1}{16}$m	70		47^{27} $1{:}11^{84}$ $1{:}41^{95}$	FrntRnnrG1	107	5 3 $1^{\frac{1}{2}}$ $1^{\frac{1}{2}}$ $1^{1\frac{1}{2}}$ $1^{3\frac{1}{4}}$	EspinozaV	122 L *0.50	American Pharoah$^{3\frac{1}{4}}$,Calculator$^{1\frac{1}{2}}$,Texas Red$^{1\frac{3}{4}}$	inside, ridden out	$180,000
090314	8DMR	ft 7f	45	◈	22^{72} 45^{23} $1{:}21^{48}$	DMrFutG1	105	1 4 1^{1} 1^{1} 1^{4} $1^{4\frac{3}{4}}$	EspinozaV	116 L 3.20	American Pharoah$^{4\frac{3}{4}}$,Calculator$^{8\frac{1}{4}}$,Iron Fist$^{\frac{1}{2}}$	speed,inside,cleared	$180,000
080914	4DMR	ft 6½f	45	◈	22^{48} 45^{04} $1{:}15^{75}$	MSW 76k	70	6 5 2^{hd} 2^{1} 2^{6} $5^{8\frac{1}{4}}$	GarciaM	118 L *1.40	Om$^{7\frac{1}{4}}$,Iron Fist^{1},One Lucky Dane^{no}	3wd to turn, wkened	$1,500

Workouts: | Oct-26-15, SA , 4F, Fast, 0:46.60, H, 2/33 | Oct-20-15, SA , 6F, Fast, 1:10.80, H, 1/8 | Oct-14-15, SA , 7F, Fast, 1:23.00, H, 1/1 | Oct-09-15, SA , 5F, Fast, 1:01.20, H, 20/38

Minimum Winning Distance: 7 furlongs
Maximum Winning Distance: 1 1/2M
Average Winning Distance: 9.28 furlongs

Auction History

Sale Price	Sale Name
$300,000	Fasig-Tipton New York Saratoga 2013 Select Yearling Sale

In United States

Blacktype Total Blacktype: 9 wins, 1 second, 0 thirds

Fin Pos	Year	Country	Track	Race Name	Currency in country of origin (Purse--Value Of Race--Earnings)
	2014	USA		Champion 2-year-old colt	(5,000,000-4,550 000-2,750,000)
	2015	USA		Triple Crown	(2,000,000-2,178 800-1,418,800)
1	2015	USA	KEE	Breeders' Cup Classic [G1]	(1,750,000-1,750 800-1,100,000)
1	2015	USA	CD	Kentucky Derby Presented by Yum! Brands [G1]	(1,500,000-1,500 000-900,000)
1	2015	USA	MTH	William Hill Haskell Invitational S. [G1]	(1,500,000-1,500 000-800,000)
1	2015	USA	PIM	Xpressbet.com Preakness S. [G1]	(1,000,000-1,000,000-600,000)
1	2015	USA	BEL	Belmont S. presented by DraftKings [G1]	(300,000-301,000-180,000)
1	2014	USA	OP	Arkansas Derby [G1]	(300,000-300,750-180,000)
1	2014	USA	DMR	Del Mar Futurity [G1]	(750,000-750,000-450,000)
1	2015	USA	SA	FrontRunner S. [G1]	(1,600,000-1,600,000-270,000)
1	2015	USA	OP	Rebel S. [G2]	
2	2015	USA	SAR	Travers S. [G1]	

MISCELLANEOUS INFORMATION
	2015	USA	KEE	Set new track record	10 furlongs in 2 07

Career Statistics

Starts: 11

Firsts: 9

Seconds: 1

Thirds: 0

Earnings: $8,650,300

Earnings Per Start: $786,391

APPENDIX G:
AMERICAN PHAROAH'S
LIFETIME WORKOUTS

Date	Track	Distance	Course	Track Condition	Time	How	Dogs
10/26/2015	SA	4F	Dirt	Fast	:46.60	Handily	
10/20/2015	SA	6F	Dirt	Fast	1:10.80	Handily	
10/14/2015	SA	7F	Dirt	Fast	1:23.00	Handily	
10/09/2015	SA	5F	Dirt	Fast	1:01.20	Handily	
10/03/2015	SA	5F	Dirt	Fast	:59.80	Handily	
09/27/2015	SA	5F	Dirt	Fast	1:00.00	Handily	
09/21/2015	SA	4F	Dirt	Fast	:49.80	Handily	
08/23/2015	DMR	7F	Dirt	Fast	1:23.20	Handily	
08/16/2015	DMR	4F	Dirt	Fast	:47.60	Breezing	
07/28/2015	DMR	4F	Dirt	Fast	:48.80	Breezing	
07/23/2015	DMR	6F	Dirt	Fast	1:11.00	Handily	
07/18/2015	DMR	6F	Dirt	Fast	1:11.40	Handily	
07/12/2015	SA	5F	Dirt	Fast	:59.20	Handily	
07/06/2015	SA	4F	Dirt	Fast	:47.60	Handily	
06/29/2015	SA	3F	Dirt	Fast	:36.40	Handily	
06/01/2015	CD	5F	Dirt	Fast	1:00.20	Breezing	
05/26/2015	CD	4F	Dirt	Fast	:48.00	Breezing	
04/26/2015	CD	5F	Dirt	Fast	:58.40	Breezing	
04/05/2015	SA	6F	Dirt	Fast	1:11.60	Handily	
03/29/2015	SA	5F	Dirt	Fast	:58.60	Handily	
03/06/2015	SA	6F	Dirt	Fast	1:10.40	Handily(G)	
02/27/2015	SA	7F	Dirt	Fast	1:23.80	Handily	

Date	Track	Distance	Surface	Condition	Time
02/21/2015 SA	6F	Dirt	Fast	1:12.40 Handily
02/15/2015 SA	5F	Dirt	Fast	1:00.40 Handily
02/09/2015 SA	3F	Dirt	Fast	:36.40 Handily
02/02/2015 SA	3F	Dirt	Fast	:36.20 Handily
10/26/2014 SA	5F	Dirt	Fast	1:00.00 Handily
10/20/2014 SA	5F	Dirt	Fast	:58.60 Handily
10/14/2014 SA	6F	Dirt	Fast	1:11.80 Handily
10/08/2014 SA	4F	Dirt	Fast	:47.60 Handily
09/21/2014 SA	5F	Dirt	Fast	:59.60 Handily
09/15/2014 SA	4F	Dirt	Fast	:47.80 Handily
08/27/2014 DMR	5F	All Weather Track	Fast	:59.00 Handily
08/18/2014 DMR	4F	All Weather Track	Fast	:48.00 Handily
08/03/2014 DMR	5F	All Weather Track	Fast	:59.80 Handily(G)
07/28/2014 DMR	5F	All Weather Track	Fast	:59.00 Handily(G)
07/22/2014 DMR	5F	All Weather Track	Fast	1:00.20 Handily
07/16/2014 DMR	5F	All Weather Track	Fast	1:00.20 Handily(G)
06/29/2014 LA	5F	Dirt	Fast	1:00.60 Handily
06/22/2014 LA	4F	Dirt	Fast	:47.20 Handily
06/12/2014 LA	4F	Dirt	Fast	:48.20 Handily
06/05/2014 LA	4F	Dirt	Fast	:48.00 Handily
05/29/2014 LA	3F	Dirt	Fast	:36.80 Handily
05/22/2014 LA	3F	Dirt	Fast	:36.80 Handily
05/15/2014 LA	2F	Dirt	Fast	:24.80 Handily

NOTES ON SOURCES AND SELECTED BIBLIOGRAPHY

I have covered horse racing for nearly two decades and have spoken, interviewed, and written about Bob Baffert countless times in the *New York Times* as well as a previous book, *The Race for the Triple Crown.* He, along with Ahmed Zayat, has kept the lines of communication open throughout the years even when sometimes those conversations were difficult or contentious. I appreciate it, and thank them both.

Likewise, Victor Espinoza and his agent Brian Beach are always generous with their time and candor and insight, for which I'm grateful. Tom VanMeter, Kevin and J.B. McKathan, Jeff Seder and Patti Miller, Mark Taylor, John Hall, and Martin Garcia all provided key details of American Pharoah's early days. A special thanks to Frances Relihan, who patiently explained to me how Thoroughbreds are cared for long before they reach the racetrack and why it is vital.

Her love and passion for horses are contagious.

Gary Stevens and Jerry Bailey, both Hall of Famers, are among the most insightful observers of the sport and have always been willing to share with me. D. Wayne Lukas and Bill Mott, two more Hall of Famers, also have taught me much. Larry Collmus, Arthur Hancock, Dr. Larry Bramlage, and Cecil Seaman always tell me something I don't know.

Likewise, projects like this do not come together without the tireless work and expertise of the marketing and publicity staffs of organizations: The Jockey Club, the Breeders' Cup, and the National Thoroughbred Racing Association. Along with the folks at the New York Racing Association, the Stronach Group, and Churchill Downs Inc., they generate a wealth of access and information that helps people like me better tell readers how the Thoroughbred industry works and why it matters. Again, you know who you are, and I am beholden to you.

For a niche sport, horse racing has a passionate and talented group of writers and broadcasters who care deeply about it. Year after year we assemble each spring, and usually come summer we are disappointed. Not this year. There were many excellent written and broadcast pieces surrounding American Pharoah that I not only enjoyed but that tipped me to another illuminating aspect of the horse and the people around him.

The *Daily Racing Form,* the sport's Bible, has assembled its fine coverage at http://www.drf.com/events/american-pharoah-coverage, and is well worth a visit. It also is worth going to https://www.youtube.com/watch?v=QFbhU5_fVao to watch the video of American Pharoah's workout as a two-year-old at the McKathans' farm. While you are at YouTube, watch the video of the colt's gallop before 15,000 people at Saratoga Race Course from the perspective of a Go-Pro camera attached to exercise rider George Alvarez.

Ray Paulick pushes harder for transparency in the sport and the www.Paulick Report.com is a must-read. Eric Crawford, Pat Forde, Dave Grening, Steve Haskin, Tim Layden, Tom Pedulla, and Tim Wilkin are terrific writers and excellent company to kill time with outside barns and inside press boxes.

Baffert, Bob. *Baffert Dirt Road to the Derby.* Lexington, Kentucky: Blood-Horse, 1999.

Crawford, Eric. *American Pharoah: Snapshots from the Triple Crown.* Louisville,

Kentucky: WDRB News, Amazon Digital Services, 2015.

DePaolo, Joe. "Pony Smokey a Loyal American Pharoah Sidekick." *Blood-Horse,* June 4, 2015.

Forde, Pat. "American Pharoah Caps Off Historic Career with Storybook Ending at Breeders' Cup." Yahoo Sports, October 31, 2015.

Haskin, Steve. "Kentucky Derby Recap: American Idol." *Blood-Horse,* May 5, 2015.

———. "Preakness Recap: Pharoah Glow Brightens the Day." *Blood-Horse,* May 18, 2015.

———. "Belmont Recap: Phait Accompli." *Blood-Horse,* June 11, 2015.

Hoppert, Melissa. "Turn-Ons: Peppermints, Cool Breezes. Turnoffs: Mares Who Move Too Fast." *New York Times,* June 5, 2015.

———. "Longtime Assistants Relish Ride with American Pharoah." *New York Times,* June 8, 2015.

Layden, Tim. "Baffert Fortunate to Be at Another Derby Following Dubai Emergency." *Sports Illustrated,* April 30, 2012.

———. "One More Time: American Pharoah Wins Preakness, Nears Triple Crown." *Sports Illustrated,* May 16, 2015.

———. "American Pharoah's Triple Crown

Obliterates Years of Disappointment." *Sports Illustrated,* June 7, 2015.

MacDonald, Michele. "American Pharoah: The Early Development of a Champion." *Thoroughbred Daily News,* April 27, 2015.

———. "American Pharoah vs Secretariat vs Seattle Slew vs Affirmed: How They Actually Measure Up." *Thoroughbred Commentary,* December 17, 2015.

Oakford, Glenye Cain. "Zayat Wears His Heart on His Sleeve." *Daily Racing Form,* April 2, 2010.

Palmer, Joanne. "We've Got the Horse Right Here . . ." *Jewish Standard,* May 14, 2015.

Paulick, Ray. "He Lied Like Nobody's Business: A Racing Con Man and His Trail of Deception." ThePaulickReport.com, August 11, 2014.

Pedulla, Tom. "After Heart Attack, Baffert Plans to Keep Winning Big." *New York Times,* October 31, 2012.

Serby, Steve. "American Pharoah's Jockey's Divine Inspiration for Triple Crown." *New York Post,* June 4, 2015.

Simers, T. J. "Thoroughbred Trainer Bob Baffert Still Has Heart of a Champion." *Los Angeles Times,* October 29, 2012.

Sullivan, Tim. "How Baffert Got Pharoah." *Louisville Courier-Journal,* June 2, 2015.

Wilkin, Tim. "Paynter Beats Odds, Illness. Recovered from Disease That Threatened His Life, Colt Set to Run in Woodward." *Albany Times-Union,* August 29, 2013.

Wincze Hughes, Alicia. "Derby Champion's Sire Emerges as Top Stallion from Humble Beginnings." *Lexington Herald-Leader,* May 9, 2015.

Witz, Billy. "Divine Intervention Is a Hope, Not a Horse, in the Belmont." *New York Times,* June 6, 2015.

PHOTO CREDITS

ABOUT THE AUTHOR

Joe Drape is an award-winning sportswriter for the *New York Times*. A native of Kansas City and graduate of Rockhurst High School, Drape earned a Bachelor of Arts degree in English from Southern Methodist University. After reporting for numerous local papers and winning awards, Joe came to the *New York Times* in 1998 to cover college sports and horse racing. A *New York Times* bestselling author, Drape's work has been honored nationally by the Associated Press Sports Editor. He is a two-time Eclipse Award winner for outstanding coverage in thoroughbred racing. He lives in New York City with his wife, Mary Kennedy, and son, Jack.